RICHARD KEARNEY'S ANATHEISTIC WAGER

INDIANA SERIES IN THE PHILOSOPHY OF RELIGION

Merold Westphal, *Editor*

RICHARD KEARNEY'S ANATHEISTIC WAGER

Philosophy, Theology, Poetics

Edited by Chris Doude van Troostwijk and
Matthew Clemente

Indiana University Press

This book is a publication of

Indiana University Press
Office of Scholarly Publishing
Herman B Wells Library 350
1320 East 10th Street
Bloomington, Indiana 47405 USA

iupress.indiana.edu

The paper used in this publication meets the minimum requirements of the American National Standard for Information Sciences—Permanence of Paper for Printed Library Materials, ANSI Z39.48-1992.

Manufactured in the United States of America

Library of Congress Cataloging-in-Publication Data

Names: Doude van Troostwijk, Chris, [date] editor.
Title: Richard Kearney's anatheistic wager : philosophy, theology, poetics / edited by Chris Doude van Troostwijk and Matthew Clemente.
Description: 1st [edition]. | Bloomington : Indiana University Press, 2018. | Series: Indiana series in the philosophy of religion | Includes bibliographical references and index.
Identifiers: LCCN 2018006095 (print) | LCCN 2018003215 (ebook) | ISBN 9780253034014 (e-book) | ISBN 9780253034007 (hardback : alk. paper)
Subjects: LCSH: Kearney, Richard. | God. | Religion—Philosophy.
Classification: LCC B945.K384 (print) | LCC B945.K384 R53 2018 (ebook) | DDC 210.92—dc23
LC record available at https://lccn.loc.gov/2018006095

1 2 3 4 5 23 22 21 20 19 18

For Emma and Nathan
and
for Dominic and Jonathan

Contents

Part III. Poetics of the Sacred

Acknowledgments

A BOOK LIKE this would not be possible without the support and effort of a great number of people. First, our contributors who put their time, talent, and energy into making their pieces as strong as they are. And, of course, Richard Kearney whose generosity and encouragement has been a constant source of reassurance. The excellent staff at Indiana University Press—especially Merold Westphal, Dee Mortenson, and Paige Rasmussen. Sheila Gallagher who provided the artwork for our cover. Fr. John Panteleimon Manoussakis who has been a mentor and a friend. Lee Oser, Peter Kreeft, Vanessa Rumble, Gary Gurtler SJ, Thomas Miles, and Donald Brand. The Luxembourg School of Religion & Society, the Boston College Philosophy Department, the College of the Holy Cross, UniLib: Atelier de réflexion théologique, Le Promontoire (www.climont.eu), the Tolle Lege Literary Society, and Duo. Our wonderful families, especially Maarten Doude van Troostwijk, Robert and Marie Clemente, and Rob Clemente. And, most importantly, our wives without whose constant support and understanding we would not have been able to finish this project. Alexandra Breukink and Tracy Clemente, thank you.

Abbreviations of Kearney's Works

Anatheism (A)

The God Who May Be (GWMB)

On Stories (OS)

Poetics of Imagining (PI)

Sam's Fall (SF)

Strangers, Gods, Monsters (SGM)

The Shulammite's Song: Divine Eros Ascending and Descending (SS)

Walking at Sea Level (WSL)

RICHARD KEARNEY'S ANATHEISTIC WAGER

Introduction: The Risk of the Wager

Chris Doude van Troostwijk and
Matthew Clemente

I

The notion of faith necessarily implies risk. Faith entails the possibility of the loss of faith. It entails the possibility of faithlessness. A faith that is comfortable, that is not threatened by insecurity and instability, that does not grapple with doubt, is no faith at all. It is evidence, science, gnosis, or the system. Perhaps it is blindness. And though all of these ways of relating to the world can be subjected to the same type of skepticism and critique as faith itself, none is faith. No, with faith, there is something different at stake. Something at once awesome and awful. Something primary, foundational, fundamental. Something that can only be authentically approached in fear and trembling.

For a person of faith, the risk of the loss of faith is ever-present. It is an inherent part of faith itself. However, one does not lose one's faith as one loses a conviction. Convictional belief is an expression of faith. It is an expression of an existential, prereflexive disposition that comes from within. It echoes a radical, archaic, primal experience—the experience of the question of faith. And if this experience is always already precarious, if it is never secure, never stable, always uncertain, then the question of faith necessarily implies two possible answers and the primordial experience provides two viable responses. Faith and faithlessness are equally valid options. Belief and unbelief are their respective articulations. Both attempt to provide an answer to an original call. Both attempt to express the radical, foundational moment of human experience—a moment both primary and unending, a moment at the heart of the human condition itself.

Throughout his corpus, Richard Kearney has attempted to examine this very experience. Making use of both philosophical and theological approaches to the question of faith—methodologically, he operates within the French hermeneutic tradition of Ricoeur, the continental phenomenological school of Levinas and Merleau-Ponty, and the poststructuralist deconstructionist tradition of Derrida and Caputo—Kearney offers poignant reflections with the sense of urgency that his subject demands. In his work over the last decade—most notably, *Anatheism: Returning to God After God* (2010) but elsewhere as well—Kearney has put forth the proposition that faith is a wager. Faith, he claims, is a response to a question posed to us, even forced upon us, by those limit experiences that make religious and poetic discourse possible.

The debt that this development in Kearney's thinking owes to other philosophers of the wager—Pascal, Kierkegaard, and James come readily to mind—is clear. Yet as this volume will show, Kearney offers us a wager all his own—one that demands serious attention, engagement, and critique. Along these lines, one question that we, the editors, have grappled with time and again as we have delved deeper into Kearney's work is, what is at stake in Richard Kearney's anatheistic wager? What can be lost and what is there to gain?

II

In the well-known formulation of his theistic wager, Pascal emphasizes the fact that the stakes are high. Choosing rightly has the potential to save one from the grips of death, destruction, and despair. Choosing wrongly might very well lead to an eternity spent in hell. Bliss, torment, or nonexistence—these are the possible outcomes with which man is presented. And for that reason, Pascal insists, one ought to wager belief in God. God is the only one who can save us from damnation and the void.

Like Pascal, Kierkegaard presents us with a wager that entails real risk and real consequence. He proposes a double existential wager which forces the question of faith onto the individual. After all, according to his Lutheran tradition, the individual alone is responsible before God. To become a Christian, Kierkegaard insists, one must first become oneself. But how can one do this? At first, one wagers between the life of the aesthetic and the ethical life. Neither option, however, leads to a life lived authentically. The first wager fails; it ends in despair. The individual is condemned to an inauthentic existence. Thus, it is only by the introduction of a second, paradoxical, impossible wager—the wager of faith—that the individual can be saved. But from our finite human perspective, this wager is absurd. It is, as Kearney might say, an impossible possibility. Metaphysical calculation provides no answer to this existential wager. One must leap into the anxiety and terror of the absurd.

Yet the risk inherent in wagering is not limited to a specific set of confessional beliefs. The pragmatic wager of William James, for instance, is also dependent on one's willingness to set aside absolute certainly and make a dangerous leap. William Kingdon Clifford's quasi-positivist credo that "it is wrong, always, everywhere, for anyone, to believe anything on insufficient evidence" was famously refuted by James who, in his refuting, offered perhaps the first pragmatist justification of religious belief. He claimed that sometimes, and especially when the stakes are high, one is permitted or even obliged to adhere to a faith that is based on insufficient evidence. Some decisions simply cannot be based on purely logical or scientific grounds. Some rely on passions and existential aspirations. At times, it would be a prudential failure not to believe. For instance, when one declares one's love to another, one must take the risk and trust, without knowing, that the other will respond in kind. Love cannot be proved; it can only be trusted. Love demands faith.

And so it is with these risks and wagers in mind that we ought to address Richard Kearney's anatheistic wager. In place of the reductive, simplistic dichotomy set up between dogmatic theism and militant atheism, anatheism opens the possibility of addressing theological questions in a nondoctrinal way. It does not try to overcome the uncomfortable experience of the in-between. It does not try to escape the either-or dilemma. Rather, anatheism proposes a faith haunted by the risk of faithlessness, and vice versa. The anatheistic wager is a constant not-knowing. It is a cloud of unknowing—a problem posed to us by those limit experiences that confront us and demand of us a response. Therefore, it is not simply a metaphysics of probability and calculation, à la Pascal. Nor is it a risk that prompts an existential leap or pragmatic prudence. It appears at birth, is present throughout life, and disappears only with death.

The goal of this work, then, is to raise the question: what kind of risks or uncertainties are at stake in Richard Kearney's anatheistic wager? If the wager is ever-present, if it confronts us and demands of us a constant wagering, a constant choice, if we are always being asked to decide between hospitality and hostility, the open hand and the closed fist, and if this decision cannot be gotten rid of, cannot be overcome—why then choose one and not the other? Why faith and not faithlessness? Why God and not the void?

III

The anatheistic wager confronts us with a fundamental paradox. If the wager is inescapable, how then can we apply to it the concept of a wager? For, as Kearney himself readily admits, the anatheistic wager is deeper and more originary than the wagers detailed above. It has about it a kind of quasi-ontological status. If, in the confrontation with the other, not-choosing is already a kind of choosing, if not-choosing is not a real possibility, if I cannot not choose—then the wager is prior to any sort of binary optionality. It is no longer an issue of "to be or not to be"—to be with God or to be without God—but, as Lacan rewrote Hamlet's famous exclamation: "to be or not, *to be* is the question." Being itself is a question and is questioning. And before we can calculate or leap or make any kind of practical consideration, the wager is always already there—wagering in and through us. As long as we live, the wager will be there. It cannot be gotten rid of.

This anatheistic wager is both an archi-onto-logical tension and an individual or collective decision. It exists before any choice, and yet it finds its expression in a variety of choices, answers, and engagements. The authors in this volume attempt to illustrate how this original, quasi- or proto-ontological anatheistic wager becomes manifest in thought, belief, and art. This text, therefore, follows Kearney's own hermeneutic example by considering the implications his work has on the spheres of philosophy, theology, and poetics. The collected articles are arranged according to the method of their exposition: dialogue in Part I, commentary and critique in parts II and III. The section called *Conversations After God* examines how anatheism problematizes and transforms the classical dichotomy between faith and faithlessness into dialectics of wagering. The articles in *At the Limits of Theology* explore the consequences of anatheistic wagering for the philosophy of religion and theological discourse. And *Poetics of the Sacred* reveals how the inescapability of the anatheistic wager makes it a never-ending story. From the anatheistic wager a straight line must be drawn to anatheistic theopoetics. Thus the wager continues in and through art—and above all: the art of living.

CHRIS DOUDE VAN TROOSTWIJK is a Dutch philosopher and theologian. He is Professor of philosophy and ethics at the Luxembourg School of Religion & Society and works as an affiliated researcher and lecturer at the Protestant Theological Faculty of the University of Strasbourg (France). He holds the Mennonite Chair for Liberal Theology at the Free University in Amsterdam (The Netherlands). His current research project "Philosophies, Theologies and Ethics of Finance" is concerned with providing a phenomenological hermeneutics of money.

MATTHEW CLEMENTE is a husband and father of two. He is a Teaching Fellow at Boston College specializing in philosophy of religion and contemporary Continental thought. He is the author of *Out of the Storm: A Novella* (2016) and is the coeditor of *The Art of Anatheism* (2018) and *(mis)Reading Nietzsche* (2018).

Part I: Conversations After God

1 Theism, Atheism, Anatheism

James Wood and Richard Kearney

I

JW: I'd like to ask you about the personal nature of your relationship to God—your own religious path.

RK: Sure. I'll tell you a story about something I did on Irish radio. It's a program called *Miriam Meets* that's on every Sunday. Usually two members of a family are invited. So I did it with my brother, Tim, who works with the *Communauté de* l'Arche, founded by Jean Vanier. Vanier is a very committed Christian who works with disabled people—kind of a hero and a saint. I played the "bad guy" and my brother, Tim, was the "good guy." We get along extremely well, but we were teasing each other and so on. He was being pitched as the theist and me [*sic*] as the more wayward one—in other words, the anatheist. A week later, I was walking in the fields near our house in West Cork, and I came to the top of this hill. I was trespassing on a farmer's land, and he drove up with his tractor and hopped out, and I thought, "Oh dear, he's going to get me for trespassing and disturbing his cattle." But he just wanted to talk about God. "Are you the atheist?" he asks right away. So I said, "What do you mean?" And he said, "I heard you on the radio. Your brother—he was very good, but you were very confused." In Ireland, an "anatheist" is an atheist—and atheists are very confused.

JW: Is there a tension between the openness, the emptiness of the name, "God"—God as the name for the "more," the "surplus," the "surprise," that humans seek—between that emptying out and the need to keep on talking of "God"? In his book *Saving God: Religion after Idolatry*, the Princeton philosopher Mark Johnston says, in effect, "Let's stop using the word 'God.' I will call him 'the Highest One' from now on"—which is good, proper anti-idolatry, but nevertheless he's managed to write an entire book about this indescribable Highest One. So if there are all sorts of words that we have to retire because language is too absolute to adequately represent this unfinished, unfinalizable, God, then from a nonbeliever's point of view, a question quickly emerges: "Well, why not just retire God himself? You've retired most of the language; why not retire the concept itself and just stop talking about God, the Highest One, and all the rest of it?" Which is another way of asking, "Why does Kearney need God in order to achieve his ethics?"

RK: I'm sympathetic at one level—doing away with the word "God" and eventually doing away with the terms "theism" and "atheism." Anatheism is just a term for the critical revisiting of that language in order to try and upset it, challenging the old dogmatic antithesis between theism and atheism. Anatheism is no more than a strategic, terminological tool to carve open a middle space that is, as the prefix *ana-* suggests, both before and after the theism/atheism divide. In a way, its unfamiliarity as a neologism serves initially to confound readers' expectations—some people think it's theism, others atheism ("an-atheism," as it sometimes mispronounced), and others again something altogether different. It depends how you read it. But at the outset, confronted with the term, no one is meant to be entirely sure—perhaps not even me. And the fact that it also means "back" and "forward" interests me. The "ana" is not readily locatable in either time or space. It is a special moment, a strange space that I do not hesitate to call sacred. So I'm using this odd prefix, *ana-*, to try to trouble the old dichotomy of God versus anti-God, and to do this in favor of a middle realm, a *milieu*, where some new kind of thinking about this ageless yet still urgent question might occur. Such a middle space is not some wishy-washy, lukewarm ambivalence—which one would be correct to "spit out" as Scripture suggests. It is not facile syncretism—a little bit of this and that without ever committing yourself to anything at all. The doubleness of "ana" is not duplicity, but rather a deeply productive tension. The idea of "ana" with its double *a* can be read in two ways: as in the colloquial *a-dieu*, it can mean both "hello" and "good-bye." One connotes a moving away from or a departure, the *a* of the *deus absconditus*—or, more radically, atheism (mystical or secular). While the other *a* is the "adieu" of "hello"—*ad deum*. Excuse the Latin, but one finds echoes of this in the colloquial usage of French and English also. And for me this double *a* says something important about our contemporary relationship with the sacred.

JW: Why keep the word "sacred"?

RK: I use the word "sacred" because it is generous—or, at least, more capacious than the often-exclusivist understanding of terms like "theism," "religion," and "God." Many people who might have a real problem with the traditional notions of God have little trouble saying "This is sacred to me" when referring to a certain person, place, or time. So the initial *a* of *ana* signals a first movement of abstention and absolution whereby one absolves oneself of the preconceptions of the old God of power and might, in a sort of apophatic (negative theology) or anti-idolatrous (iconoclasm) gesture. And this preliminary move, akin if not identical with a certain salutary atheist scruple, may then open the possibility—never the necessity—of a return to something more, other, transcendent: a surplus that was always there though we didn't see it. This is what I call *ana-theos*, or the *God after God*. Something "called" God—for God is a name that means different things to different people. The best response, at least for me, to the question "do you believe in God?" is, "It depends what you mean by God." In other words, "Tell me what you understand about God, and I'll tell you whether I believe it."

JW: So, tell me something about what God means to you. Tell me something about your own childhood in religious terms. Your father was a sort of observant Catholic, wasn't he?

RK: Yes, he was. Silently observant. He never came to mass with us.

JW: Oh, he didn't?

RK: No. He went often to his own mass. He was a silent observer and rarely took the Eucharist. He felt unworthy and would go on a penitential pilgrimage to Lough Derg in Northern Ireland once a year; only then would he take communion. Whereas my mother was very devotional and very partial to the sacraments. So to put it in terms he would never have used himself, my father was more "apophatic"—he rarely spoke about religion and never about theology. He was educated and intelligent—a professor of surgery—but never articulated his religious or spiritual beliefs. In fact, at his funeral, a medical nun from one of the Cork hospitals came up to me and said, "You know, every day we saw your father at the back of the chapel. He never went into surgery without saying a prayer." But it was like a revelation to us. We would never have imagined it.

JW: He went on his own?

RK: Yes.

JW: Interesting.

RK: By contrast, my mother was full of spiritual pathos and very involved with helping suffering and homeless people in the city. Both parents were incredibly tolerant—moral but never moralistic or moralising. My mother would say, "Just be good to people." To take a somewhat dramatic example, when contraception was outlawed in Ireland, she would encourage all six of her sons to bring condoms when we dated girls. She knew that boys would be boys and wanted us to be responsible and never cause our girlfriends any harm. My sister became pregnant when she was still in her teens and suffered the consequences of a punishing Catholic community. But my father and mother stood by her and her baby, right through the terrible ordeal when she had to give up her studies and lost her first job as a trainee teacher in a girls' school for "fear of scandal." My parents were amazingly strong and protective. I respected that and learned early on that religious people could be the best as well as the worst.

JW: So your mother was a churchgoer and took you along?

RK: She took all seven of her children. My brothers and I were altar boys. We went through the whole thing, and it was very beautiful. Sacramental, richly liturgical, something magical, not at all censorious or punishing. It may have been somewhat atypical of most Irish Catholic culture of the time; I don't know. But when I later heard and read about what so many of my contemporaries lived through as young Catholics—a punitive, fear-filled, guilt-ridden religion—I felt fortunate to have had the parents I did.

JW: The punitive element, that wasn't there at all for you?

RK: For the most part, no. I was, of course, beaten by the Christian "brothers" in primary school—nobody escaped that—but fortunately, my parents sent me to secondary school in a Benedictine Abbey called Glenstal. The monks there had a deep culture of tolerance, an openness to interreligious dialogue inspired by pioneering Benedictine missionaries like Abhishiktananda and Bede Griffiths in India; and a real sense of critical questioning informed by Vatican II theologians like Yves Congar and Henri De Lubac. Glenstal Abbey was also a place of ecumenical reconciliation in a sectarian Ireland, where the Northern troubles smouldered and raged in the late sixties and seventies.

JW: As a teenager, did you struggle with inherited belief or was the inherited belief not a large enough pressure that you had to struggle with it?

RK: It was a mixture of inheritance and struggle. Glenstal Abbey, where I went when I was twelve, provided a forum for this that was not, as I mentioned, very typical of Ireland in the late sixties. And then there was my equally atypical family situation—with a very apophatic father and a very cataphatic mother. And, of course, my mother's devotion to the poor and needy—we'd pray for them and for my father's critically ill patients every night before bed. It was basically my mother who shared my father's work with us. He never said a word about it himself. And then three of my brothers started working with the disabled community as teenagers—they were much better than me in that regard. I was reading Nietzsche and Heidegger while they were pushing wheelchairs in Lourdes and Knock. They were very inspired by Jean Vanier's movement *L'arche*, which was set up to care for the mentally disabled by taking them out of awful psychiatric hospitals, known as "looney bins" in Cork, and living with them in ordinary houses. Vanier, originally a philosophy professor in Canada and a good friend of the family, was extremely liberal, open, ecumenical, wise, and caring. So I saw all the good side of Catholic caritas and caring for the broken and wounded—along with the more oppressive side infamously epitomised by some perverted clergy in Ireland, as elsewhere, and in much of the Catholic-imposed social intolerance (regarding divorce, homosexuality, premarital sex, unmarried mothers, contraception, abortion, and so on). So, although I remained informed by a spiritually rich religious life on a personal level with my own family and educational experience, at a public level, I was extremely angry with the official Church. But my antiecclesiastical indignation did not prevent me from struggling to retrieve what I considered to be certain valuable—perhaps invaluable—treasures of my spiritual heritage. I felt I could be furious with the bishops while continuing to worship something called "God."

JW: You weren't struggling through theodicy questions?

RK: Of course, but not for long. Theodicy never made sense to me. I was incensed by the very idea from early on. I could never believe in a divinity that willed or allowed evil if it had the power to do otherwise. That seemed like sheer cruelty or casuistry. I never gave credence to a deity of omnipotence. My God was one of nonsovereignty, vulnerability, fragility, and unknowability. A God of service, who preferred washing feet, healing the sick, giving bread, dying for his friends and enemies alike. In fact, the washing of the disciples' feet was always my favorite Easter liturgy. Jean Vanier used to do that. He'd go around and wash the feet of those—both abled and disabled—at his Easter table. That to me epitomised the divine as a servant—not servile, but in the service of others, strangers, outcasts. So, when you mention Mark Johnson defining the monotheistic God as the Highest One, I would rather say the "lowest one." My God is an anti-God in that sense, God as outsider, guest, vagrant, the one who hungers and thirsts for justice—"the least of these," as he says in the gospels, the *elachistos*. Not the God above us but, as Paul Claudel put it, the God *beneath* us.[1]

JW: Now, what if an ethically, politically engaged atheist had turned up alongside you while you were doing those good, Vanier-inspired works? And this ethical chap was as ethical and motivated as you but turned out to have a Dawkins-like lack of belief. Where, then, do the distinctions fall? What would separate you, if anything, from him? What would be the difference?

RK: Well, the first thing for me would be what *doesn't* separate us—the fact that we're both in service to something radically other than ourselves. If you look at Matthew 25 . . .

JW: It is a foundational text for you, isn't it?

RK: Yes. Matt 25:31–44 is radical. But its radicality is so often neglected in practical and theological terms. It's crucial. Christ identifies here with the *hospes*, the stranger in the street, the last person in the world you think could be God. And that is where and how the kingdom comes—incarnate in the one who gives or receives a cup of water. I mean, that is the exclusion of exclusion par excellence. So if the worst of religion is its exclusiveness—"we have the revealed truth and the rest of you are damned"—the great thing about this passage (and I believe one finds certain equivalents in Judaism, Buddhism, and other religions) is that *no one* need be excluded, except those who exclude themselves by choosing not to give or receive bread. Atheists are not at all excluded here—but I will come back to this. In fact, the asking—acknowledging one's need for bread and water—is as important as giving the bread and water (or wine, as the case may be). So anatheist practice, as I understand it, would be the *exclusion of exclusion*, not the contrary. Or, to put it in more technical terms, when it comes to serving strangers, orthopraxis trumps orthodoxy.

JW: I see.

II

RK: But let's get back to your example of the nonbelieving student who is doing the same thing as the believing student. What is the difference? When I'm washing people's feet with this guy as we're working together with the homeless in downtown Dublin or out in Somalia, the first and most important thing is that we're *doing* the work (*facere veritatem* as Augustine says, "*do* the truth"); the second thing might be that, as we are working, we have a conversation. And the conversation begins with the questions, "What do you say that you're doing? And why are you doing it? What is your narrative about this shared action?" In short, what is the story behind your being here? Or the history behind the story? The why, who, wherefrom, whereto? I recount my story and listen to the other's story as well.

JW: You trade narratives.

RK: Yes. We trade narratives, and then we ask questions about those narratives: The atheist might say, "Why do you call that God?" And the anatheist would say, "Well, actually, I call it the suffering servant." And the reply might be, "But that's not my view of God." And then I could tell the story, as I understand it, of Abraham and Sarah feeding the hungry strangers under the Mamre tree and of Isaiah as the suffering servant and Christ's washing of the feet at the Last Supper (perhaps using the more unusual term "the Nazarene" rather than "Jesus" or "Messiah") and the feeding of the hungry with loaves and fishes and the healing of lepers (the one who came back to give thanks was an outsider, a Samaritan) and the later testimonies of Francis and Claire, and Teresa and John of the Cross, and Etty Hillesum and Vanier and so forth. I would explain that these are some key stories from my own Abrahamic Christian tradition, but that one could find analogous (though not identical) stories in other spiritual or religious traditions—some of them occasionally called "atheist," like Buddhism. I would express my belief in the radical ethos of hospitality to the outsider, the excluded, and the estranged as being central to my notion of the name or metaphor "God," which, for me—as an anatheist—radically includes atheists equally committed to love and justice for the stranger. And having said all that (or preferably a fraction of it), I would simply stop and listen to what the atheist had to say. I would be totally open to the fact that his or her story might be just as convincing and moving than mine, if not more so, or that our stories might overlap in some interesting and surprising ways, producing a more open theism and atheism—that is, novel variations of the anatheist option.

JW: So, for you, it comes back to narratives in the end?

RK: Yes. But in the case of religion—religious narratives are literary narratives but not just literary narratives—this does not have to mean illusion, fiction, untruth, or flight of fancy (as Freud, Marx, and Nietzsche said). It can also mean testimony—a witnessing to the truth: "you shall know them by the fruit" (Matthew 7:20), the fruit of their actions as recounted through stories and histories. And these fruits of faith might be called second actions that are inspired by the sacred stories initially inspired by first actions. It is a hermeneutic circle, as Paul Ricoeur puts it—prefiguring actions of sacred figures configured as oral and written narratives that can then be refigured by believers of those narratives. In other words, you begin with a sacred life or history that calls for a story that configures that holy act (hospitality, love, pardon, and revolution) and that, when read or heard by others, gives rise to another sacred act that reprises and re-enacts the story. And so on, ad infinitum. I think that is what the infinite means—the call of the good constantly reinscribing itself in finite acts of history and stories without end. Christianity for me is that tradition of transmission through the lives of the saints, beginning with those who visit the empty tomb or share bread in Emmaus and then down through the lives of ordinary Samaritans and saints in the lower case as well as the upper case—like St. Francis and Mother Teresa and Dorothy Day and Martin Luther King. And this is still going on every day where guests and strangers exchange actions and words of compassion. Hannah Arendt says that if someone asks you who you are, you tell your story.[2] If someone asks me why I believe, I do just that. I tell my story.

JW: Yes, it seems tremendously important. I find that whenever I write about theological issues, I'm almost forced to admit some element of myself.

RK: As in your novel, *The Book against God*—that is quite autobiographical isn't it?

JW: Well, yes and no. I had a pretty strange upbringing religiously. My parents are Anglicans, and I grew up in the north of England, in Durham. But in the 1970s, when I was about twelve, the church we worshipped at underwent charismatic renewal. My parents fell quite hard for this Anglicised American evangelicalism (because that's what it was, really), despite the fact that my father was a scientist—he taught zoology at Durham University. I spent my late teenage years struggling pretty hard with my parents' evangelical Christianity, and in some ways my very concept of Christianity—even as I reject religious belief—is ultimately an evangelical one (which is a kind of tribute to my parents, I guess). In fact, when I wrote *The Book against God*, which is about an atheist who has religious parents, I tried hard to make those fictional parents very different from my own—I gave them a very easy-going, tolerant, undogmatic, centrist kind of Anglicanism, which is quite far from the evangelical form of belief. I did this because I wanted to get a true novelistic narrative going and not merely produce memoir. But if I didn't quite portray my parents in that novel, I certainly portrayed their world.

RK: The circle of narrative-testimony-praxis is the crux for me—the heart of the whole thing. Theory comes after (though it is not unimportant). So, to repeat, I would begin by saying where I am coming from and then listen to where the other is coming from. And what interests me is to learn of the journey that brings my interlocutor to say, "No, I cannot call that God," or "Gosh, I never thought of that before. I thought of God as the almighty one, not the three strangers coming out of the desert or the hungry, thirsting outcast on the wayside or the Shulammite woman lusting for her lover in the streets at night, asking to be kissed with the kisses of his mouth (as in the Song of Songs), or a voice crying in the wilderness." So we would listen to each other and hopefully learn from each other. I would hopefully learn more about atheism and so deepen my anatheism. In the final analysis, such dialogue comes down to the question, "What is God?" And I very much enjoy Joyce's answer to that in *Ulysses:* "A cry in the street."[3] For me, *Ulysses* is a holy book, ending with a cry in the street and a cry in the bedroom—a woman crying out "yes," as Mary did in Nazareth. And several works by Gerard Manley Hopkins, William Blake, Fanny Howe, and other poets are sacred texts too. But that is another story.

JW: In that exchange, would you consider yourself engaged in some process of anatheistic conversion? I wouldn't like to use that word, but you know what I mean.

RK: I wouldn't use the term "conversion" either—I dislike the idea, as I do anything that smacks of evangelism or apologetics. I would hate to think I am trying to convert you now. God forbid. But I would say that in any meaningful exchange of narratives on religion, there might be some kind of mutual transformation. I distrust the current academic fashion of so-called neutrality. As if questions of God could be conducted without any concern for personal and existential issues of faith or truth. In the beginning is hermeneutics. We all have our presuppositions and wagers. If we were to put things in theist or atheist terms—I am actually becoming less and less satisfied with these tags—I would say that in the anatheist space of mutual exchange and question, the relation between service and faith, between the divine and human goodness, between God and the stranger, I would say that in the space of reciprocal opening to each other, one of us might describe himself as an anatheist theist (me, for instance) and another as an anatheist atheist (you, for instance?). That is more or less how I would see my relationship with you in the anatheist discussion we are having right now. When I read Nietzsche, Freud, and Marx as a young student, for example, my understanding of theism was deeply transformed in good ways. Though for obvious reasons, the relationship with those atheist interlocutors was not mutual (alas, they were dead). In my dialogues with you—now and on previous occasions, and in reading your writings on literature and belief in *The Broken Estate* or in your novel—these intellectual encounters are challenging and opening up my thinking about religion, God, and spirituality. I would also add that it is largely in my recent exchanges with you—and also in my exchanges with Buddhist thinkers—that my dissatisfaction with the very terminology of theism/atheism has become more pronounced. But theism and atheism are the terms we have to deal with, at least in the West where the monotheist/pantheist/antitheist debates have raged—sometimes with very violent results. As Heidegger said, we have to use the language of metaphysics to get beyond metaphysics. I have to use the language of

Christian onto-theology to get beyond the limits of onto-theology. It is in this sense that *ana* is, for me, an alternative to the theist versus atheist polarities, the "us versus them" exclusivism. For me, Christ, genuinely understood, is the exclusion of exclusion. But there are many Christs before and after Christ. As he himself said in that wonderfully self-multiplying kenotic way of his, "before Abraham was I am" (John 8:58) and "I must go so that the Paraclete can come (John 16:7)."

III

JW: So, where would you place yourself on the Christian spectrum?

RK: I must confess that I even find the identifications of Christian and non-Christian very limiting at times, especially as one progresses in genuine interreligious dialogue with others. I would say that I am post-Christian in the sense of ana-Christian, by which I mean that I go beyond certain aspects of my Christian church and heritage while also going back to it *after* I have left it. Having abandoned my childhood faith, I keep revisiting, retrieving, and reviving what I find there as an inexhaustible remainder—the surplus, the gift, the "always more" that remains an endlessly rich resource for hermeneutics.

JW: I'm attracted to this because it makes human sense. It makes human sense and it makes a narrative sense as a way of honoring the mixture of one's traditions, not least because even if you stop believing in God—and for better or worse, I would define myself in that language—you can't really get beyond the God you inherit; you're always—as you put it—"after," you've been marked, and indeed you don't want to get beyond God, in a way. However, let's stick with that hypothetical atheist encounter. I'm going to lob a couple of questions. First, is there some element of *command*—divine command in the orthodox sense—to do good that separates you from the atheist? The second related question would be, suppose the atheist says, "Look, I like your narratives, and what you've told me is that you have an inherited tradition that is a collection of stories—it's a literary tradition, a radical literary tradition about strangeness, hospitality, and kenosis. But I've got a literary tradition too." Let's say this atheist starts talking about George Eliot and Marx. And he continues: "I think there's a lot of common ground here. I've got my philosophy and my fiction. You've got your Bible stories. But please, let's just stop talking about this whole God thing, because we're just fiddling about with varieties of metaphor." I suppose this is another version of my earlier question: "Why not stop talking about God?" Suppose the atheist says, "Yes, your biblical stories are truly great stories, as great as the ones told by Eliot and Marx (or Hardy and Adorno, or what have you), but don't make them into more than that, because I don't believe that you believe they *are* more than that."

RK: Well, first, I would respond that it's not just the Bible that's my story. I see my story as participating (very humbly) in the story that continues on well after the Bible—that includes St. Francis and St. Clare, Jean Vanier, Martin Luther King, John Hume, Mahatma Gandhi, and so on. Do you know what I mean? It's a whole history of stories that are testimonies and testaments to people who, in the name of this particular God of *kenosis, caritas*, and *gravitas*, have done good things. So I start from Augustine—I don't always like Augustine, but he said two things that resonate with me a lot. First, *God* is the name for what we hope for. It's what we hope for and it is, to use the language of the Alcoholics Anonymous (AA) program, the impossible. Being cured of an addiction that nothing else—no medicine, therapy, or psychopharmacology—can seem to heal. Nobody knows why AA works. But somewhere along the line, you begin with the admission that you're totally helpless before this addiction. Nobody goes to AA unless he or she is at rock bottom. And then out of that confession of emptiness, out of that total surrender—"costing not less than everything" as T. S. Eliot, in his last quartet *The Little Gidding*, would say—the addict hands over his or her powerlessness to what's called a "higher power"—however that may be defined. It doesn't have to be a transcendent God. It doesn't have to be a metaphysical or biblical "God." But there's something *else*, something *other*, something *more, extra, strange* in the sense of not-me, beyond me, more than me. And this is what I'm trying to get at.

JW: And that something other is *beyond language*, yes? I'm trying to press this distinction, because that is the point you would press against the atheist.

RK: That something other is beyond language but is accessed through language. And what I share with the atheist is the second Augustine phrase mentioned earlier—"do the truth." You don't first think the truth, say the truth, profess the truth, defend the truth. You *do* the truth.

JW: I like that.

RK: So you know them by their actions, by their fruits. Now, the atheist might say, "Well, what about my fruits? I can list as many people as you who were doing good things in the name of man, not God." I would acknowledge that and would want to respond in several ways. First, one could cite Karl Rahner's idea of the anonymous Christian. You do the Christian thing without knowing you are doing it. You give the cup of cold water, you just don't see that you're giving it to Christ every time you give it to the stranger. You call it something else. And that is fine. It doesn't matter what we say; it matters what we do. When you see something other in "the least of these" that commands you, solicits you, calls you to do something that you don't naturally do—something "impossible," like giving up your life in the service of others—you're a Christian whether you like it or not. It's a clever bit of ventriloquism, albeit generous in its inclusiveness to "nominal" non-Christians. And I do like the response of the Buddhist monks when Rahner visited them in Kyoto and called them anonymous Christians: "And you, Professor Rahner, are an anonymous Buddhist."[4] Touché. And well meant. Leaving aside Rahner's term, I do believe that we can be summoned by children, friends, neighbors, and enemies, to do the impossible every day of our lives. For me, another word for "God" is the "impossible." What is impossible for us is possible for God. So if the only way of making the impossible possible—that is, healing me of my addiction—is invoking a "higher power," then why not? We do need to find other words—like "the impossible" or "the possibility of the impossible"—for God. "God" is such a controversial hold-all that can mean a thousand things and has been subject to so much misinterpretation and violence down through the ages—particularly the God of sovereignty and power. "Absolute love" or "impossible hope beyond hope" are other terms. We need poets who give us new ideas again and again (Joyce's "Cry in the Street," Hopkins's "Pied Beauty," Virginia Woolf's "It," and Proust's "Petit Miracle"). We perpetually need new words, images, names, stories to fill in the space of "God"—which Jews and apophatic mystics are right to want to leave empty in its transcendence and otherness—so that we can fill it in with hundreds and thousands of little names. Like the Hindu's five hundred names for God, that's a start and a good reminder to us of the modest limits of our naming powers. Who dares reduce God to one name or idea? The more names we have, the better. Derrida and I agree that "absolute hospitality" is a good name—as a term that names the solicitation to do what is, to respond to this or that stranger, here and now, as an incarnate someone who calls me to do the impossible.

JW: So is there a *command* as such?

RK: Yes, there is. But the divine command comes in the form of a question: "Where are you?" In other words, "Now that I need you to feed me, clothe me, love me, heal me, hold me—where are you?" And I answer: "Here I am." It seems to me that Levinas gets this right when he brings together the key summons of Biblical ethics and the key principle of humanism in a wonderful philosophical insight. In the first and last instance, it is the surprising voice of the stranger, the transcendent call of the other, that says, "Where are you?" And what is belief or faith here? It's the belief in the other, in yourself, in life on this earth here and now—that the impossible can become possible. It is *credo*, the "I believe"—as in, I trust; I have confidence; I give credit to the other; I wager that the other is truly other and not just me talking to myself. That act of faith as trust and truth is also a creative act. The common French term *créance* bears witness to this. That command can mean do not kill, share your food, love the loveless, or simply peace, love, hospitality, hope, pardon, forgiveness—the emptiest words in the book. In any book, aren't they? But—*faute de mieux*—they are also the best words we have for God once we understand them in an unconditional, absolute, transcendent way—which doesn't take them out of the immanent world for one instant. In the work of the Guestbook Project, I have learned over the years that hospitality is holy, sacred, precisely because it means doing the impossible: *facere impossibile*. And I have had the extraordinary sense—witnessing concrete instances of hospitality in divided communities like Mitrovica, Jerusalem, Derry, and elsewhere—of the impossible happening, of an event where something surprising and unpredicted emerges, some dimension of otherness in the other person, of strange grace in the until-then-hostile stranger. In those impossible moments, one witnesses a transcendence surging up in the immanence of the moment, a divine excess, surplus, extra in the human, of the human, through the human, beneath the human, beyond the human—and whose very divinity does not take anything away from the humanity. *Au contraire*. It deepens and rarefies it. The same experience of this "more" that makes the impossible possible can also happen in our relationship with nature. But that is another question.

JW: Is that responding to otherness—to the surplus, the "more"—is that where you'd locate the command? Because command is fraught in two ways. It's fraught in the sense that the atheist might say, "Well, you have told me about the command, but the fact is that you just happen to have read these so-called sacred stories as a teenager; they moved you immensely and inculcated the idea of ethical engagement and decency and so on. This is all very moving, but it's not quite a command, exactly." And command is vulnerable from another atheistic or antitheist position, which defiantly asserts that one should do good because it is right, not because one is told—commanded—to love one's neighbor. I tend to agree with this defiance.

RK: I agree with Hitchens on those two points, but I don't see the stranger—the sacred stranger, the stranger as sacred—as browbeating me to do the good or as some imperial power ordering me from above, *ex cathedra* or *ex machina*. I see it as a "thin, small voice," like the one that spoke to

Elijah in the cave—a call, rather than a command. A solicitation from utter powerlessness: "Where are you?" Not: "Give me food or be damned in hell." But rather, "Can you feed me so I can live?" The summons is not a diktat but a question. As when Jesus says—at the ontological level of food, offering his life and body as bread for his followers—"Who do you say that I am?" it's the opposite of a command as injunction, while simultaneously being a voice or call that commands our attention and, by extension, commands our care. It provokes and persuades. It is, in the lingo of speech act theorists, "perlocutionary." It desires our response in word and action, but we are entirely free to say no. The "commanding" voice (if one wants to retain some sense of "commandment") is vulnerable, fragile, or, as St. Paul says, "weak," which does not mean it is nothing. It's not "squishy" (to use one of your words). No, the very vulnerability of the naked call has its own special strength, its own authority—what Vaclàv Havel calls the "power of the powerless."[5] That power is stronger than the mightiest of armies, for thoughts that come on dove's wings guide the world, as Nietzsche wrote in *Thus Spoke Zarathustra*. That's what I would say to the angry or defiant atheist.

JW: You are quite close to Levinas here.

RK: I am. I learned a lot from Levinas's writing and teaching when I was a student of his in Paris in the late seventies. Along with Heidegger, Ricoeur, and Merleau-Ponty, I would say that he had the biggest philosophical influence on my thinking about God. The idea of a divine summons coming through the "orphan, widow, and stranger" is a deeply Judaic idea, as I try to show in my own chapter of *Anatheism*, and it extends throughout the Abrahamic tradition—and I would argue, beyond. The call of the stranger for me is quasi-universal. It can occur in any culture, religion, time, or place, albeit differently in each case. Because its universality only comes through the singular: It is not some abstract, transcendental, metaphysical principle or idea, but rather a concrete, lived, carnal experience between persons—and doubtless also between persons and things, places, animals, plants, planets. To come back to the biblical narrative for a moment, I would say that the command of the stranger in the street—invoked by Jesus in Matthew 25—doesn't have any power. There's no army to back him up. No triumphal fleets of angels. No imperial powers. Just a cry in the street. The voice of an utterly exposed, naked body full of need and desire. And that body, I would hold, is in everybody. And if it has any "authority," it is that of Jesus at the end of his exchange with the grand inquisitor in Dostoyevsky's *The Brothers Karamazov*—which you write so wonderfully about in *The Irresponsible Self*—when he approaches the cardinal of power and might and plants a kiss on his lips. That's the call, and it is the very opposite of the temptation to trump weakness with might that Dostoyevsky identified, rightly, with the three temptations of the devil in the desert. These temptations have all been yielded to in history, as we know from the appalling consequences of triumphalist Christianity, Judaism, and Islam. Hitchens, Dawkins, and the recent anti-God squad have a good point here, and I would not dismiss them, like some, as "undergraduate atheists." That is too easy. For me, anatheism is the complete overturning of triumphalist religion in all its forms. I don't believe that is impossible for God—God who works in and as humans, as word made flesh again and again, every time a cup of cold water is called for and given. And I don't believe I'm making it all up. It's there in the great stories of people who have changed the world—the sages and saints, the prophets and pilgrims, the endless heroic rebels and revolutionaries who transformed our earth into a better place, time and again. I repeat my list of twentieth-century anatheists: Mahatma Gandhi, Martin Luther King, Etty Hillesum, Dietrich Bonhoeffer, Dorothy Day, Nelson Mandela, John Hume, Jean Vanier, and many, many more. But these are just uppercase "Holy Ones" (who would be the first to refuse the capitalization). For every one of these names, there are millions who go unrecorded and unnoticed: lowercase "holy ones." But they are there, and we all witness them at different times and places in our lives, don't we? Anatheism is about the hallowing of such everyday acts of agents of goodness. Not sentimental niceness, but hard-core hospitality—possible beyond the impossible. The sacred, in and through the secular. Or, as Gerard Manley Hopkins puts it, "the poor potsherd matchwood immortal diamond is immortal diamond."[6] If the devil is in the details, so is God.

JW: The thing you privilege is this miracle of the impossible—this event of strangeness or otherness that makes the impossible possible. But what if the atheist says, "Look, the thing that separates us is not theological difference but a linguistic one. Kearney has a greater faith in metaphor and symbol than I do. He revels in metaphor. He's always using these words like 'sacramental' and 'anatheism,' and I can do without them. But it's really language that he believes in." I presume, and I don't want to put words in your mouth, that you wouldn't want to just rest there. You'd say, "Hang on. I'm not going to be defined simply as your standard issue postmodernist. What I do privilege is something extra-linguistic, some otherness beyond language." Would that be fair?

RK: Absolutely. And that otherness has, in my view, gone by certain names in different biblical or religious narratives. In *The God Who May Be*

(GWMB), I try to look at how the other, who promises Moses liberation, refers to himself in Exodus 3:14. *Asher yaheh asher* in Hebrew. This it usually translated as "I am who I am". But there are alternative translations offered by Rashi, and later by Franz Rosenzweig and Martin Buber and Erich Fromm: I am who may be, who can be, who will be. I am the one who will be with you and who will come to be in history, in the life of this earth, if you bring it about, if you show up, if you answer my call and you make it—make me—happen in the world. In *The God Who May Be*, I call that (in technical terms) onto-eschatological otherness. Ontological is the pledge, the commitment to *being* (Greek, *ontos on*). This means that the transcendence of the other, the stranger, the impossible, does not reside in some Platonic otherworld but in a coming-into-being, a being-toward-being, which in Christian theology is called *kenosis* (the emptying of God into being) and *ensarkosis* (word becoming flesh). We witness this most immediately in the transcending gesture of otherness, strangeness, moreness, surplus, in the other person. I would also add the "other thing" because like Hopkins, I think it can happen in nature as well as in humanity. There is a "more" in nonhuman nature as well as in human nature. Western humanism (both Greek and biblical) has often been too anthropocentric, ignoring the alterity and mystery of animals, plants, fish, and planets. But ethics sometimes excludes that because you just think of the truly human person and not the rest. So the term *onto-* tries to capture this fidelity of the sacred to the being of all things.

JW: And the term *eschatological*?

RK: Eschatology refers to last or ultimate things, and I like the term because it is much broader a term than theology. You can have different kinds of eschatology. Paul Ricoeur uses it at the end of his Freud book to refer to the "sacred" in general philosophical terms. He doesn't talk about the divine, the theism, God, revelation, or salvation here—he talks about the eschatological dimension of the sacred as that which comes before the beginning (archaeology) and after the end (teleology). It's the ultra, the ultima, the not-yet, the still-to-come. And this overlaps with the kind of messianicity one finds in posttheistic thinkers like Walter Benjamin, Ernst Bloch, Jacques Derrida, and Giorgio Agamben. So the question is: Does this kind of language—of the sacred, of eschatology, of transcendence, of otherness, of moreness, of messianicity—actually help one *do* the impossible? Does faith in the more-than-possible, in the impossible becoming possible, give one more hope to keep going, to keep waiting for God—like Beckett waited for Godot—and preparing a space for God to appear potentially in each person or thing? I believe it does. We're back to the question of the efficaciousness of faith, the power of the powerless handing over to a "higher power"—which actually reempowers us to do something we could not otherwise do.

JW: But if one doesn't want to call that "God"?

RK: Fine. And one might even construe such reticence as a certain apophatic scruple, a refusal to speak about what one cannot speak, what is beyond speech. Think of Ludwig Wittgenstein's famous conclusion to *The Tractatus*: "Whereof one cannot speak, thereof one must be silent." Wittgenstein calls this unsayable, unnameable realm of silence *das Mystische* (though that is, I suppose, another kind of name, isn't it?) "The mystical" is what cannot be said, what goes beyond what is the case, what we know, what we can represent in thought and language. "I'm going to do the truth, but I'm not going to speak about it." I respect this. I even admire it. But the difficulty here, as I see it, is that it makes for a very solitary struggle—like Kierkegaard's silent, single one on Mount Moriah with no one to talk to, no one to share his impossible summons. Derrida's Abraham is alone on the mountain. It's just too hard; it's not liveable. One goes crazy in such absolute isolation and silence. So one of the reasons I propose a certain anatheist retrieval of religion is its *shared* language. It's about shared stories, commonly inherited narratives, translatable traditions and transmissible memories—albeit radically reinterpreted and retold (in accordance with poetic imagination and ethical sensitivity to each new historical situation). By contrast, one of the things I am a little wary of in our postmodern culture is its isolationism in the midst of a pseudo-collectivism (Facebook and the immediate availability of the social media). Where is the possibility of genuine community? Can one believe in the impossible on one's own? I am not sure. Religion in its etymological sense of *religare*, a *binding* to the other, the one beyond and beneath us, the stranger as an impossible guest rather than the enemy, is perhaps important here. The beginning of Abrahamic religion is the moment when Abraham welcomes the three strangers into his tent—turning hostility into hospitality—and the three turn out to be God. Genuine religion is the repetition of that gesture: war becoming peace. I fully endorse the idea of a "religionless Christianity," espoused by Dietrich Bonhoeffer and Paul Ricoeur, if we understand religion in the sense of dogmatic institutional imperium but retrieved as a genuine *auctoritas* that links us to a larger tradition and a historical community beyond our isolated, individual selves. I think something like that is still very valuable. Perhaps even indispensable.

IV

JW: I wanted to ask you about prayer—whether this other, this otherness who could be called God but you are happy not to call God, is a presence.

RK: One could call it by that name too.

JW: Exactly. Is it a presence one could or can pray to? That's a general question. And a more personal one is the presence *you* pray to. For example, Terry Eagleton's book, that I reviewed in the *New Yorker* a couple of years ago, *Reason, Faith, and Revolution*, trots out some perfectly acceptable Aquinas.[7] I like Eagleton's ethics, I like his anti-idolatry, and I like his Jesus of the gospels, who sounds a bit like Terry Eagleton, except doing better works than Terry Eagleton. But not once in the book does Eagleton mention prayer, and one is forced to conclude in the end that he has something like the philosopher's concept of God—partly because he is philosophical in nature, but partly because he actually needs that "God" in order to bash on the one hand idolatrous evangelicals and on the other hand the idolatrous atheists who mirror the evangelicals.

RK: Are you saying his approach lacks prayer?

JW: I'm just observing that Eagleton never really mentions any personal relationship with this God that he's always on about. And fine, I have no problem with the spadework necessary to get rid of the idolatrous God. But then, if someone writes a book about God and there's no sense of presence and prayer, what kind of "God" is it? That's my question. I think your answer would generally be, "Yes, absolutely, this otherness is a presence that one can pray to and meditate with." And my more personal question is whether you are inclined to pray like this.

RK: Well, yes and yes. I do believe in such a presence, and it is what I call the power of the powerless. It is something "out there" (beyond imaginary projections or linguistic tropes)—it is something sacred, someone sacred that one can pray to and that I do pray to. So that is the short answer. And the longer answer is that I get weary of philosophies of religion that are just intellectual games. (I am not accusing Eagleton of this, but there is a certain postmodern play with divine-sounding signifiers that exhausts and frustrates me). I agree with Marcus Aurelius (and Wittgenstein) that philosophy is therapy—healing, caring, responding to pain and anxiety, seeking justice and goodness—and that if it is not, then it's a waste of time. It's just a game with ideas and bashing one argument against the other. So for me, it either does good—by doing the truth—or it doesn't. And it is known by its witness, its fruits, and its stories that transfigure our lives. "Wisdom is vindicated by her children (Luke 7:35)." And might I add that this witness is not just a matter of ethics; it is also poetics. A poetics of presence that involves prayer. At least prayer understood in Simone Weil's beautiful phrase about prayer being the absolute attention of the soul. So for me, the poetry of Dante, Herbert, Blake, and Hopkins is as real a form of prayer as the caring actions of St. Francis, or Teresa of Calcutta.

JW: You have some lovely stuff on "sacramental poetics" in *Anatheism*, where you write about Joyce and Woolf.

RK: In most of my writings on religion, I try to engage this crucial relationship between poetics and ethics. Poetics is very important because it embraces the splendour and pungency (to use one of your favorite words) of flesh. I believe this is a central aspect of the sacred often ignored in contemporary religion, which tends to observe a puritanical apartheid between sacred and profane, even in Christianity, which is supposed to be based on the radical incarnation of *logos* as *sarx*. This poetics of sacred carnality is, I believe, indispensable—word made flesh. Kenosis descending from the highest to the lowest. So the miracle of the impossible can happen in the flesh—not just the spirit. The good that commands and calls does not come from some Platonic otherworld, some transcendental form, but from our lived ordinary universe. Beauty—or pungency—is the extraordinary in the ordinary, the more in the less, transcendence in immanence, otherness in everyday "thisness" (Hopkins's riff on Duns Scotus's *haecceitas*). Poetics responds to the sacred that shines and seduces through the flesh. It's a form of sacred seduction, and thus poetics is essential for ethics. Otherwise, it becomes cheerless moralism. *Miserabelisme*, or as Nietzsche said, cruelty. So the good is beautiful—Socrates was right about this—and it incites desire. *Agathon* ignites *eros*. It's not a matter of saying: "I must do the good thing by going against my nature which is wicked and fallen." And here I strongly disagree with Levinas, echoing Pascal, when he says that *le moi est haissable*—that ethics is unnatural. There is no room for an aesthetics of holy desire in Levinas—not to mention a divine pungency or sacred imagination. His ethics of the other does not allow for a poetics that mobilizes desire and imagination, that appeals to the good in our nature, the word in our flesh, the stranger within us as well as without. There are no icons in the Levinasian universe, no Bach or Blake, no Raphael or Rilke. Just the accusing and persecuting call of the other.

JW: So to come back to prayer, are you saying prayer is connected to a poetics of presence?

RK: I am saying that when I pray, I pray to something *there*. You cannot pray to Derrida's or Levinas's Other because it is not there. The Levinasian face of the Other has no color in its eyes, no redness in its lips, no saliva in its mouth, no smell, no *pungency*. It is placeless, timeless, sexless. A quasi-transcendental placeholder. So disincarnate it only has a voice, a summons, but no fingers, hands, or feet. It does not touch us and is not touchable. The anatheist stranger, by contrast, is radically embodied and appears to us in concrete historical, spatio-temporal contexts, even if its holiness exceeds these multiple incarnations and epiphanies, as something supra-human breaks through its humanity. It is *there*. But where I do agree with Levinas (and Derrida after him) is that the other is not just my projection or alter-ego; it is someone who comes to me from beyond me even though it may also surprise me from within. But either way—whether it comes from without or within—it is more than me; it transcends me. That's why it is more than humanism—why it is the more-than-humanism that keeps humanism human in a way by never allowing it to close up in itself.

JW: So, in terms of names, who do you pray to?

RK: My mother first taught me how to pray. I am sure I share that with many. So as a child, I prayed—like most Catholic children of in the 1950s in Ireland—to Mary, to Jesus as her son (more than as Messiah), and to the saints. There was a saint for everything: St. Anthony, for lost things; St. Christopher, for journeys; St. Francis, for compassion; St. Jude, for hopeless cases; St. Blaise, for sore throats and illness; St. Martin de Porres (the Peruvian slave), for fairness and justice (one of my younger brothers was named after him); St. Teresa the Little Flower, for little things. There was someone for everything—even tying your shoelaces. A sort of hallowing of the ordinary universe with someone always there to talk with. It was like I grew up with the communion of saints, and I still find myself praying to holy people rather than to gods, as such. I didn't pray much to God the Father growing up, though that changed a bit when I heard Jean Vanier speak about the prodigal father and son as depicted in Rembrandt's extraordinary painting. One more example of poetics bringing religion back to life. Shortly before my mother died of melanoma some years ago, she said she would like an interreligious funeral service. She herself was a Eucharistic minister toward the end of her life and very active in the local parish. Nothing like this had ever been seen in the village church in West Cork. And when the day came, my bother Philip, a priest who works with Vanier's *L'arche* communities, said a mass, and my different brothers and sisters and nephews and nieces said different prayers from the Buddhist or Vedentin traditions. It was really very moving and in keeping with my mother's belief that, in her own words, while "Jesus and Mary were her people, there were other people for other people." No hint of exclusivist superiority of her holy ones over other traditions and paths. No trace of supercessionism—other religions have little bits of truth but mine is the one with the "whole" truth. There was never any "My God is greater than your God" kind of talk. There are many mansions of faith and many rooms in each of those mansions and those rooms are populated with many names.

JW: Do you use any special names when you pray?

RK: I do, in fact. When I am in West Cork in the summers, for example, I pray a lot to St. Brigid. Our house is located just opposite of Bridget's Island, and there's a holy well there which was a place of pilgrimage for centuries. She was called *Muire na Gael* (Mary of the Gaels), because local Irish people revered her as much as—if not more than—Mary, the Mother of Jesus. I pray to the local saints, Brigid and Finbar and Fachna. And I pray to Benedict when I return to Glenstal Abbey where I was educated—a Benedictine Monastery. And I pray to St. John when I am with Jean Vanier, as he has a special devotion and understanding of his special mission and grace. And I pray to Teresa of Lisieux when I am with my French wife and family in Normandy and St. James when I am doing my annual pilgrimage on *le chemin de saint Jacques de Compostelle*. There are not many saints in Boston, mind you; but my local churches are St. Ignatius and St. Bernard's—so they do quite well. And I have to admit that I have a special devotion to Mary, the Mother of Jesus, and Mary Magdalene, because my mother was a marvellous mix of both—in a totally unpretentious natural way. I loved her dearly. I should add that when I visit a Hindu temple like Aranachula in India or the Buddhist White Monastery in Kathmandu, I pray to their saints and holy ones too: to Ramana, to Choqui Nyma. Not in some "spiritual tourist" way, but seriously, deeply, respectfully. It's not squishy or opportunist. It's not New Age consumerism. I mean it. But while I believe in the equality of all holy names—as pointers and prayers to the sacred—I do not believe they are all the same. They are neither the same in themselves or in me. On the contrary: Buddha, Shiva, Isaiah, Jesus—they are all radically distinct and unique. My own special choice of names is distinctive, accordingly. This is your question, right? It is deeply Christian, as the above list indicates. Why? For the simple reason that Christianity is the religion I grew up in, the holy narrative (with all its unholy betrayals and misreadings) that I learned to love and respect from my genuinely devout family (both parents and siblings), my wonderful Benedictine and Jesuit teachers and, later on in life, my incredibly impressive Christian friends (most recently here in Boston, people like Fanny Howe, Sheila Gallagher, Mary Anderson, Bill Richardson, and the list goes on). It is actually quite important for me to name them as they are for me secular-sacred saints in their respective unique ways. But perhaps I am getting too personal now.... The point I am trying to make is that the saints who matter are the ones under your nose in space and in time. Apart from praying to saints in their special incarnation or dwelling place, I also like to pray to the saints on their feast days. There is one a day in the Catholic calendar. I believe in the community of saints in a very incarnate way—a bit like the way Thich Nhat Hahn and the Mahayana Tibetan Buddhists speak of the Boddhisatvas. They are all around us. If you can't smell God, it is not a divinity worth its salt. Saints are the salt and smell of God. Without them, there is no God to speak of. God is dead. And as Nietzsche's madman rightly says—announcing God's death in the *Gay Science*—"Gods too decompose, you know."

V

JW: I'm interested in the Cambridge theologian, Denys Turner, who is a theist really, and is very interested in Meister Eckhart.

RK: As am I.

JW: In his book *Faith, Reason and the Existence of God*, Turner ultimately argues that although Eckhart is obviously a kind of mystical deconstructionist, there's actually a sort of orthodox set of beliefs underpinning that negative mysticism. I guess this is what makes Derrida a little suspicious of such mysticism.

RK: It's atheism in drag.

JW: Right. The last chapter of Turner's book circles around the "ultimate question": "why is there anything?" Turner imagines an exasperated atheist saying to him (I paraphrase): "It is all very well, you embarking on a project in which you re-educate me in what I'm supposed to deny. But if you, the theist, won't affirm anything comprehensible at all, then why would the atheist need to do any denying in the first place since you theologians have already done all the denying there is to be done? Does not your so-called negative theology amount to little more than a strategy of evasion, which kills God off with the death of a thousand qualifications?" Turner admits that this objection has some force and he tries to reply to such an atheist with a kind of bedrock definition of what he, Denys Turner, does believe. He writes, and here I am quoting from Turner:

> As an atheist response to the theist, this line of attack though promising is not yet quite fair. There is something which the theist affirms—asking the

question 'Why anything?' just is its affirmation—but it is something affirmed about the world, namely that the world is created. That, as we have observed Thomas to think, is our starting point for talking about God, and so long as we remain resolutely anchored in the implication of that starting point—that in speaking thus about the world the theist is always speaking about the ultimately ungraspable, that we do not know what God is—the theist can feel justified in all manner of talk about God, and can safely and consistently allow that everything true of creation, everything about being human, is in some sort grounds for a truth about God. For in saying that what the theist affirms is something 'about the world' we are not denying that the theist is talking about God: saying that the world is created is, on the contrary, how to talk about God. The negative theologian still has plenty to say about God, more than enough for the atheists to get their denying teeth into. Negative theology does not mean we are short of things to say about God, it means just that everything we say about God falls short of him.[8]

Now, in many ways, that is clearly different from your position because that seems to me to be a fairly orthodox negative theism. But it interests me because Turner offers a bedrock, and I suppose it's not necessarily your bedrock. Turner's bedrock is the creator: to talk about "God" is to affirm that the world was created. It's precisely this bedrock that I find difficult to affirm, and it's why I don't call myself a believer because I do think, with Turner, that if there is an extra-linguistic presence that means anything (a power worthy of worship, love, or fear), then such a force or power must be a creator. Yet unfortunately, such a concept takes me back to theodicy, and I can't stand the implications of theodicy (i.e., the cruel, indifferent, or weak creator-God). Is your extra-linguistic presence such a creator, and if so, can you see a way out of what I was just talking about—the theodicy problem?

RK: Wow. That is the best "last" question I've ever been asked. A lot to be thought and said. But let me just jump in and move around in no particular order. The bedrock, yes. I do believe there is a bedrock, but it is not a given bedrock. It is a giving bedrock. In other words, if creation is a story of theodicy, then I'm 100 percent with you: out, out with God. I'm an out-and-out atheist. Anatheism means reinterpreting the notion of creation—as a metaphor but also as something more than a metaphor. It is, of course, a metaphor for what I call "giving" (what Heidegger, in *Being and Time*, called "*Es gibt*": the giving of being and time); and this metaphoricity, of course, entails imagination and narrative (as I have tried to show in much of my early work on these subjects). But I would want to claim that is also more than just a figure of speech, an anthropomorphic projection of our human creative powers onto some higher Being (as Feuerbach, Marx, and Freud so brilliantly described). The reason we have to speak of creation as metaphor, in my view of things, is that we can't jump outside of language to get at that thing, whatever that thing is, whatever "it," to use Virginia Woolf's language, is. We use language, so we are constantly reinterpreting what language is trying to say and to depict its figural attempts at trying (always impossibly) to say what can only properly be "shown" (as Wittgenstein realised in the *Tractatus*, when he said that the mystical can be shown but not said). For me, these reinterpretations of "it" in metaphors and stories of creation are not to be taken literally, but figuratively. And yet not "just" as fictionally (qua illusions) but anatheistically—as making certain hermeneutic claims to something "real." To say that life is creation is to speak metaphorically in that it is saying that life both is creation (the gift of a giver) and is not (literally) creation, as creationsits or theodicists wrongly claim. For me, theodicy is a form of idolatry by refusing this second aspect of the "is not." It takes—I would say mistakes—God's power as that literally of a king, sovereign, emperor of the universe (and so Hitchens, Dawkins, Marx, etc., are perfectly correct in rejecting it). But the power of theodicy, that remains human freedom and creativity, is not, for me, the true power of divine creation—which is the power of the powerless, "possibilisation," the god-who-may-be (which is how I translate Exodus 3:1, following Cusanus notion of *posse* and Rashi's notion of the "one who will be"). No caps allowed. So I say an unequivocal no to the creator God of theodicy. And then we can ask, we are free to ask, if there is some sense in the stories of "creation" in the great wisdom traditions (it is not just the Abrahamic tradition—even Plato has a creation story in his *Timaeus*), which can be read in terms of hospitality—that is as an offer to enter the world and history as a calling to peace, justice, and flourishing. And to ask if this alternative (anatheist, posttheodicy) reading can be shared with others who hail from the great wisdom traditions, and even many who don't but still have a sense that there is something potentially "gracious"—and not just fortuitous—about life. Something holy in the habitual, something to be hallowed as sacred even in the very lowest and least of things—a shared or shareable story of life as a gifting. Even Nietzsche recognizes, after his timely declaration of the death of God, that if someone gives you something, you receive it; you do not ask who gives. There is a mystery that life surprises us with, beyond our planning and control and autonomy, beyond the mere calculative economy of give and take, credit and debit, mercantile trade and reciprocity—some meaning in and through things that is greater than what we merely put into things. A meaning is revealed to us in life in addition to the meaning we project or interpolate onto life. I read creation accordingly not as an imposed theodicy of necessary causality but as a "*petit miracle*" of hospitality—the marvel of the impossible becoming possible when the strangeness of the stranger surprises us. The strangeness of what Heidegger and Freud called—in different but fascinatingly complementary ways—"the uncanny" [*das Unheimliche*]. So for me, "the mystery of creation" is not something you believe—as if it was a proposition of logic, evidence, argument, causality going all the way back to some supreme superintendent cause that would explain everything. It is not a matter of belief, but of faith—faith that there is some meaning in the impossible giving and receiving of a gift. Faith as trusting. *Fidens* as *confidens*. And the *con-* implies another, a cocreator, a stranger who is not oneself. It is a wager based on incalculable, noncomputable odds. That's why it is a risk. The risk of hospitality. That the impossible becomes possible with the creation of the new, the hitherto unthinkable and unimaginable. A matter of faith rather than belief or knowledge.

JW: So just to jump in for a second, because I don't want to disturb your flow–would it be fair to use the phrase, not just of hospitality, "the miracle of hospitality," but also of creation—"the miracle of creation"?

RK: Yes, the miracle of creation, if that means the miracle of the gift, that there is a giving that is not a given—something taken for granted. Do you know what I mean? Creation can never be a given. As soon as it is considered so, it becomes an idol: a fact, a piece of evidence, *quod erat demonstrandum*. And we are back to theodicy: creation happened and everything is predetermined and preordained. That idea is as abhorrent to me as it is to you. But that is not how I would read the idea of creation. I prefer the radical (quasi-heretical) idea of mystics like Meister Eckhart, who says that creation is an endless gifting and birthing in every moment of existence as it surges and bubbles (*ebulutio*) up from nothing into something. So when he says, "I pray to God to rid me of God," what he means is that there's a letting go of the God of theodicy in order that the God of natality can be born: a moment of conaissance, of cocreation where the human and divine, the secular and sacred, give birth to and through each other. It's startling and beautiful. For an anatheist appreciation of sacred beginning, in each moment, there must be an evacuation of the old God—the knowable, familiar alpha-God of causal creation, omnipotence, and theodicy. Adieu, bye-bye to that God. So then, out of that evacuated space, out of what Eckhart calls the empty bowl, the vacant (a-theist) womb, a new divinity can give birth to itself through us, can begin again out of nothing, its nothing, our nothing. The God after God gives birth to itself through the void. But apophasis and negative theology are not the last word, though they are indispensable. There is also, for me at least, the affirmative possibility of a God who-may-be, being reborn through us. And here I would want to interpret the notion of the empty womb, the void, the nothing as the *khora*, which is what Plato calls (in the *Timaeus*) the origin before the origin, and that Christianity reinterprets as the womb of Sarah and of Mary. Let's go back to the beginning, at least in the Abrahamic story. We have the image of the bowl that Abraham offers to the three strangers who appear out of the desert in Mamre. He gives them a bowl of food and water, and in so doing, a scene of potential hostility (they are *hostes* as ostensible enemies) becomes one of hospitality (they become *hostes* as divine guests). But it is Abraham and Sarah's faith that makes this miracle possible, that the bowl might become full with food just as Sarah's own womb (until then, barren, empty) can become full with child. The impossible becomes possible. Sarah laughs (which is what you do when faced with the impossible if you don't despair or shoot yourself). And a child, a new beginning, an impossible birth, happens. Isaac (meaning laughter) is born. In the annunciation, in the Abraham story, there is this openness. So it's a second creation, if you will. The Christian annunciation repeats this scene of Abrahamic creation/birthing/gifting/hospitality/faith (they are all one). A womb that cannot have a child has a child. The impossible becomes possible (*adunaton* becomes *dunatoni* as the angel-stranger says to Mary in Nazareth in Luke), but these impossible birthings from nothing are going on all the time. For creation thus understood is not about one big omnipotent bang at the beginning of time, which fixes things once and for all for the rest of time, but rather a series of endless multiple rebirthings. I'm very Eckhartian in that sense. It's happening all the time. In every moment. If we allow it to happen, whether we call it "God" or not. And what we chose to call it is obviously a matter of language—a matter of what special images and stories we have to describe it. Because we don't have facts. We don't have evidence or proofs. It is not verifiable or falsifiable. It is not about knowledge, but faith. Faith in a story, but a story you can choose to believe is true, in the sense of *troth*, something you trust, espouse as your spouse, betroth as your betrothed, love as your lover. It's all in the Song of Songs. The only God worth its salt is the God of the Shulammite woman.

JW: But is there something beyond the language, a reality beyond the stories?

RK: For me—for anatheism as I understand it—yes, there is. And that is why it is not just fiction, though it relies on and presupposes fiction. One cannot bypass narrative and metaphor on the way to the sacred. But the sacred is something more than the stories we tell about it. As in the old Buddhist example, they are fingers pointing to something beyond the hand itself.

I have faith that sacred narratives—the scriptures, the lives of saints, the testimonies of holy people (and they are everywhere to be found)—refer us to something other than ourselves, bigger than ourselves, more loving than ourselves. This could be read as purely pragmatic at one level: let people believe this if it makes them do good. But I happen to think it is more than pragmatism. I believe it and am prepared to pray to that other in others.

JM: Could you say more about the notion of *khora*?

RK: Yes. Let me return to the Christian narrative here, since it is the one I know best. (Derrida and Caputo will explore the mystical potentials of the Greek Platonic *khora* for example—and I have had critical exchanges with them both on this in *Strangers, Gods and Monsters*). Mary, in the annunciation scene and afterward, is described in Greek Orthodox liturgy as the *khora* of the *akhoraton*. She is the figure of the womb, the bowl, the empty space through which the divine, the littlest of things, the lowest of the low can be born. And the visitation of the three kings from afar echoes the three Abrahamic strangers in the Biblical imagination. It's all part of what Northrop Frye and Paul Ricoeur call a "great code" of figurations—prefigurative, configurative, refigurative. A yes that goes from the first chapter of Genesis through the stories of Sarah and Mary to the reveries of Molly Bloom. (Think of Bloom recalling Molly's "yes" at the end of *Ulysses*. Coiled up in bed beside Molly, he is described as "man-child weary, child-man in the womb," signalling the possibility of rebirth through Molly's "yes" of desire, of affirmation through new life). And in addition to literature (sacred and secular), there is also visual art; and I think particularly here of the Greek Orthodox images of the *perichoresis*. Take Andrei Rublev's icon of the three persons, the canonical image of the Trinity in Eastern Christianity. *Perichoresis* is the image of three strangers moving in an endlessly open circle. This is not some static, omnipotent, fully accomplished God at the end of history. It is the image of the eschaton—the last of things—as three people moving around an empty bowl: Mary's womb as the *khora akhoraton* (which means the "container of the uncontainable"). So Mary's *khora*—at the heart of the *peri-khora*—is imagined as the core of an uncontainable divinity, newness, strangeness, moreness. This womb is the empty, ever-renewable open (to cite Rilke) at the heart of the Godhead, the a-theist space that makes anatheism possible. So when Levinas says atheism is Judaism's best gift to humanity, he means the carving open of this space. And in the eschatological imagination, it is this space, this *u-topos*, which keeps the three *topai* moving in a circle, a circle in which each of the figures plays host and guest in turn, saying to the other "After you, after you, after you." And in this dance (*khora* also has the sense of *khorein* as in a Greek chorus) we rediscover the double ana-theist movement of a-dieu, as each person leaves its place for the other and takes the place left to it by its other. We find this twofold movement of departing (*ab*) and approaching (*ad*), of leaving and arriving, of transcending and incarnating, beautifully captured in the Latin translation of *perichoresis* as *circumin-cessio*—which can be spelled with a *c* meaning *cedo*, to cede one's space or with an *s* meaning *sedo*, to occupy or receives one's space. That, for me, is why I believe in the poetics of the sacred—narrative, imagination, metaphor, icon. I think if you stop creatively rethinking and renaming the words and the concepts of the divine it dies. The *perichoresis* goes on and on.

JW: It sounds as if your response to Denys Turner might be, "Yes, I do believe in a creator God, but the creator God I believe in is rather different than your creator God. You seem to believe, Professor Turner"—forgive me if I am putting words in your mouth—"in a creator God who is pretty much the founder of the world, the spark of the world, who providentially in some way manages the world, even though you can't speak about it. Whereas my God, my creator God, is, as I see it, an endless gifting." Would that be fair?

RK: That would be fair. Since the sacred story I personally hold by—the Abrahamic narrative—does speak of a God of genesis in its opening chapter, it would be a stretch for me to shed that right off; but how I reinterpret it is an endless gifting (beyond the merely given). I would want to speak of the radical importance of the seventh day of this on-going genesis of word into flesh. The Sabbath is crucial because it is the day when nothing happens. When God stops and we start. When the divine withdraws (*zimzum*) and we take on the promissory work of cocreation. The seventh day, though it seems to come at the end, is actually there from the beginning as the gap in God. It is the time of *kairos* and the space of *khora*. And here I return to the empty bowl at the heart of the trinity, the free zone at the centre of the Godhead. The call to make the impossible possible and the possible actual. If you get rid of this space of loving cocreation you have theodicy. You lose God as the one who *may be*, who *can be*, if and only if one responds to the call of the stranger. One no longer hears the cry in the street. "What is God? A cry in the street" (*Ulysses*).

JW: That's beautiful.

RK: Because that's the cry of powerlessness. But it is also—I would add—Molly's cry of "yes." So it's a cry that solicits the food of life—"Give me bread"—and it's also the cry of love.

VI

JW: When, if ever, you think about this inconceivable beginning of time, the big bang—something that physicists themselves don't know that much about—do you, can you, envisage, imagine, your creator God, your "extra-linguistic presence" present at this big bang? Can you imagine your extra-linguistic force there? Right there at the beginning, right there—not just beyond language, but *before* language?

RK: I must confess, it is not the kind of question I ever ask. Physics and metaphysics are two languages of causality that I do not apply to the question of the sacred. To think of divine creation as causality—the first, supreme, final cause, or the *ens causa sui*—is already theodicy in my view. I utterly respect the thinking of science and physics but am not comfortable, personally, with trying to explain "God" in those terms. I think it is perhaps a case of what certain analytic philosophers, following Gilbert Ryle, would call a category mistake. I'm not competent to go there, and I don't. So let me come at it from another angle, from the claim that in the beginning was the word. There are two things about this: in the beginning was the word, and the word was the promise and desire of flesh. History—human history, cosmic history—can then be viewed as a beginning that never ends, as a constant rebeginning, an endless remaking and rebirthing of word as flesh. But for anatheism, the word is first and foremost a cry. So we could reformulate Scripture as saying—in the beginning was the cry. The double cry of "yes" and "Where are you?" The first is a cry of love and desire, the second is a cry in the dark, a cry in the street, a cry in absence and pain and in separation and loss that says, "Where are you?" Both are repeated as the cry of the child at birth. So one is summoned into existence by a call that asks us "to be." To be there for the other. To show up as the other shows up. We're called "to be" by a cry for existence. So God *is not*, God *may be* if we respond to the cry and make God (as call, promise, hope, and desire) incarnate by bringing it into the flesh. Now, I know I am going back in language when I speak of the cry and the word made flesh, but I also intend this as testimony to what happens in the street. Everyday voices, gestures, and solicitations, as when someone phones up and says they need help with a paper or problem, the cry is ordinary. The word and the flesh are that quotidian (which is why I am very reluctant to capitalize them). Quite a number of contemporary philosophers are returning to the realist and causalist metaphysics of Aquinas—McIntyre, Eagleton, and, it seems, Turner too, from what you are saying. But while I have huge respect for the brilliant synthetizing author of the *Summa Theologiae*—that is not my path, and his proofs for the existence of God are not my proofs. I don't have any; I don't believe in a God that can be proved, in a God of whom one says, "I believe that God exists." Faith is not *believing that* but *believing in*, as I said previously. In contrast to the metaphysical notion of God as first cause of the universe, as pure act without possibility (*actus purus non habens aliquid de potentialitate*), anatheism wagers on an alternative notion of God as what may be—as *posse* rather than *esse ipsum subsistens*. My first book, *Poetique du Possible*, ends with the statement "Dieu n'est pas mais peut être." And this *God of May-be*, this sacred *Perhaps*, is not an invention of mine. It goes right back to a radical messianic reading of Exodus 3:15 through Nicolaus Cusanus's notion of *possest* right up to contemporary notions of sacred possibility (Etty Hillesum, Franz Rosenzweig, and Ernst Bloch). It is a counter tradition, if you will, often linked with a certain mystical anarchist current sometimes dismissed as atheist, as Leibniz and Derrida rightly acknowledged, or a subtradition, the God beneath rather than beyond. The more in the less. When Cusanus (the brilliant fifteenth-century Christian thinker) tried to describe this mysterious *possest* he compared it to the fragile voice of a child in the street. We are back to Joyce.

JW: And back to the first cry of creation.

RK: Yes. And that is the *perichoresis*—which is, of course, itself a poetic image expressed in an icon. I would say that the cry of creation—the cry of the beginning and the end—comes from the middle of the *khora*, what I call the "fourth dimension" of the sacred. In the metaphor of the trinity, there are three persons, and then the fourth dimension is the khora. That's also the neglected and repressed feminine dimension. It is the dimension of history, desire, birth, time, space, and finitude, which most orthodox causalist metaphysics expel from the patriarchal plenitude and purity of the deity. It's what Derrida calls "phallogocentrism." The cry of khora is a fourth forgotten dimension which challenges the perfectly self-contained, self-sufficient, omnipotence of the supreme being. So, to return to the relationship of all this to physics, I should mention that I recently had occasion to ask a great astrophysicist at Harvard, Leon Golub, about the fourth dimension. And he went away and thought about it—he's very careful, he doesn't spin into metaphors and narratives like me. He's a very thoughtful atheist fascinated by these questions—which to me is far better than a theist who isn't fascinated. He sent me some wonderful notes on the ways of thinking about a fourth dimension in physics and mathematics. I was delighted. I realized I'm not just alone with my metaphors; there may be something out there physically. A dialogue might be possible at some level between metaphor and matter.

VII

JW: That's a very nice line. I'm going to have to quote you on that. I have a question of the gossipy kind. I would assume, given all that we've discussed and what I know of your belief, your faith, and your work, that it doesn't bother you at all that our mutual friend, the artist Sheila Gallagher, who is a committed Catholic believer, probably thinks you're more of a believer in her terms than you actually are. And that I might say to Sheila at a dinner party, "Well, I think Richard is actually much more of an atheist than he would like to admit." This contradiction doesn't bother you?

RK: No. On the contrary. It means I may be getting something right. I'd be worried if that conversation didn't happen. I do like differences; the fact that when we have our exchanges about God—at BC, at Harvard, here—it is a real dialogue in the original meaning of *dia-legein*, welcoming the difference, a respectful, creative difference. I have that in a special way with Sheila too. If you are my favorite atheist anatheist, she is my favorite theist anatheist. Anatheism can handle both. As long as these dialogues continue—at the level of personal and intellectual friendship and witness—I realize, once more, I am not totally on my own with figures and tropes. I am bound again, reconnected, *re-ligare*, to a community of minds, bodies and souls. And that brings me back to the communion of saints. Which for me is not about saints in heaven but concrete people on earth.

JW: How would a Derridean thinker like Caputo react to all this? I presume he would pounce on your mention of a presence that is something more, something extra-linguistic.

RK: Yes, I suspect he would. And even within my use of language, he might take issue with my frequent recourse to narratives. For a deconstructionist, that would be too hermeneutic. Too much deferring and referring to traditions, memories, communities, to a whole legacy of previous interpretations. He'd be suspicious of that because he's deeply committed—and I totally respect this. His Derridean position that you're alone in the desert (like the anchorites) and on top of the mountain (like Kierkegaard's and Derrida's Abraham). It's not just narrative imagination and tradition; even metaphors are suspect because, as the etymology indicates, they are transferring meaning, transiting and transferring from one meaning to another. In contrast to such hermeneutic mooring, bridging, translating, deconstruction claims (as I read it) that you should be alone, inconsolable, and disconsolate before the radical absence of meaning. You should stay with the dark sonnets, with the dark night of the soul, and not move beyond them. I fully acknowledge the mystical annihilation of self, the total abyss of loss, but with John of the Cross and Hopkins, I also want to take the second step, though I fully respect those who don't. It's a brave choice. Uncompromisingly lucid and honest.

JW: And if you're a solitary in the desert is there, for you, still someone else there?

RK: There's an other, an otherness—yes.

JW: I am thinking of what Caputo said to you in your Harvard dialogue in 2011. He said something like: "I go to colleges all around America and people come to me and say, 'My life really changed because I took Jesus Christ as my Savior and I really believe in God as creator and redeemer,' and what do you have to say to them?" For me, that question is always the pressing one. And I am always coming back to that. We've just explored this whole question, but for Derrida and the deconstructionists, is there something else?

RK: There's an alterity out there that is coming at you. But it's utterly anonymous, it's utterly uncaring. As Derrida says, it does not care, it's not love, it's not grace; it's something fortuitous that confounds and interrupts. It's not humanism, it's not messianism. It is a structural messianicity: of pure event, without messianism—that is, without face, flesh, content. It's khora without the persons.

JW: Is it this antihumanism which differentiates Derrida from Levinas?

RK: The difference between Derrida and Levinas is complex. I am close to Levinas in holding that the face of the stranger is the trace of transcendence, but I part company with his exclusively Abrahamic-Judaic reading of transcendence. He is radically anti-incarnational and has no real dialogue with Islam, not to mention with what he refers to as "paganism"—Buddhism, Hinduism, Toaism and other non-Abrahamic spiritualties. Religions outside Judaism are basically forms of idolatry. There is only one true form of transcendence: the *Tout Autre* of divine creation understood as radical separation from nature, immanence, history, imagination. This total other is contaminated and betrayed in incarnation. There is no possibility of gracious translation or transition from sacred word to profane flesh. That's where he stops short of anatheism, though his adherence to an anti-idolatrous atheism as crucial to Judaic ethics comes close at times.

JW: So if someone says to you, "My Lord and Savior has changed my life"?

RK: When I hear people speak like that, I try to listen and understand where they are coming from. My basic line would be—and this leads us back into hermeneutics—if your faith in what you call your "Lord" leads you to follow Martin Luther King or Etty Hillesum or Dorothy Day, I am with you. And if it leads on the opposite path of Rush Limbaugh or Rick Santorum, then I'm against you. These same words can be deeply enabling or profoundly disabling. They are neither black nor white. Anatheism reads between the lines and makes its wager. You shall know them by their fruits. It is ultimately a matter of tasting, eating, living. God is what we eat, or God is nothing at all.

JAMES WOOD is a staff writer at the *New Yorker* and Professor of the Practice of Literary Criticism at Harvard. His most recent book is *The Nearest Thing to Life*.

Notes

1. Merleau-Ponty quotes Claudel in *The Prose of the World*, 83–84: "God is not above but beneath us—meaning that we find him not as a supersensible model, which we must follow, but as another self in ourselves which dwells in and authenticates our darkness."
2. Arendt, *Men in Dark Times*, 97.
3. Cf. Kearney, "Eucharistic Imagination in Merleau-Ponty and James Joyce."
4. Rahner, "The One Christ," 219.
5. See Havel, *The Power of the Powerless*.
6. In his sonnet from 1889 "That Nature Is a Heraclitean Fire and of the Comfort of the Resurrection."
7. Wood, "God in the Quad: A Don Defends the Supreme Being from the New Atheists," *The New Yorker*, August 31, 2009.
8. Turner, *Faith, Reason, and the Existence of God*, 236.

2 A Conversation After God

Chris Doude van Troostwijk and
Richard Kearney

I

CDvT: Let's start with the fact that people sometimes misunderstand what you mean by *anatheism*. Anatheism, if I'm not wrong, is not so much a going back to "God" as it is the condition of possibility of a religious attitude, and thus the possibility of God. If so, could we characterize anatheism as some sort of "theory of religion" or a theory of the genesis of religion?

RK: I would say that anatheism is not just a theory but a wager. Or a faith before faith. There are many theories of religion, as you know—religion as an expression of ritual and social consensus (Durkheim); of periodic blood sacrifice (Girard); of wish-fulfilling projection onto a supernatural being (Feuerbach/Bloch/Marx); of compulsive pathologies of fear, illusion, power, and consolation (Freud and Nietzsche); and so on. These are all very interesting theories, but anatheism begins with the experience of a wager shared by all human beings from the beginning of time: the wager of hostility or hospitality when confronted by the stranger. Faced with an unknown other—guest, foreigner, refugee, adversary, the other without or within—we are all capable of responding with violence and mistrust or with openness and empathy. Human history is a story of murder and war; it is also a story of impossible hospitality, of acts committed by great people from Abraham, Jesus, and the Buddha down to contemporary figures like Mahatma Gandhi, MLK, John Hume, Etty Hillesum, and Nelson Mandela. And also, let us not forget, by lots of little people every day of the week, who perform what Proust calls "*les petits miracles*" of sympathetic imagination. These anatheist acts inform and motivate theories. But existence precedes speculation. Anatheism is *praxis* and *phronesis*—to use Aristotle's terms—before it is *theoria*.

CDvT: So there seem to be two ways of understanding the wager. One is anthropological—the human power to put another human being ahead of oneself. Another is more theological—involving a response to something more than human both in and through the human, a surplus of love that makes the impossible possible. You say that the encounter with the stranger is a universal human experience, but does it have to involve God *per se*? Could we not speak of it in purely humanist terms? That is James Woods's question to you: "Why bring in religion?" In the history of philosophy, the Enlightenment enabled us to rid ourselves of God. Then, with Levinas, we were introduced to talk of the stranger as the trace of God—the so-called "theological turn in phenomenology." Suddenly, God came back again.

RK: I agree. The anatheist wager can be interpreted anthropologically or theologically, humanistically or religiously, atheistically or theistically, or both. For some (like James Wood), it is an either-or (and he chooses the former). For me, it is a both-and. The wager is primarily about treating the stranger as friend or enemy (from the double term, *hostis*), not about believing or not believing in God. It is existential before it is propositional. In many wisdom traditions, "God" is the term used to describe the conversion of enemy to friend, of feared adversary to guest. "God" is a common name used by millions of people for millennia to denote the impossible move from hostility to hospitality. And there are, as we know, multiple names for God—and sometimes no names at all. Certain spiritual and mystical traditions share with humanism the option to refuse all names for God. As when Eckhart prays to God to rid him of God. They suggest abandoning all conceptual rights of the sacred so as to let the miracle happen. Eckhart calls it in a prayer *Abgeschiedenheit*: letting go to let be, letting mystery happen, letting come what promises to come. Anatheism is this radical alertness and attention to the call for transformation; and one could cite as a practical example here the twelve-step program that, in curing addiction, talks of a "higher power." Proust talks of "little miracles"; Joyce of "a cry in the street"; Woolf of a "match struck in the dark." The poets have great images when it comes to talking about the sacred (*sacer* has the same root as "secret," alluding to what is intimate and ultimate, an unnamable dimension of strange otherness). And we too often forget that some of the most holy scribes and sages were poets. Theology is very often a theopoetics, which forgets this fact. So the important thing, ultimately, is not the name as such. That is why anatheism proposes an open space and time before and after the binary division of theism versus atheism, beyond religious-secular wars and ideologies, in favor of an existential experience of the impossible becoming possible, of hostility being transformed into hospitality, of violence becoming peace. "Ana" signals a moment of grace, trust, and change, a metamorphosis where something strange happens—something given, not made, a receptivity to the stranger that comes out of the blue. But the moment is invariably modulated by spiritual wisdom traditions. Anatheism has a history, a genealogy, a tradition. It is a hermeneutics of memory as well as a phenomenology of experience. We make hermeneutic sense of the anatheist event as best we can. Some read it as a God moment, some do not.

II

CDvT: So anatheism is less a theory than an interpretative option or experience? But the *anthropos* takes part in experience; *theos*, by contrast, isn't an empirical fact.

RK: You're right. *Theos* is not a fact, but it is, as the Greek term reminds us, a certain way of seeing (*theaomai-theoro*) things, experiencing the divine in people and things that exist—a vision of divine movement. That is why the root verb *theo* can also mean "running," as Socrates suggests in the *Cratylus* (397d)—like a river or electrical current, a power of constant motion and transformation—contrary to the old metaphysical notion of God as an immutable changeless supreme being. John Scotus Eriugena picks up on this wonderful notion when he says that the one who sees is the one who runs through all beings. "When *theos* is drawn from the verb *theo*, it is rightly interpreted as signifying *the one who runs* (*currens recte intelligitur*). Because God runs across everything that exists and is never impeded, he fills all in his course, conforming to the verse of Scripture: 'His word runs with haste' (Ps. 147:15). Or again: 'If God is called the One who runs (*currens dicitur*), it is because he causes everything that exists to run from a stage of nonexistence to that of existence'."[1] In that sense, we could say that we run into God, and God runs into us. The sacred is therefore that which refers to the secret and the strange, the ineffable and unnamable stranger in our everyday midst. The one we run into when we least expect it. And sometimes even, the stranger in ourselves—as Kristeva and Freud describe our encounter with the "uncanny" other in our unconscious or as Augustine and the mystics describe our most unfathomable inner depths (more intimate than our most intimate selves: *interior intimo meo*). Gerard Manly Hopkins puts it well: "Oh the mind has mountains / sheer, frightful, no-man-fathomed / hold them cheap may / those who ne'er hung there."[2] He is referring to the sublime abyss within, where void calls to void as the Psalm reminds us: *abyssus abyssum avocat*. I agree with the contemporary Franciscan Richard Rohr when he says that the real distinction is not between the sacred and the profane, but the sacred and the desecrated, and we are the ones who do the desecrating; we are the ones who desacralize what is intrinsically sacred in all living beings. How? By refusing the call of the stranger to change what is, by resisting the summons to run from nothing (our self-enclosure) to something, from ourselves alone to someone or something other than ourselves that solicits love and change. The call of the stranger may be experienced as epiphany or trauma—two ways of registering the other—and it is often a mix of both. But the bottom line is that it bids us "change our lives" (like the artwork in Rilke's famous poem). This is part of our existential experience, but it is also part of our hermeneutic heritage—our available traditions of stories and revelations. If one looks at the history and culture of religions, one finds a special language and liturgy that advocates for this welcoming of the stranger. You find it in Abraham receiving the strangers at Mamre, Mary welcoming Gabriel, and Jesus and the Buddha welcoming the sick and the seeking. That is why it is so helpful to be inspired and informed by our great wisdom traditions. But we are, potentially, equally informed and inspired by the call of the stranger each day of our lives. The wager is constantly called for. That is why anatheism refuses to oppose our existential experience and the hermeneutic inheritance of our spiritual traditions.

CDvT: If we take seriously the psychoanalytical approach to trauma as a nonretrievable wound, it is not an *either-or.* In epiphany, something like a traumatic undertone continues to sound. Abraham never will forget the horrible day he was ready to kill his son, even if the story relates that God sent a ram as a substitute.

RK: You're right. And the story of Abraham and Isaac at Mount Moriah is a good example of how trauma (the temptation to murder his son) is but a whisker away from epiphany (the revelation that he must not murder his son, but rather replace the cult of blood sacrifice with the way of mercy and love). The call of God comes in the implied call of Isaac to his father: "do not kill me," and Abraham makes a genuine anatheist wager: he listens to the stranger/angel/other calling from the face of his son and abandons the old god of blood sacrifice. He runs from the old image of God to the new. Abraham opens himself to the God who comes, who runs toward him. God *after* God. Ana-theos. There is always someone or something that resists evil and bloodlust, that calls for something else—the sacred still to come.

CDvT: Is it a matter of choice and imagination, then?

RK: Both—a choice to be chosen by the call of love and justice, and imagination as a response to the call to create and recreate anew. Anatheism is not voluntarism or subjectivism. It is not just about "me"—but me (or us) faced with the stranger. Therefore it is radically interpersonal. I cannot respond to the call of the stranger without imagination and choice. The modalities of this response differ from one spiritual tradition to the next. The Judaic and Islamic religions, for example, tend to emphasize a transcendent God where words and scriptures—the Torah, Talmud, Koran, Haddith—are more important than plastic images, statues, paintings, liturgies (though there are exceptions—Sufism for instance). Christianity, Buddhism, and Hinduism are more on the side of the immanent, declaring certain persons and places sacred—teachers, saints, gurus, mountains, rivers, planets, and so on. But *stories*—works of narrative imagination—are central to all the wisdom traditions, transcendent and immanent. Think of the foundational role of sacred stories in the Abrahamic tradition: Genesis, Abraham meeting the strangers at Mamre, Jacob struggling with the angel, the healings and parables of Jesus, or in Buddhism, the Jakata stories and images of the wanderings of the Buddha in search of wisdom. It is only later that these sacred-spiritual narratives are institutionalized and codified into what we now know as "religions." And these religions often tend to close down the role of sacred imagination and narration into exclusivist rituals, credos, dogmas, and doctrines. In so doing, they provide a sense of religious identity and belonging for a particular group—which is compelling and important; but this is sometimes at the expense of interreligious curiosity and generosity—namely, interreligiousity. The spirit blows where it wills. It defies spiritual closure and self-certainty. Remember, the Greek for "sacred" is *mysterion*, meaning literally a blinding experience of verticality and strangeness bringing about a transformation of self, a questioning of identity. And when thus blinded by the sacred, our imaginations go to work. They turn the darkness into light.

CDvT: I noticed that you often use the terms "God" and "sacred" interchangeably. As a Protestant theologian, of course, this automatically sets off alarm bells in my head. God and the sacred are two different concepts.

RK: They are. I agree. But for me, the sacred is a more capacious and inclusive term. Buddhists, for example, can readily speak of persons or things being sacred, but they do not accept the idea of a transcendent God. You can say this person, this place, this time is sacred to me, and it doesn't necessarily posit a belief in a theist God. Lots of nontheists, humanists, and agnostics can say, "This is sacred to me" in the sense that it is irreplaceable or that there is some special value or mystery about it. Can one explain why? Not easily. There are reasons of the heart that reason does not understand. Different wisdom traditions provide rich treasuries of witness, art, and imagination concerning our experience of the sacred, and one can also access the sacred without a theist theology. One can experience the sacred without proceeding to an affirmation that God exists, without espousing a church of particular confessional beliefs and doctrines. Anatheism is a space that allows for both a theistic and an atheistic experience of the sacred stranger—and of the hospitality or hostility wager that arises from that. It acknowledges a sacred-spiritual moment before a leap of religious faith as such. A sort of faith before faith, if you like. Or a faith after faith. Derrida and Caputo refer, for example, to a messianic desire that precedes all propositional doctrines and opens us to some sense of the impossible, the gift, the perhaps, the event to come, the kingdom. One can choose to call the impossible by an atheistic name like "chora" (as Derrida says, he "rightly passes for an atheist") or by a theistic name like "God": defined, as I say in *The God Who May Be*, as the "possibility of the impossible"—the sacred possible beyond the impossible. Anatheism allows for both theist and atheist dispositions and fosters dialogue between them.

CDvT: So "God" comes after the experience of what is sacred for me or for you?

RK: Yes, if you chose to take the step from the sacred to God. The sacred is always concrete and contextual, singular and experienced in some way. We speak of *something* or *someone* sacred: a sacred time, a sacred place, a sacred person or stranger in relation to you or your community. Mecca is a sacred place for Muslims; Varanasi is a sacred place for Hindus. Even though these are not sacred places for me as a Christian, I can respect them as holy places for others. But this sense of multiple particular sacred places and persons invites me to interreligious compassion and dialogue, so the sacred doesn't have to be just "for me." I can recognize a sacred place for others, too, and go there with reverence.

CDvT: Should we also distinguish between the sacred and the spiritual?

RK: Yes, I think it is important to acknowledge the difference between the spiritual, the sacred, and the religious. The spiritual is everybody's search for something special, a *surplus* of meaning. And I am not sure I have ever met anyone not open to that. One can easily say that one is spiritual without implying a relationship to any particular sacred person or place or to any particular religion. Literature, poetry, art, yoga, and meditation are all spiritual practices. They can be individual spiritual choices without involving commitment to any shared sacred experience, tradition or religion. They are human experiences, acts, searchings. One can do yoga without being a Hindu and walk the Camino de Santiago without being a Christian. The sacred takes spiritual practices to a more incarnate, shared level of special times, places, stories, persons, and invariably involves some element of community, while religion, for its part, takes it all the way to codified doctrines, dogmas, rites, ceremonies, and beliefs. The three levels—spiritual, sacred, and religious—comprise a series of options one can take or leave (at least in our secular western democratic culture) and I am not setting up any claim to progression or regression from one level to the next. Personally, I am happy to embrace all three, but I equally respect others who chose one or another.

CDvT: You start with making choices and wagers.

RK: Yes, and in that sense, it is a human point of departure. But anatheism is not limited to the human. It is a human response to something more than human, in and through the human. Each sacred wager is centrifugal; it runs beyond the self. The sacred is something you want to run toward because it is other than you and solicits you in some way. And then the religious is a further option, if you wish to take it—that is, to commit to a particular shared set of doctrines, rites, and traditions. And finally, God, one could say, is above all religions as the name for the divine X-factor: the name for what cannot be named. And it is because God is an apophatic, unnamable in essence, that—paradoxically—one finds multiple different names for God in multiple different religions. Eloihm, Yawheh, Abba, Kyrios, Allah, and so forth, in the Abrahamic tradition and several hundred names in the Hindu scriptures. "The non-nameablility of the divine is its omni-namability," as Eckhart, according to Stanislas Breton, rightly says.[3] There are many names for God, and they all aim at something more than the name—the more in the less, the infinite in the finite, the radical grace of transformation, the possibility of impossible hospitality to the stranger.

III

CDvT: Jean-Luc Nancy, in a discussion with Jean-Luc Marion, articulates the question about God in terms of an exclamation, an address: "my God." And in that same text, he remarks that "God" is as much a *nom propre* as it is a *nom commun*, a noun.

RK: Yes, the intimate, personal "my God" is one of many names, and as soon as one says "my God" or "our God," one has already made the apophatic into the kataphatic—part of one's own experience of the sacred. Not just a name, but the experiential event of a name in one's own being (personal or communal).

CDvT: What then is "God"? A concept? An idea?

RK: God is a word, a name, an idea, but an empty one that we need to fill in and flesh out with images, narratives, liturgies, actions, and embodiments.

I mean, if I pray to X, that prayer means nothing to me. But if I say a prayer to Jesus, to Mary, to Saint Francis . . . I do not pray to some empty abstraction—I pray to someone. So God is always a crossing of the name of God into flesh, a running toward us as we run toward God. The name needs to constantly fill and empty itself again and again, God after God after God anatheistically. I think again of Eckhart: "I pray to God to rid me of God."

CDvT: But that is because you are a Catholic.

RK: But you Protestants pray to Jesus, don't you? And to the Father in heaven?

CDvT: I remember in my church, there was a discussion about that. Some said you can't pray directly to God, but only to Jesus. Which is, dogmatically speaking, nonsense. If you use the name of Jesus Christ, then you're already praying to a crossing of the name. In a sense, the godly Christ is the cross over the human name of Jesus. But the point for us is, I think, that you have to wager: theists may call to God or to one of his many other names; atheists refer to some other concept. But the wager is inescapable.

RK: I agree.

CDvT: Do I understand you rightly, then, when I say that for you, anatheism indicates the moment of hermeneutic decision: in what language are we going to articulate the experience with the stranger? Either chora or God? Either philosophy with Plato or theology with, let's say, Augustine? Chora is a notion of openness, purely formal, whereas "God" is loaded and has strong spiritual and religious connotations. When pondered carefully, the two concepts do not have equal weight.

RK: For theologians, yes, God is more loaded than chora. But theology comes after religion which comes after the sacred.

CDvT: Could we say "eschatology," in the sense that there is no original experience that is not oriented to some final horizon of interpretation?

RK: Yes, I think so. I often use the term "eschatology," which I have preferred to theology in previous works like *Poétique du Possible* (1984) and *The God Who May Be* (2001). Ricoeur uses eschatology in his conclusion to *Freud and Philosophy* to denote an ontological sense of the sacred—sacred understood as the surplus, the other, the strange: the beginning before the beginning and the end after the end. In this sense, he distinguishes an eschatology of the sacred from both an archeology of the unconscious (Freud) and a teleology of absolute consciousness (Hegel). The eschaton precedes and exceeds the Freudian *das Ding* and the Hegelian *telos*, while admitting a proper role for each of them, and their resultant disciplines—namely, psychoanalysis and dialectics.

CDvT: So anatheism denotes that which exceeds comprehension, while remaining the condition of the possibility of it. But is your eschatology the same as Paul's eschatological expectation? "For now we see only a reflection as in a mirror; then we shall see face to face. Now I know in part; then I shall know fully, even as I am fully known" (1 Cor. 13:12). It seems to me you are talking about something like an *ana-eschatology*, if you accept that neologism. A return to the moment of excess, both in the beginning and in the end?

RK: I like the term ana-eschatology. I see it, with Ricoeur, as transconfessional and therefore conducive to interfaith dialogue. The question "what is the eschaton?" can be answered in different ways. I am thinking again of Ricoeur's hermeneutic question: "*D'ou parlez-vous?*" My own personal hermeneutic answer is: I come from an Irish Catholic, pagan, Christian tradition, and my wager—my interpretation of the wager—is deeply informed and inflected by this. This existential-cultural framework affects my reading of spiritual, sacred, and religious experience. My atheist friend James Wood might say: "I read the same phenomena from a secular-humanist hermeneutic." And Derrida and Caputo chose to read it from a posthumanist messianic one. There are many ways of reading the eschaton.

CDvT: And Heidegger tried to get rid of Christian theology altogether.

RK: He tried to replace it with a new mythology inspired by Schelling, but I am not sure he ever fully succeeded. I think William Richardson is right about that. And here again I think we may find anatheism useful in challenging the old dogmatic distinction between theism and atheism. People were burned at the stake for such dogmatic disputes. Anatheism, by contrast, presents theism and atheism as variable and sometimes exchangeable options, as hermeneutic interpretations, but deeply heartfelt ones.

IV

CDvT: Take James Wood again. He says something like, "Look, I believe in opening my arms to the stranger, but I do not need God to do that; I do it as a human being."

RK: I tried to address this question in the postscript to *Anatheism*: "why is the wager of hospitality not just glorified humanism?" And my answer is, because the anatheist moment remains open, disposed, vigilant toward something more than human, which can call to us through the human (or nature)—a sort of in-finite which shines through and exceeds human finitude [*Dasein*]. In that sense, there is something posthumanistic in my reading. Nonetheless, the more-than-human in the human is a total vocation to become more human. As Chesterton says somewhere, when you die and go to heaven, God will not ask you why you were not more like him, but why you were not more like yourself. What I call the more-than-human in the human is the stranger in ourselves that goes beyond ourselves, the transcendent in the immanent, the possible-impossible in the actual. This posthumanism can either take the form of an *anatheist theism* (which, in recent debates in *Reimagining the Sacred* and elsewhere, I would identify with thinkers like Charles Taylor, Jean-Luc Marion, John Panteleimon Manoussakis, and Catherine Keller) or take the form of an *anatheist atheism* (Julia Kristeva, Jean-Luc Nancy, Giorgio Agamben, and Jacques Derrida).

CDvT: The traumatic moment of the encounter provokes the anatheistic wager in that it calls for inscription in already existing discourses. Levinas, like you, talked about the *infinity* of the other: at once articulated *in* finite discourses and resisting radically any reduction to finitude, therefore *infinite* (not finite).

RK: It provokes discourses about events—epiphanies or traumas—which come before or after our language. But we can only access them through our language, right? Even if it is a proto-linguistic language of the senses—what I call "carnal hermeneutics." I agree with Levinas that this primordial *sensibilité* involves some kind of "existential trauma": a primal *wound* as it were, but one that does not have to mortify and injure but can also be experienced, as Gregory of Nyssa put it, as a "beautiful wound." Or to play on the common root of wonder and wound—from the Germanic *wunde—a wonderful wound*. Such a wound, if the wisdom tradition narratives are to be believed, is first registered as fear and trembling since it is radically strange and unfamiliar. That is why the holy figures of scripture are "troubled" and even terrified by the encounter with the stranger—in whatever language you chose to name it: the *ger*, the *hospes*, the *xenos*, the *gast*. Abraham and Sarah, Jacob, Mary of Nazareth, the shepherds at Bethlehem—"Every angel is terrible," as Rilke says. And the first thing such angelic strangers say to their human recipients is, "Do not be afraid. Nothing is impossible to God." It's there from the time you are born—this traumatizing call and response. It's there from the very beginning. Your first cry is a response to a trauma that Levinas calls *le traumatism original*, and your last cry before death. From the moment we're born to the moment we die we're being addressed by a call; we're responding in one way or another—we are wagering, carnally or cognitively.

CDvT: But we can't suppose an active will power for an infant. Might we say that the wager is wagering in us?

RK: This is an interesting question. Can babies wager? Take some recent research in developmental psychology, indicating that since birth, we have two ways of responding to the world. One: you connect. Two: you disconnect. The "original trauma"—with a small *t*—of natal life is such that one either withdraws or makes a movement out of oneself, toward the other—who, of course, has also experienced trauma and has her own kind of call and response. We are always going back and forth between the movement toward and away from the other. This designates the precognitive carnal-natal options and vacillations of association or dissociation, which remain throughout one's lifetime. Laplance and Klein offer a fascinating psychoanalytic reading of the infant's different ways of fantasizing the breast, interpreting it symbolically rather than biologically—though, of course, the breast is both a source of nourishment, warmth, and milk, as well as of primal eros and thanatos projections.

CDvT: But surely at birth there is no "I," no self, nothing like a subject. Yet there is still the call and the response. The wager is not, in this case, an active decision. Kristeva quotes Winnicott in your interview with her: "Consciousness is not just cerebral. Consciousness is somatic."

RK: Winnicott is right. For the newborn, the existential wager is never, of course, a case of a cerebral choosing subject—à la Descartes or Sartre. It is a play of active-passive interfusion between two beings: mother and child. Kristeva calls this primary natal relation *reliance*, declaring it to be one of the most underestimated of all human relationships, and she reckons we ignore this primordial bond at our own peril, for it is deeply humanizing and formative. It is curious, but I have come to believe that birth is already baptism, the baptism of desire. I discuss this with Emmanuel Falque in another conversation in this volume. From the moment you are born, you desire something that you cannot have; you're suddenly exposed in your nakedness, in terror and fear, to this strange world—at once potentially hostile or hospitable. You respond.

V

CDvT: Richard Colledge wonders in his contribution whether the wager implies something like a Kierkegaardian leap, with the risk of voluntary and subject-bound fideism. But it seems that, for you, the wager is primarily not an active, subjective choice, but rather a bodily and relational event.

RK: Subjectivity is anachronistic here. We retrospectively project that onto the child. Anatheism never happens with one person. It is always between persons, always in relation, transfusion. And from the moment the child is born, she is already in relation—sensing, fearing, but also desiring—searching for connection and direction (the primary sense of *sens*). Then, as the child develops, she reiterates and accentuates the moments of attraction or retraction. Those initial wagers happen between two people—mother and child as host and guest. The first person you encounter is your host, and you are the guest.

CDvT: That implies that your host, at that moment, is determining your wager. *Après coup*. I am thinking of Lyotard's concept of *enchaînement*. The sheer *quod* of a phrase does not yet have a determined meaning; it all depends on the phrase that follows. Yes, the baby is a guest to the mother, but only if the mother accepts the child in hospitality. But the newborn could equally appear to be a *host* if the mother rejects her, for instance, in postnatal depression.

RK: It is a both-and situation, wavering between connection and disconnection. I remember Levinas telling me once that he'd been watching TV the previous night and had seen a doctor put his finger on the foot of a new born child. The foot moved backward and forward, and that very double-response of withdrawal and offering was, Levinas suggested, already a form of language, where the first wager begins. Contact or retract. Cry out or remain silent. Already we're sensing the world through our senses. That is where carnal hermeneutics originates. The first natal wager is *carnal*, not *epistemological*, which is why anatheism is not agnosticism. Agnosticism says, "I don't know" in epistemological terms. Anatheism is prior to questions of knowing and not knowing, but it is precognition before cognition, sentiment as presentiment. So that all cognition is, strictly speaking, always recognition, the working over and working through of sometime that has already been sensed. Once again, the double sense of "ana" as *pre-* and *re-*, before and after.

CDvT: Would you frame this original anatheistic wager as more proper to hermeneutics or to phenomenology? The carnal side I associate with the latter; the epistemological and religious with the former.

RK: I would say that hermeneutics goes all the way down and is therefore *already*, from the start, also a phenomenological experience. What I call carnal hermeneutics is phenomenology as proto-hermeneutics. When we're sensing, we're already *directing* our senses, like the French question "*dans quel sens*?" Do you go toward the other or retreat from the other? Sense means not just sensing a sensation, but rather looking for sense as meaning, a sense of direction, an orientation in the world with others, or finding your way in a strange new world.

CDvT: So the wager is about sensibility—about closing or opening? In fact, some sort of deep hermeneutics?

RK: Yes, a sort of primal phenomenological hermeneutics where you are prefiguring your world. You may be born in the desert, like Ismael, and all you can do is cry out and there is no one to rescue you. Abraham, your father, has cast you out. He doesn't hear you, won't hear you. Will someone else come to rescue you? Will anyone answer your cry: "Where are you?" The cry of a child is a wager in the sense that when it cries out, it prays, hopes, trusts, and believes somebody will come.

CDvT: Again, this wager is happening to you more than you are consciously responsible for it . . .

RK: Yes, it is happening to you, but you are also participating in what happens. As a day-old infant, you are, of course, not responsible for what happens to you, but you are responding. You're responding to trauma or love. Or both. And as soon as you're responding, you're already on a threshold, an in-between transitional space, an *entre-deux* between self and other, in however primitive and inchoative a sense.

CDvT: This recalls a proximity to William Desmond's metaxology (*metaxu*—between) as Richard Colledge suggests in his essay.

RK: I am very partial to my friend William's metaxology—the transitions and mediations between divine and human, the natural and metaphysical. That is also why I don't want to draw an unbridgeable dualist gap between the animal and the human, because we are responding as human animals—or "humanimals" as my colleague, Kalpana Sheshandri puts it. Again, this is something I develop in my dialogue with Falque. So when it comes to the question of anatheism, there is a metaxoglical moment when we respond to the call of the stranger, a reaction to the presence of the radically other. We don't translate that experience into theories or doctrines about theism or atheism until we go to school or church and learn about religion. But the wager is operative at birth—a sort of carnal *connaissance* as *co-naissance* (cobirthing) between two beings. Religion and theology are methods and codes for thematizing and institutionalizing that experience *après coup*. One rearticulates the primary ontological first faith (*fides*) and trust (*confidens*) into scriptures, rites, representations, and doctrines. If one is a Christian, one rereads one's primary sense of carnal orientation vis-à-vis strangers in terms of Mary and Gabriel, Jesus, and the Syro-Phoenician woman. If a Hindu, one speaks the life of Krishna; if a Buddhist, one speaks the life of Siddhartha. These are different and equally legitimate (which is not to say equivalent) ways of responding after the event, *nachtraglich*, to the trauma-epiphany of first fear and first faith—and the struggle, the wager, the journey between them, which I call the anatheist journey.

CDvT: Are there successive wagers, then?

RK: Yes. There is a primary wager between hostility and hospitality regarding the stranger and a secondary one between belief and nonbelief. Anatheism works back and forth between these two levels of wager, of call and response. Hence the double *a* of anatheism as "ad" (toward) and "ab" (away from). Advance and absence. Advent and abandon. The two senses of *a-dieu* as moving toward or away from the other, which many chose to call God, and many prefer to call by some other name or no name at all.

VI

CDvT: Let's try to dig deeper into this journey and focus on prayer. Wasn't it precisely Jesus who, calling himself the "son of God," taught his disciples—and thus us—to pray to "our father?" Didn't he want all of us to engage in a journey of transformation, to become sons of God?

RK: Yes, he did. One can read the entire life of Christ, right up to his death on the cross as a radical rejection of the Alpha-Patriachal God, who demands substitutionary atonement of his son. By contrast, Jesus (and Isaiah before him) invites everyone to be a "son of God," like him. "You can all follow me," he announces. A theopoetic calling to everyone to become a son or daughter of the divine, to become a *hospes* as he revealed himself to be in Matthew 25. Anatheism reads Matthew 25 as an open call to everyone to become host or guest. An endless call to rebirth, as God after God after God, stranger after stranger after stranger …

CDvT: But when Jesus prays on the cross, his prayer seems to be much less confident. It is more like a complaint: "My God, my God, why have you forsaken me?" (Matthew 27:46).

RK: Christ's cry from the cross brings me back once more to the double *a* of anatheism. The cry represents the *a* of abandonment, replicating the first natal moment when we abandon the womb and are abandoned to life. Thrown or ejected into life, as Heidegger might say: *Geworfenheit.* One's first experience entering naked and exposed into the world is one of forsakenness, but it is immediately and simultaneously accompanied by a second or double experience of yearning to reach toward someone or something "other" than oneself, to survive, be salvaged, saved—the second *a* in ana, which signals advent: Christ's "unto thee I commend my spirit." The first cry of the child captures this double sense of *a-n-a*. Both moments—abandon and advent—are equiprimordial. We spend the rest of our lives going back and forth between them, reinterpreting our earliest beginning in light of our last end. In that sense, we are at once both natal and mortal. Just as the kingdom reinterprets creation, eschatology repeats genesis, and so on. Now, in any good anatheist debate regarding the second "religious" wager, the atheist might say to the theist, "I respect your need for religious faith, but I'm not going there. I'm staying loyal to the first *a* of absence—abstention, separation, natal beginning, eventually leading to autonomy and individuation (what Lacan calls 'symbolic castration')." Atheistic humanism doesn't have to be seen as deficient or defaulting. The atheist has every right to say, "We can handle things among ourselves; we don't need to appeal to God." Whereas the theist chooses to translate the moment of primary trust into a religious belief, a holy scripture, a theology, a set of ritual ceremonies, prayers and practices which identify the stranger as God.

CDvT: We make that second religious wager when we are praying, don't we? To whom do we address ourselves when praying, if not to God?

RK: The anatheist theist says that there is something out there in which she confides, has confidence, to whom she expresses fidelity and faith qua divine other, which she calls God. To which an anatheist atheist like Derrida or Nancy might reply, "Well I too am prepared to say that there is something more—but it is something more in human life itself, a *sur-vivant* of life in life. An alterity and excess here and now. Within the finite. We can find that in art, in literature and culture, in everyday life. We don't need to go to some transcendent deity. I can see the need for trusting in some ultimate goodness that is inexplicable, but I do not want to put the name 'God' on that."

CDvT: I would agree that, yes, we need to admit the excess or the surplus. But to me, it's not enough to merely indicate that there is something or, if you want, some sort of spiritual energy "out there." The need for "gods" is felt at all times in all places. It has some sort of necessity in it. Why? Maybe because of an inescapable need which I feel in myself.

RK: What Kristeva calls "*le besoin incroyable de croire.*"

CDvT: Exactly. But why this unbelievable need? Because of a split. Because human beings are only able to experience trauma at a distance—not when the trauma actually happens but only in the awareness that a trauma has happened. Thus I'm conscious of my inability to experience that which I have experienced in trauma. In a sense, I find myself in two places: in the presence of a trauma that I do not realize and, at the same moment, in the realization that I do not realize it. This double position reveals that, in some ways, I'm already heading for something like a vision *sub specie aeternitatis*—something like a bird's-eye view of the world, of my world. It is as if my own experience of my inability to experience trauma is already a going-out, a going-above the world—an experience of transcendence. But the one who is looking down at himself "from above" is stuck in the presence of trauma without knowing it. There is in human subjectivity this striving for transcendence, this moving force to go beyond, and the concomitant desire to address.

RK: Again, this sounds to me like Kristeva's "incredible need to believe."

CDvT: It prompts us to propose something like a divine individual, a god—I mean something with anthropomorphic features. God becomes the name for the more-than-human experience of the unexperienceable. In myself, in being conscious of myself, I'm always already heading for some sort of subjectivity that is larger than I am, larger than this Augustinian intimate untouchability of myself that so interested Lyotard at the end of his life. And this "more-than-me" captures the features of otherness and irreducibility that were revealed to me in the traumatic experience with myself in relation to the other, the stranger, both hostile and welcoming.

RK: I see what you are saying, and perhaps that is why anatheist wagering is a wondering and wandering, a fluid crisscrossing between atheism and theism. I think atheism without theism is unhealthy, and vice versa. The anatheist wager has nothing of the all-or-nothing of Pascal's or Kierkegaard's fideist wager. Healthy atheism grounds and complicates eschatology: that is what Jesus came to do. He was an atheist, defying the existing religious authorities, before he redirected his anatheist faith toward God. He reinterpreted the divine (against theodicy). That is what he meant in his cry: "My God, my God, why have you forsaken me?" "Do you know why you have forsaken me? Because you—the God who has forsaken me—are the alpha-God of totalizing omnipotence, and I'm here to prove that we have to get rid of you. You are an idol. I have to fully carnate you to show that the true God is your 'face in ten thousand faces,' as G. M. Hopkins has it. My calling is to manifest you in and as every singular son and daughter of God who gives or receives bread or water in your name—that is: in the name of love." The anatheist Christ says: "This is my vocation—to announce the death of an excarnate God and the birth of an incarnate one. A God of flesh." "Unto Thee, I commend my spirit" is the opening of consent to a Thou that is beyond, because beneath, the omni-God of theodicy. As Merleau-Ponty put it so well, citing Claudel: "if there is a God, it is a God beneath us, not beyond us."[4] Christian incarnation means that the more is in the less, the infinite in the infinitesimal.

CDvT: Have we identified here a second argument behind the anatheist hypothesis? First, we said: I have had an experience that exceeded my ability to experience; but, paradoxically, I am aware of my own inability to experience that experience. So we're staying on the level of ego. But this ego is a stranger to himself, as Kristeva would have it.

RK: Or a "wounded cogito," as Ricoeur puts it—a self that's haunted and obsessed by the stranger.

CDVT: Yes, and the second argument has to do with the phenomenon of "addressing"—the miraculous experience of prayer. The original wager provokes us to respond in a very carnal and incarnate way. But responding is addressing. Therefore, the original wager calls for a "name," an "address." Again, something like a "God" born out of the impossible experience of excess. Addressing myself to God implies that the other to whom I am addressing myself also has subjectivity. So, if the phenomenon of looking to this traumatic moment "from above" or sub specie aeternitatis, it implies the idea of a super-consciousness, the address "reinvents"—and here I think of Derrida's reflections on invention—this super-subject as the other. That is why I believe that we'll never entirely be rid of the anthropomorphic or, better, the personal God. At the most minimal level, we'll stick to some sort of divine name: we interpret our own cry in relation to trauma as an address. Psychology might call it projection. But I refuse to admit that it is a simple mirroring process. It is more like an expulsion of strangeness and thereby a reiteration of it on another level. Trauma begets trauma by "projecting" the impossible experience onto some sort of exteriority that bears the name God.

VII

RK: I think I see what you mean. I suppose anatheism occurs when we make the wager to ensure that we dwell in what Keats called "negative capability"—a remaining in radical mystery and uncertainty, refusing to reduce the wonder of the other to myself, resisting the temptation to limit the irreducible stranger who calls to a merely subjective projection.

CDvT: Yes, and thus also respecting the "split" in ourselves—our subjective incompatibility, the other in ourselves. *Soi-même comme un autre* (Ricoeur).

RK: Indeed, anatheism is there to ensure that I don't say, "This mysterious other is *me*." The stranger is precisely *not* the same as me. The other in me is not reducible to me. It is more than an alter-ego. In terms of eschatology, that implies that we need the father to rescue us from the anthropology of the son by reminding us that there's always something different, always a kingdom still to come.

CDvT: You mean that the Father stands for the traumatic moment, the real otherness? Not the projection of my self in a super-subject, but the projection of my *trauma* onto that subject, my experience of not coinciding with myself?

RK: Well, it's a way of responding to it in a certain language, a very psychoanalytical language, about the relation between father and son. The one thing that precedes and eludes us at birth is the father. We know the mother, but we don't know the father. It's about a beginning before I begin, a genesis of becoming before I am. I began before I begin. I was begotten before I was born. And that experience of unknowable paternity—whether you call it the Creator on the first day of creation or Joyce's "epical forged check," the "blind rut in the dark"—we all share that in common. There's something else that precedes and supersedes us—that comes *before* and *after* us. We don't have any control over it, and that is expressed in Christ's words, "I must go so that the Paraclete can come." In other words: the son becomes the father to the next "son," who is the Paraclete as endlessly reproducible sonship—filiality replicating itself as endless hosting and guesting (Matthew 25). Perichoresis once again. Father birthing son birthing spirit ad infinitum. We have to be careful of gendered language here, of course, but I am merely citing the terms of scripture, which are hopelessly masculinist. We could say something like this: by eschatologizing the language of creation, we rescue it from narrow naturalism; we take it out of the chronological determinism of *natus* and *genus*, toward a spiritual sonship and daughterhood.

CDvT: So anatheism is, for you, also a way of rethinking theology in modernity or, if you like, postmodernity? If so, would you agree that in classical theodicy, a spatial paradigm of thinking was presupposed, spatial in the sense of a simultaneous, metaphysical, hierarchical, unfolding relation between the one and plurality; whereas in *anatheism*, a different scheme, a paradigm of temporal succession without final comprehension, is presupposed? I noticed that you refer repeatedly to notions of achronic seriality, successivity, and historicity. And this time beyond and before time seems to relate to a traumatic moment that escapes temporality. I see some resonance here with Levinas's analysis of the birth of time, from the relation to the face of the other, and maybe also with Lyotard's analysis of Newman's "The Sublime is Now."[5] Trauma is the enigma of beginning. So the only way of speaking about it is by coming back to it, retrospectively: the trauma will be noticed only after the event has passed. And this moment is constantly passing, which would make the grammatical mode of anatheism the *future antérieur*?

RK: You are right: anatheism is *ana*-chronistic. But I would modify your suggestion. Theism and atheism follow chronological time, whereas anatheism upsets that model in a basic sense. According to Freud and Marx—and the Dawkins anti-God squad—religious people are delusional and infantile: they should accept the scientific enlightenment and become secularized, rational, responsible grown-ups (albeit, for Freud, at the price of neurosis—the "discontent" of mature civilization). That is a model chronological "progression" which anatheism challenges. Anatheism accepts certain aspects of the atheist critique of religion but it introduces the vertical into this horizontal notion of time. Modernity is not some ineluctable march of Progress.

CDvT: I would relate that discussion to the paradigm of simultaneity. Time, *chronos*, as expressed in the attitude: "Once we had theism; now we have atheism." But when you propose anatheism, you propose to come back time and again to that unpredictable "thing" that will always only become articulated *afterward*, in the *future anterior* tense. Hence: sheer successivity.

RK: Let me try to clarify. Kairological time breaks open chronological time. It is a temporality of the strange (traumatic or epiphanic, sublime or sacred), which is always already there and always yet to come. Derrida and Agamben got this right—following Benjamin—in their analysis of messianic temporality. Bergson also had great insights into this deep temporality, as developed by Deleuze in his magisterial work on cinema and time. The time of cinematic montage is, curiously, isomorophic with that of eschatology.

CDvT: So ana-time as the *future anterior* once again: what is will only be articulated when it has already passed away.

RK: Yes, but that does not take us away from the moment. The moment is always potentially traumatic and epiphanic because it escapes us. And chronological time and history are attempts to put that back into some sequential casual order. That is, if I understand you correctly, what you entitle the simultaneity paradigm. Such order can be a particular temptation for theism and atheism alike. Both risk conceiving time in terms of causal regress and progress.

CDvT: You mean, institutional theism puts the experience of time under the dictate of *logos*. Would then *anatheism* be the inscription of *logos* into the impossible experience of time?

RK: It depends, again, what kind of time. I insist on this distinction between chronology and ana-chronology (kairological-eschatological-traumatic time). In Greek mythology, Chronos devoured his sons. He wanted everything to come back in line with the cause, to return to the paternal origin. He couldn't let the other—his children—go. By contrast, *ana* indicates that time is uncontrollable, untotalizable, and that we are always too late for the moment, but also that it is always still to come because it is an excess. The excess is interpreted apophatically by mystical theism; there are no words, names, narratives, images for it. It is interpreted kataphatically by theism, through teachings, theologies, liturgical calendars. Anatheism says that the apophasis and kataphasis need each other.

VIII

CDvT: When you say "need," you mean that kataphasis and apophasis are mutually corrective? I remember Derrida's reflection on the mystical question "*How to avoid speaking?*"[6] The silence pierces through the words. The mystical moment prevents any discourse from closing in on itself, from totalizing or adequate repetition.

RK: In that sense, one could say, provocatively, that Derrida needs the church and the church needs Derrida. Why? Because the church without deconstruction risks reducing messianism to triumphalism. And Derrida on his own is a lonely voice crying in the desert with no one to talk to. I asked Derrida once, "How do you pray?" And he answered, "I pray in Hebrew because I have no other language." Even the apophatic needs a bit of kataphatic help when it comes to the crunch.

CDvT: As a Jew—but what is it to be a Jew?—Derrida has his linguistic, Hebrew community.

RK: Yes, and Derrida is very helpful on the relationship between concrete historical "messianisms" like Judaism and Christianity and what he calls "messianicity"—the more formal condition of possibility of all messianisms. In this deconstructionist sense, one might say that *anatheism* is not a belief or disbelief but, to come back to your opening question, the condition of possibility of both. When you disbelieve anatheistically or believe anatheistically it is always a wager that expresses the fact that you don't know: the fact that it is, at bottom, always a matter of faith and trust in the stranger, however that is defined (as they say of the "higher power" in the AA movement).

CDvT: You have been doing some interesting recent work on Duns Scotus. Is anatheism a version of Scotism—I mean a radical acceptance of contingency?

RK: In a sense, yes. The contingency of human existence makes every wager free. And there I remain a Scotist existentialist, a believer in freedom, but not arbitrary freedom. I would say, rather, a responsive, interrelational, summoned freedom.

CDvT: The risk of skepticism is there too.

RK: Of course, and that's why anatheism always harbors an element of skepticism and doubt. Call it what you will: *docta ignorantia*, the dark night of the soul, not-knowing, anguish, questioning. It also informs the first step of the twelve-step program of AA: the admission that I am radically abandoned—forsaken. The realization that you are not in control but are radically helpless regarding your attachments and illusions, your addictions, and repetition compulsions. You are now ready to appeal to the other—the higher power beyond your ego, which is the second step of AA. In short, you realize you cannot do this on your own; healing is impossible without recourse to a community. You need the other—your sponsor, your group. You need to tell your story, to hear the story of the other. Nobody can do it alone. Kierkegaard couldn't. He was miserable. Derrida couldn't. They were both spiritually and intellectually miserable.

CDvT: But maybe one is only miserable if one refuses to accept that one's always already in community?

RK: I agree, and it is complex. Because even to the extent that Kierkegaard was miserable, he still had a church to fight with, a language to speak to and to speak against. *The Lilies and the Birds* and all those sermons. He had a common discourse, however controversial. He belonged to a messianic-Abrahamic tradition, much more explicitly than Derrida, but he lived it contentiously, as the "single individual" devoid of congenial partnership or community. Even the "single one" is in relation to some community it resists or rejects.

CDvT: Then, does Derrida too need to come to religion? To a faith community?

RK: Not necessarily. An example: I have a friend who went to AA meetings and said to me, "Oh dear, I'm going to have to come to the God-moment; I can't stand it." And I replied, "You don't have to. You can interpret the 'higher power' agnostically, in human terms, if you wish." But then, of course, you get a definition of the human that enlarges the human. I would say then: "In the human, there is something more than human."

CDvT: Before addressing this theme of the inhuman or the more-than-human, tell me: do you think there is an intrinsic link between faith and community?

RK: If you ask people, "Why do you go to church?" many say because of community. Now, humanist atheists may say, "I don't need to find my community in a church. I find it in the human race. I find it in my neighborhood peace group, my local protest march for liberty, justice, housing, the right to choose, gay marriage, LGBT rights, or whatever. I find it having dinner with my friends." And that is all very true. The difference with communities based on something that is more than human—usually called God or spirit or the sacred—is that they acknowledge that we're not the only active agents involved: there is something bigger than us at work. There is something "higher" or "deeper" beyond or beneath us.

CDvT: Someone might pose this challenge: the Greek vision of the gods was that the gods suffer like human beings. They're kind of super human beings, but they have comparable problems. And that creates a solidarity, a community in suffering between the gods and men. Whereas in monotheism, this projection of the vulnerability of humanity into the sphere of the divine is lost.

RK: I'm not sure that the God of Abraham and Judaism is always such an indifferent God. I think that there is a lot of passion and compassion in the wisdom books, in the Song of Songs, in Hosea, and Isaiah. And Jesus is a suffering servant par excellence. In Sufi Islam too—think of the poems of Hafiz and Rumi where God is the guest, the drunk, the lover, the dancer, not some abstract impassive impersonal force. Which is why Salafism—at the root of Isis and Al Queda—persecutes Sufis. The Sufis have no time for abstract ideologies.

IX

CDvT: Can you say more about what you call the "more-than-human." If we take Nietzsche's *Übermensch* as this "more-than-human," for example, we can't even say it is human.

RK: It may also include what Lyotard called the "inhuman," and then the line between atheism and theism becomes very porous and fertile. Each of us has a theist and an atheist inside. From the beginning, since the moment of birth, we experience both the sense of "I belong" and "I do not belong," and we can emphasize one moment or the other: either our desire to connect with the other, to communicate with the other, or our desire to be on our own, independent, sovereign. Both are important. And each involves taking a stand, saying, "Here I stand." You find these alternating positions even in the monastic tradition: *ora et labor. Labor* is going out and working with your community. *Ora is* prayer, contemplative life as *monos*, alone, abandoned to the spirit. And then comes, once again, the call of the other: I need confidence and faith in the other, who will recue me from my loneliness, and who, in turn, needs my care and attention. I take my stand.

Hinenee. Me voici. Here I am. Anatheism is not wishy-washy indifferentism; it is not lukewarm oscillation and procrastination. It is about making bold and committed wagers while always remaining open and attentive and refusing the tyranny of certainty—the lure of absolutism.

CDvT: That is on the side of the encounter with the other, but we spoke already about self-transcendence, about an immanent *dépassement* of the human subject who is always there where he can't be, as Lacan said. Otherwise and more-than-human.

RK: And God is, I admit, one traditional name for this more-than-human in the human. Just as God is the more-than-animal in the animal. And the more-than-natural in nature.

CDvT: I'm not quite sure about the last two. Your thesis is similar to that of Pierre Gisel, who talks about the excess as the differential trait of the sacred and of God. But yes, God is the more-than-human in the human that I discover in myself as the thing I cannot put into words.

RK: You discover it in yourself, and you discover it in the other.

CDvT: Yes. Perhaps first in the other, before it reveals itself in me. But how do we discover the "more" philosophically speaking?

RK: In philosophy, we have only phenomenology, existential hermeneutic phenomenology of the other, of the face, what John Manoussakis calls the *prosopon*. That is the most convincing philosophical way, it seems to me. Unless one leaves philosophy and turns to a theology of revelation; but even revelation is conveyed and communicated through narrative witness, with different confessional interruptions. The Talmud tells us there are ten ways to read each line of the Torah, and Christianity was transmitted by four gospel narratives. Again, we are faced with differing versions of carnal or scriptural hermeneutics—from top to bottom, there is no escape. You wager every time you read—the face of the stranger, the text of tradition—and respond.

CDvT: In this sense, you could say that the idea of excess, of the *over-man* projected onto some sort of "being" that still keeps some anthropomorphic elements, can also be found in political ideologies. In that sense, Marxism might be a replacement for religion.

RK: That is the claim of atheistic secular humanism—a humanism that also includes Nietzsche, Feuerbach, and Bloch. It says that the more-than-human comes only *from* the human. I would say that the more-than-human also comes *to* the human. It manifests *through* the human, but it is not something we own or limit or predetermine. It arrives out of the desert. It is immanent in the human world, but it is not of the human world. That is what we mean by the term "sacred" (in Greek *mysterion*, meaning blindfolded): something mystical and mysterious in our most mundane experience. We cannot see it with our ordinary eyes, but we can, nonetheless, feel and taste and touch it as coming to us from without—from the holy stranger and the strange. And that experience of the sacred is available to everyone, atheist and theist alike.

CDvT: You mentioned it already, but I find the tension between theism and atheism that can exist in one person a fascinating thing. Take the words of Jesus on the cross. I see a chiasm in the juxtaposition of his two exclamations. "My God, why have you abandoned me" implies that in the address, in the performative, Jesus paradoxically affirms what he denies on the level of signification: God is there, even if Jesus says he has been abandoned by him. As if he is crying for God to help him, to do something—which is impossible, because God has abandoned him. So he is asking for the impossible. In the question, as such, there is something like the possibility of the impossible. And then in the second move, in a kind of symmetrical way, there is also a paradox: "Into your hands I command my spirit." How could I commend my spirit? Isn't it the other way around? I need the other—life and death—to take my spirit from me. How could I do it myself? Which spirit, which subject could commend himself to stop living? So there is the chiasm: when Jesus cries out the first time, he is crying for the other, whom he needs but who is absent; in the second cry, he is pretending to be able to do it himself, but can't: death comes from without. And therefore, he is presupposing the presence of the other.

RK: Again we find the paradox of "ana": I am abandoned by the other who goes as I consent to the other who comes. God gone, God back again. Fort/Da. I think, in death, we reach a moment of "I am alone." Everybody dies alone. Nobody can die for you. It is the most singular [*eigenst*] experience, as Heidegger rightly says. But Heidegger failed to acknowledge the accompanying gesture. The call to the other: where are you? And the response: here I am. This is the second *a* of ana—the ultimate letting go, the radical openness to the stranger and the strange.

CDvT: In an ultimate sense, I can't let go of my life because that would presuppose my subject and thus my life. Finally there is something that takes my life. "Take my life, Lord ..."

RK: But you can consent to that.

CDvT: You can try to be prepared, maybe—by opening yourself to the ultimate moment. But this impossible death experience resonates with my thoughts on what I would call *para-theism*: we can't get rid of God. We cannot be abandoned completely. When we are still crying out, when we are still addressing ourselves to that which is beyond our capacity of comprehension and interpretation, we are not alone—not entirely.

RK: All right. Maybe you can never get rid of God, but you can get rid of the idols that get in God's way. God goes by many names, as we've said, and some of these can be read as pseudonyms, not just the five hundred Hindu names for deities, but even more secular, ontological, and colloquial terms such as *mystery*, *depth*, *being*, *ultimate meaning*, and *chora*. Very few people would refuse to admit that there is some deeper dimension to their lives, and further that that dimension—in nature, in particular human beings, in special times, places, spiritual experiences—is "sacred" to them—even if they don't use the word "God." Stanislas Breton once wrote that the truth of monotheism—the belief in an unnamable God—is actually polytheism—the belief in multiple names for God. Anatheism is polynymity.

CDvT: Derrida speaks of something like this in his *Spectres de Marx*. . . . A ghost is present-in-absence. Or even Lyotard had his philosophy of religion, in which God was the name for the unnamable event, only graspable *après coup, nachträglich*.[7]

RK: Yes, *spectres* are something extra, excessive, uncanny, indeed *nachträglich*. We should go back to Derrida's reading of Marx to see how eschatological he is. There is something there where humanism mixes with mysticism. I think if you dig down into any great atheist thinker, you'll find some gap opening to the sacred. The sacred in the broadest sense. It's like you excavate, and suddenly someone is knocking from the other side. That's the sacred as *secret*, because you don't know who is there. It is a stranger in the dark.

X

CDvT: Shifting gears now from death to birth, we said that anatheism inscribes itself in time—it is immanent. And trauma is irreversible. So what would you make of Christian ideas of rebirth and reconciliation which seem to imply that a blocked situation opens up again?

RK: Well, I think rebirthing—perhaps we could call it "ana-naissance"—is what we are doing all the time. I am all for serial sacramentality. For me, the Eucharist is not some special thing. It is an exemplary liturgy, a paradigm for something that is happening all the time: the sharing of hosts with guests, of bread with neighbors, in a way that makes the simplest morsel of matter into the flesh of the world—the on-going incarnation of word as flesh. Just like what I was saying about birth being a universal baptism of desire. Nobody is excluded from the rite of passage into the holiness of human community. Baptism is just a Christian sacramental way of saying something very simple and applicable to all Christians and non-Christians alike—you go under water to rise again; you die to be reborn. Everyone dies to be reborn. The infant is traumatized by birth—the terror, the cold, the naked air—at the same time as she rises into an epiphany of postnatal life. Death and resurrection are not confined to Christ—they are parts of everyone's experience, which is why nearly all wisdom traditions have their equivalent version of Christ-figures undergoing transformation through loss and abandonment, finding light through darkness, dying unto self in order to be reborn anew. Think of Siddhartha, Isaiah, Shiva, Chiron, and more.

CDvT: You mean that religion is a staging, an affirmative and reaffirmative *mise en scène* of original and universal human experiences of natality and mortality? A creative and affirmative hermeneutics of existence? But surely religion does more. It promises reconciliation, forgiveness, peace.

RK: To respond more personally, I see the work of Guestbook as relevant here—as an art of pardon and forgiveness it implies an impossible moment, a wager of hospitality. Pardon is always a wager of trying to break the obstacle of passivity in order for the impossible to come. Now, that may sound very utopian, but it is actually very practical. I believe that if you venture an anatheistic wager, the impossible can become possible in one's work with others in community. Exchanging stories, changing histories. You cannot do it alone. The AA healing of addiction and trauma is a powerful case in point. The "little miracle of forgiveness" (Ricoeur) can only come through others, through witness, shared testimonies, exchanged narratives, wise elders, sponsors and peers who are prepared to walk part of the way with you. There can be "big miracles" of forgiveness too, of course—think of Esau and Jacob, think of Christ with his thieves and crucifiers, think of Mandela and his jailors, or Hume with the IRA. It can happen, and such healing witness is contagious, whether it be by direct experience or narrative transmission. It can go viral, change the world.

CDvT: Could you say then that "God happens" when the miracle of forgiveness takes place? And maybe also the other way around—from the experience of forgiveness when it is needed, but there is no way to bring it about. Miracle is a condition of possibility of the God call, and vice versa.

RK: The reason why religion should remain anatheistic in its roots is because it should remain true to a faith in real community, not in commodity fetishes, fads, and fanaticism. By always allowing a moment of a-theist doubt at the heart of anatheist faith one remains immune—or at least resistant—to the lure of fundamentalist idolatries. Being hospitable to the stranger keeps one safe from the totalizing and scapegoating ideologies of collective religious egos.

CDvT: I'm a bit hesitant here. It is not black and white. We need a comfort zone—social habits, rules, and maybe even ideologies. Maybe even some inhospitality. Why? Because otherwise, every single moment and place would be loaded with ethics and sacredness. Then we would lose the sacred, because the sacred—and I believe the same counts for ethical engagement—has its specific places and times. It would be a terrible, undifferentiated life if everything was sacred! If every encounter was ethically charged and we were always all entirely responsible, we would be submerged.

RK: Yes, there are limits, boundaries, finitude. From the point of view of God, if we put it like that, every moment is indeed potentially sacred. But that is not possible for us finite human beings. Walter Benjamin said we should treat each instant as a portal through which the Messiah might enter. Every moment the Messiah is knocking, but most of the time we are just not capable of hearing, seeing, or handling it. Our finitude is such that too much infinity would blow our minds, blind us, traumatize us into speechlessness, strike us dumb. So we can only let in a little at a time. "Through a chink too wide comes in no wonder."[8] Although I do believe that saints and holy people—and that can include a neighbor down the road—are those who manage to keep the door ajar more than most of us, or at least on the latch! Through prayer, through practice, through service, through giving, through constantly hosting guests and strangers in their lives, they are actually pretty close to holiness, but never totally. I think of people like Jean Vanier, Teresa of Avila, John of the Cross—even they confess to dark nights of the soul. Their own terrible darkness. Theresa of Calcutta went dark too. Every moment cannot be holy even for the holiest of beings. Christ, too, had his Gethsemane. The holy is something constantly ventured, adventured, wagered, and we can't do it all the time. We can't be "on" from dawn to dusk. We'd be hypersaturated. We'd burn up. The world is full of wonders and wounds. Epiphanies and traumas. It's all too much. At times it can be very cruel and hostile. But it has within its cracks and fractures a constant call for hospitality. Epiphany shines through trauma. The thin small voice, the name of "perhaps," the little God of the possible. Ana-God. The Stranger who comes and goes and comes again.

CHRIS DOUDE VAN TROOSTWIJK is a professor of philosophy, Dutch philosopher and theologian. He is Senior Lecturer and Senior Research Fellow at the Luxemburg School of Religion and Society (Luxembourg) and affiliated researcher and lecturer at the Protestant Theological Faculty of the University of Strasbourg (France). He currently holds the chair for liberal theology at the Mennonite Seminary at the University of Amsterdam (Netherlands). His research and teaching project, "Philosophies, Theologies, and Ethics of Finance," is a phenomenological hermeneutics of financial crises and monetary antinomies.

Notes

1. Erigena, Periphyseon, I, 452 D as quoted in Falque, God, the Flesh, and the Other: From Irenaeus to Duns Scotus, 66.
2. Hopkins, "No Worst, There is None. Pitched Past Pitch of Grief."
3. Breton, "Kearney's The God Who May Be," 258.
4. Merleau-Ponty, *The Prose of the World*, 83–84.
5. See Lyotard, *The Inhuman: Reflections on Time*. And Newman, "The Sublime is Now," 580–582.
6. Derrida, *Psyche 2: Inventions of the Other*, 143–195.
7. See Doude van Troostwijk, "Phrasing God: Lyotard's Hidden Philosophy of Religion."
8. Kavanagh, *Collected Poems*, 110.

3 Mysticism and Anatheism: The Case of Teresa

Julia Kristeva and Richard Kearney

I

RK: Could you begin by saying something about your recent work on Teresa, a mystical believer who clearly fascinates you, Julia Kristeva, a self-confessed atheist? Why Teresa? Why now?

JK: Let me begin by saying how deeply touched I have been by the subtle existence of this wonderful baroque saint, Teresa of Avila. How I came to her is an interesting story—almost an accident, really. I had a student who wrote a doctoral dissertation on the spiritual experiences of Dostoyevsky, Kafka, and Proust. This man became the director of the Catholic press in France, and one day he called me saying they were undertaking a project of small collections—each between fifty and one hundred pages—to be written on one of the more important spiritual figures of Europe, and they were asking some authors to choose a figure. In my case, it would be my choice, and I would be taking the psychoanalytic approach. I was just finishing a book, *Murder in Byzantium*, and the main personality in this book besides the narrator is a Byzantine princess named Anna Komnene—who is, for me, the first feminine historian because she makes a chronicle of the realm of her father, Alexis the Second. She explains the crusaders, and this is the only narrative about the crusaders from the point of view of somebody who is not a part of the Crusades. And I said this to the director of the publishing house, Frederick Boyer, and he said, "It's interesting, but she's not very famous. We don't have time to discover new spiritual figures; let us think about somebody else. Why not St. Teresa of Avila?" I didn't know anything about Teresa besides the Lacan reference to her in *Encore*. In this book, he was interested not in pleasure, but in what he calls *jouissance*, and in particular feminine *jouissance*. The cover of Lacan's book features an image of Bernini's Baroque sculpture of Teresa, which is now in the Italian church Santa Maria de la Vitoria. It represents Teresa's transfixion, a particular stage of her ecstasy that she describes in a startling passage that I quote at the beginning of *Teresa My Love*. Teresa presents her ecstasy of belonging to God as an enthusiasm that embraces all the senses, and it is through the intermediary of an angel, represented by the figure of a young boy. This angel stabs her entrails with his spear and makes them fly into the heavens. She describes this in a very erotic and masterful way. And, when first approached by Boyer, this was the only thing I knew about the work of Teresa. I told him that I was particularly ignorant of her, and he said it did not matter—read about her. I decided to read her work, and my reading lasted over ten years. I said in my book that St. Teresa is the roommate I lived with for a decade. And I've read all the things she has written, but also all the things that have been written on her, including some feminist interpretations from the divinity schools in the United States. Eventually, I decided that I was unable to make a small book for the collection administered by my friend and student, so we altered our contract and I gave him another book instead: *This Incredible Need to Believe*. I thus vowed to try to write something that corresponds to this extraordinary figure that shakes all of our identities, genres, and disciplines, because it seems to me that it is impossible to bring her in contact with a modern public without giving some biographical details, some historical background, some quotations from her, and also some interpretations from the perspective of someone like me who is in contact with her and tries to represent her. So this is the way that I tried to shake the genres—biography, fiction, theology, memoire, diary, philosophy, history, case history—and to give all of my enthusiasm, a sort of ecstasy, if you want, from my own point of view.

RK: You are a philosopher, a linguist, and a writer, but to what extent would you describe your book as primarily a psychoanalytic study?

JK: Well, I am reluctant to directly impose psychoanalytic concepts on somebody else's experience, be it the experience of a writer like Marcel Proust or Marguerite Duras, and particularly on such mysterious experiences as those of Teresa. I do not follow people who try to take a concept of psychoanalysis—be it orality, anality, Oedipus complex, and so forth—and to reduce such rich experiences to these schemas. Indeed, I think it is a betrayal of the psychoanalytic attitude and of the experience. My idea in reading Teresa was to be infiltrated by her experience, to try to adhere, to be in a sort of osmosis with her, as we are when we are hearing the person on the couch, and then to try to see what this means for me and how I can use some notions of psychoanalysis in a creative way—transforming them in order to make a particular discourse that will be not psychoanalytic only, not feminist only, not sociological only, but also a discourse that is appropriate to Teresa as I read her. So, it is the consequence of a dialectic of osmosis and differentiation regarding the object of interpretation. This is why I say that Teresa was my roommate, because it is very much an everyday belonging and distancing, something that is easier to do when you have insomnia in the night and try to understand people through what I call nonthinking. It is better expressed in French by the term "à-pensée," a substantive not a verb, with the *a* being a privative preffix to indicate a drift from the cognitive rational abstract processes toward unconscious processes of sensation and affect—so it is thinking that is not thinking but is passing through thinking.

RK: So, what is the image of mysticism that results from this kind of approach, and what kind of psychoanalysis seems to you most convenient to this strange Spanish mystic? Would you be happy describing it as anatheistic? Are not most genuine forms of mysticism anatheistic in their "letting go" of the established God concepts, as Eckhart says, opening themselves up to new and often unnamable experiences of divinity? This anatheist opening enables mystics to let one kind of God go in order to welcome another. It frees minds from "conceptual idolatry" and creates space for the return of the sacred father (or mother), for further "rebirthing," as Eckhart calls it.

JK: I agree. My first impression of Teresa's particular kind of mysticism came from comparing her with my knowledge of other mystics. Everybody knows that they are so different—not only Meister Eckhart and Teresa, for instance, but also Catherine of Siena and Teresa. So, I tried to put together all those things according to the view acquired through such cohabitation with Teresa. Three years of reading and research followed by one year of actual writing. I will say that three aspects of the Christian faith in the mystics struck me. The first is the belief that there exists an ideal father, that God is an ideal father from a psychoanalytic point of view. But also because the accent in mysticism—more than in everyday faith—is that faith is love, it is a love for this father. The first is the insistence on this privileged connection of the mystic with the father. The second is that this idealization is not only ideal in the mystic's experience, but also resexualized—particularly in the case of Teresa, but in different mystics too. This is sensorial and quite disturbing sexually in the sense that some mystics—male mystics, for instance—experience themselves as women being penetrated by God. There are a lot of metaphors that touch on the sexual difference. Nevertheless, it seems to me to be a permanent trait of almost every mystical experience that Teresa epitomizes. The idealization is resexualized. The father is a beaten father who is tortured and crucified, and this experience of suffering is also aggravated in the mystical experience.

This suffering is experienced as pleasure alongside death and vulnerability and the castration of the father. He is ideal, but he is suffering and he is a source of ultimate pleasure and ultimate suffering. The third aspect that struck me is that the mystic identifies with the father through an orality, which is the Eucharist. I love him, I suck him, I am in a very-close oral attitude. With Teresa it is very strong—not just an image, but an experience: she envisions the father as having her breast and on her breast, but this orality is only an intermediary level in order to go on to the word, to the word that comes out from the mouth and is not a sensorial, but rather an abstract connection with him. I say abstract, but in the experience of Teresa, this abstraction is engulfed, penetrated by taste, by tactile experience, and by hearing. Everything is a way to self-engender the ego through sensuality. But this self-engendering of the ego through sensuality comes through language; the oral participation with the father is transformed through the Eucharist into a word participation, but the word is not a single abstract word. It is a metaphor, which is a metamorphosis. Charles Baudelaire, who was a very strong Catholic—as you know—said that for him, compared to some weak poets, words are not comparisons; words are metamorphoses. If people say, "I am like a tree" then Baudelaire would say, "I am not like a tree; I become the tree." And something like that occurs in this identification of the mystic with the father, which is oral, which is corporal. But when Teresa, in this case, speaks about him, every word becomes more than metaphorical. Every word becomes a metamorphosis that tries to make us experience physically her faith, her love. So, these aspects of the Teresian experience are, for me, stronger in her experience, though they can be found in other mystics. She pushes them to the extreme. She is a unique anatheist mystic.

II

RK: In your writing and reading of Teresa, you are mixing the discourse of religious mysticism with both literary poetics and psychoanalytic theory. Can you say what specific psychoanalytic approach you find most helpful in approaching Teresa as you are doing this—given that so many psychoanalytic treatments of religion have proved to be reductive and unsympathetic in the past?

JK: When I draw from psychoanalytic theory, I use my own concepts, but I also draw on Winnicott when he calls the early stages of mother-child behavior and some regressive stages of his patients a *psyche-soma*. This means the psyche is not only verbally expressed, but it is expressed through preverbal signs and through exacerbated sensibility of feelings, hearings, and visions. You know that Teresa speaks about her visions, but she says they are not visions given to the sight, but to the body. The sight is only one part of this. *All* the senses participate in these visions and, according to Winnicott, such stages can be observed in patients when they have some traumatic experience. When on the couch, they reach for these traumatisms; they are beneath the level of words, consciousness, communication. They try afterward—when engulfed in the psyche-soma and left only with their bodies—they try to describe these situations with metaphors that are metamorphoses. In these cases, Winnicott would say, "I wonder why people think that consciousness is cerebral. I think that consciousness is somatic." This linkage between the cerebral and the somatic, and between the abstract and the sensorial, is very, very important in Teresa's experience of the love of her father. And here, maybe her own neurological fragility is concerned because she had some very frequent epileptic fits that are described in her memoires. Teresa describes her ecstasies as traveling to God—going outside of herself to be in exile with him. These are the words she uses to describe experiences that can be very painful—experiences comparable to the epileptic auras described by Dostoyevsky as a blend of bliss and pain. Some French and Spanish neurologists have identified these kinds of mixed experiences, painful and joyful, as epileptic. Teresa claimed that she was able to produce them; they did not only suddenly happen. She could produce them when she was freed from the powers of *memory, consciousness*, and *will*. But once liberated from the conscious net of mastering possibilities, she could also go into very deep depressions. Her mystical moods could go either way—between light and darkness. In this sense, her mixed experience could be described as "anatheist" mysticism, as you understand it.

RK: Isn't the psyche-soma open to the imaginary as well as the sensorial? Wouldn't you agree that it was crucial for Teresa to not just experience the divine in her body but also in her fantasies and fictions, in her metaphors and writings?

JK: Yes. This is absolutely crucial, and I think it is useful here to refer to Husserl when he says in *Ideas* that "fiction constitutes the vital element of phenomenology as it does for all eidetic sciences."[1] Why is Husserl as important a guide for me here as Winnicott or Baudelaire? Because Teresa herself gives us a possibility to get in touch with her experience through her fiction. We have to understand what happens to this woman through what she was able to tell us about it, through her fiction. And she was very conscious about the importance of fiction for her. She writes somewhere, "I give you this fiction in order for you to understand me." She is aware of the fact that she is not a theologian, that she does not have concepts but writes in a fictional way, a different way of thinking that makes people understand. But she makes a very nice distinction between fiction and understanding. Fiction is one of the ways to make understood something that is not understandable through willing, memory, consciousness, or concepts. So this comprehension of the psychic apparatus as enabling different visions and fictions is very important if we are to appreciate the complexity of this woman who is not only given to the father, but also understands this experience and feels the necessity to share it.

RK: Was it thanks in part to her use of such a strategy that she managed to confound the Inquisition and escape unharmed?

JK: I think so. When the inquisitors wished to burn her, she managed to convince them not to by using this kind of fictional understanding. She managed to survive by seducing her contemporaries and continuing to do so down through the centuries. My attempt in my recent book, *Teresa My Love*, is to appreciate her fiction by way of living her regressions, her love affair, the importance of love in this human experience, the connection with language. Language is love, and love is language. We have to understand the connection between them. Love is the field of psychoanalysis; language is the field of linguistics, theology, semiology, psychoanalysis, fiction. So I said, let us go through all of these fields in order to apprehend the complexity of the human being. And let me add that I think that without this baroque experience of love, of faith-like love, like tremendous regression and like fiction, without such experience we would not have the Enlightenment. Baroque experience opens the way to the Enlightenment—enlightenment in the sense of Diderot, Sade, and Rousseau. Teresa opens the door to a great freedom for humanity, and because we ignore this "anatheist" experience, because we repress the dangerous aspects of it, we are becoming a type of humanity that is merchandized, that is mercantile, that leads to the market and to a global submission to finances, a type that we experience in the modern crisis. The only way to resist this, I believe, is to rehabilitate Teresian experiences and to see how we can respond to them. But I have to say that our fiction is so feeble and weak in comparison to hers, which covers such a width and depth of territory, theology included.

RK: To pick up on a question put to you by my colleague, Catherine Cornille—is such mystical experience possible without faith? In short, what's God got to do with it?

JK: What is God? What is faith? This is something that I try to answer in a very modest way in *This Incredible Need to Believe*. I think that different religions have different scopes of faith. You know this better than I—as you show in *Anatheism*—how faith is different in Judaism, for instance, than in Christianity. But if you explore the complexity of different aspects of faith and see the common ground in them, you find the universal need to believe, which is common to all of these different aspects that were built in the history of humanity—Hinduism, Chinese Taoism, Confucianism, Christianity, Islam, and so forth. Both of us are interested in this question of the singularity and universality of belief. For my part, I identify different explanations and rationalizations of this need to believe in people like Freud and, in a more simplified way, through the knowledge of my teacher of linguistics, Emile Benveniste, who wrote a wonderful book called *Indo-European Language and Society*. The word *faith* is analyzed through the Sanskrit roots of the word. The Sanskrit for *faith* is *cred sraddha (śraddhā)*, which means investment. And what is investment? When you go to this secret and sacred Sanskrit text, it means I give my heart to God, and God gives me recognition and eternal life. This transaction of giving, giving vital force, and the promise for eternity of the vital force is called *cred sraddha*; it is related to joy and suffering and gives in Latin *credo*—credo as a transaction of forces. This allows a human being to perpetuate his life. Freud, as you know, was the staunchest of atheists. But he was very interested in the question of belief. He said that psychoanalysis is an illusion as religion is an illusion, but this illusion will last. People think that he wanted to abolish religion because he wanted to abolish every kind of illusory approach to the world and subject it to the rigors of science. But that was not what he said. He thought that science would follow every kind of illusory approach to the world, and he said that, regarding the early stages of human behavior, illusion is necessary. He calls this an investment in the primordial father—the father of primordial history. The German word is *Bezetzung*, and the English word that we use to try to understand this investment is *Cathexis*. It is very interesting to see how it works in the triangle between the mother, the child, and the father. It points to a third figure in the biological dyad between child and mother, and this third figure is the father of the human prehistory, who is not the oedipal father, who is not the father of love, but the father who recognizes me and who I recognize. Maybe we can say more about this later. The Jewish notion of election is involved here, and what is important is what Freud calls the need to believe. I have to believe in the father because he believes in me. And this belief is not an investment in an object. I do not like him as an object of pleasure, and he does not like me as an object of pleasure. This is a psychic investment, a psychic recognition. This is the border where the instinctual drive is transformed into a mental representation. It is a shifting between *zoe* and *bios*, the biological and the psychical. And the agency of the third person, who is the father in the human family, is the condition of this separation between the child and the mother—the establishing of another relationship that will be psychic representation as a condition of language. When this position of the father as a loving father is established, my babbling—my echolalia, my bababa—become references to a third person, to an external object, and they change from babblings into signs and into words. So the faith, the credo, is the copresence of a third figure that elects me and that I consider as an axis of mental representation, which is a new kind of pleasure. It is not the satisfaction of eating or sucking my mother or having a bottle of milk to satisfy my urge. It is a mental, psychic satisfaction. This kind of need must be satisfied in order to develop other skills, and particularly the *desire to know*—the desire to problematize every kind of naiveté and so on. From a psychoanalytic point of view, we require both the "need to believe" and the "desire to know." Faith, according to Teresa of Avila, is this movement of cobelonging of need and desire. And she goes into both of them with great intensity, with all of her body and with all of her senses. So, if you understand faith in this fashion, I would say faith is necessary. And in this sense, I also share her faith.

III

RK: I'd like to link this question of faith and knowing to that of *writing*. You seem to suggest in your own reading and writing of Teresa that it was writing together with faith that saved her from madness—or at least from destructive illness. But might it have been possible for her to have saved herself from psychosis by other modes of expression, such as music, art, or liturgical prayer? There seems to be something in your rewriting of Teresa's writing that emphasizes the importance of *language* over other modes of expression, which operate more at the level of "psycho-soma" and what you call "the sensitive imaginary." This latter is shared by all of the arts, but you sometimes appear to privilege the therapeutic role of the written word over the nonverbal in the process of conversion and transmutation.

JK: First, I do not think that Teresa was a psychotic. She had a very strong tendency toward hysteria—or something that was very excessive, a paranoid sense of persecution that is also in a sense made real—because she was of Jewish origin on her father's side, and persecutions existed in Spain. This extravagance of her feelings made her very sensitive and may have induced a sort of hysteric epilepsy, which would be very handicapping without the possibility to quiet this crisis through verbal explanations of what she was experiencing. And that is what her confessors asked her to do.

RK: You are thinking of Saint John of the Cross and Gratian, who encouraged her to write and even helped her evade the Inquisition at one point?

JK: Yes. The role of self-analysis through confession was central. And she was also able to imagine the role of literature—literary poetics and fiction—because her mother was a great reader. She wanted not only to *speak* about her senses, her life, her sensorial conflicts to the confessors, but also she wanted to *write* about them. What I discovered was that in that period, the church invited certain women who were considered eccentric and at variance with the canon—there were many sects, illuminati, heretics—to write about their lives. There was a particular genre—*La Vie*—that women excelled in. And there were many publications, like women write novels today. But in that period, the church invited them to write about their lives, and it was considered a sort of therapeutic, natural way to quiet the excitation.

RK: So to return to my question—can different arts save us from certain neurotic symptoms and pathologies, especially of a religious or spiritual nature?

JK: Of course—in some ways, but not totally. If it were possible through arts, we would not have psychiatric hospitals. There are some difficulties that the aesthetic experience does not settle. But what we need essentially is an addressee, a man or woman who can understand this need to believe, this desire to know, to be that partner of the love affair that we need with the world. And the psychoanalyst is this partner, a fictional one, a substitute; but this remaking of the love experience through the transference and contra-transference is something very important. And, of course, not only the participation of the man or woman, but also the medium of language seems to me to be more powerful than painting or music for the therapeutic process. Of course we enjoy Bach, Giotto, and Raphael more than Céline or Marguerite Duras; but in order to be in touch with the traumas, the narrative that comes with language has more possibilities because this medium that is the word has the possibility of abstraction and of understanding. The desire to know is effectuated in the word, and it also has the possibility to be close to the psyche-soma. We can make our metaphors into metamorphoses. My book on Collette shows how the style of Collette is a sort of a cotermination of the words with sensations. And when we read her, we forget what happens but we live with her sensorial experience of the word. So the possibility of the word to maintain the closeness with feelings and the body and, on the other side, to go to the extremes of sophistication in psychoanalysis is something enormous. Catholics often understand this.

RK: So who—before the invention of psychoanalysis—would have been the analyst for Teresa? Who would have played this role of the third, the partner, the substitute lover or surrogate father? Is she analyzing herself? Or is she speaking and writing for her confessor, for her imaginary readers (us), or for God (like Augustine in his *Confessions*)?

JK: No, God is not an analyst. At one point, Teresa says, very revealingly, that "water" is her element. God is unrepresentable, but water is an intermediary between her and God—God who makes water exist for her and she is a very dry garden. She distinguishes between four types of prayer, which she describes as "four waters" that cultivate the garden of the person praying. From her writings, I have ascertained that for the cloistered nun, water signifies the link between the soul and the divine: an amorous relation that unites the dry earth of the Teresian garden with Jesus. Springing from the outside or the inside, active and passive, neither one nor the other and without confusing itself with the gardener's labor, water transcends the earth that I am and makes me into something more: a garden. Myself, earth, I only become a garden through the touch of a vivifying medium: water. I am not water because I am earth; but neither is God water, for he is the creator. In our encounter, water is the fiction, the sensitive representation—it represents the space and time of body-to-body contact; the copresence and copenetration that makes being, living being. For the fiction of water joins me to God without identifying me with him. It maintains the tension between us while filling me with the divine. It spares me the folly of confusing myself with it: water is my living protection, my vital element. Representing the reciprocating contact of God and his creature, water dethrones God of his suprasensitive status and brings him down, if not to the role of gardener, then at least to that of the cosmic element I taste and touch. The element that nourishes me, touches me, quenches my thirst.

RK: So water is essential to Teresa as element, as matter, as sensation, as metaphor. But perhaps also as medium (*metaxu*) in the sense outlined by Aristotle in his analysis of touch in *De Anima*? How does this relate to the whole psychic-therapeutic work of "psyche-soma"?

JK: You are right, Richard. It is so essential, as both metaphor and medium, because Teresa herself is also the water. She can heal herself because she is both inside the wound and outside. She has the possibility of psyche-soma and the possibility of the analysand, who makes the analytic interrogation, judgment, and also tries to cleanse the bloody wounds. But she also uses another kind of social actor—the confessor. The confessors were her "psychoanalysts," and Teresa was very subtle and, at times, vicious in her use of them. She was very critical toward some of them. They couldn't understand her. They were too rigorous. She was very grateful to others who understood her and guided her. Even when they condemned her, she followed them. So there was a very interesting ballet that she organized with all of those people, and I would be interested to know why theologians do not examine the different confessors that she had, because there is a very long correspondence with them. We might ask why, for example, some Dominicans—who played a very important role in the Inquisition—condemned her, while others protected her. Jesuits also played a pivotal role in the comprehension of her story; and maybe one of the things that brought her close to the Jesuits was the invitation of Loyola to pray through the excitation of the senses. To go with the identification of Christ to what he calls the "*loquella*," referring to a quasi-infantile nonexistent language that regresses toward and drowns itself in the sensible. Here we find a language that is not language, the dismantling of language itself, the investment of the sensorial body in the identification of the different stages of Christ's crucifixion. So this knowledge of the crossroads between feelings and language as experienced in Loyola's exercises is something quite close to her. Those Jesuits understood her well, and I think it would be interesting to see how scholars who know these methods and documents better than I—following the institutional position in the Church, the Vatican's position toward this—might shed light on how she was so competent to create this experience that seems so important to understanding human beings.

IV

RK: In *New Maladies of the Soul*, you offer a fascinating study of Didier—a troubled soul who paints, but has no response. There is no credo and even his own mother looks at his paintings and does not judge them. He has a certain "*regard de la mère*," but it is not enough.

JK: And now he is accepting the couch to interpret that . . .

RK: Yes, so the turning point in the case was when you decided to give your own responses, your own reactions to his painting. Painting or composing was not in itself enough for healing. Didier needed you to respond.

JK: Yes, in this case I allowed the patient to bring in his paintings and also some reproductions that he owned, and I saw them and we began to speak about them. First, he became very aggressive. He said, "You speak like every psychoanalyst. I thought that you, Julia Kristeva, would be much more intelligent. Why do you speak like this about my images?" And then he became more interested in what he had been suffering and described how it happened and how he might go beyond it. And he started to have his own words, a new, more sensorial language than the abstract discourse of before.

RK: This reminds me of the question Jeffrey Bloechl raised at the Boston College seminar on your work regarding the different kinds of language Teresa used—some more theological, others more psychological, some more narrative and poetic, others more analytic and abstract. Is there an order of priority or importance here? Especially when it relates back to the question of writing as therapy?

JK: It is true that there are different genres in Teresa's work. There is poetry and there are the self-analytic works—*The Life* is not the same as the *Interior Castle*. The deepening of the auto-analysis, the self-analysis is clearer in the later book. The first one is more on the surface of what happened but not in the self. But in the analysis of the psyche and the foundations, it is more historical and political. Yet even there, there are a lot of psychological elements: she speaks, for example, about a different sister with whom she was in connection; she analyses their own traumatisms, their own failures and relations. There are a lot of different styles. But her poetry is not, I believe, her most powerful mode of expression. In some respects, she is more analytic than poetic. And I think this may have something to do with her reading of Saint John of the Cross: she got the impression that his condensed way of expressing the faith through poetry, through poetic language that is a small condensed narrative, makes the faith experience closer to asceticism. And she was terrified by this when she observed how John of the Cross lived his day. She said about him, "I am horrified by you!" ("*Je suis epouvantée par toi*"). She was shocked by this, and she wanted to unfold this conversation that brought him such sacrifice. Teresa wanted to take her distance from the excessively severe and at times almost sado-masochist tendencies of John, whom she also called her "little Seneca" because of his Stoical habits. Teresa herself was quite strict in establishing the *decalced* (shoeless) Carmelites; but while she discouraged the nuns from going out of the convent enclosure and becoming too worldly, in favor of a demanding spiritual prayer life, she steered clear of masochistic extremes. For her, spiritual discipline was a way of maintaining a permanent contact with the "essence," which allowed also for "exaltation" within the enclosure of the discipline. In other words, Teresa did not want to sacrifice herself but to give herself as a love relationship to God and to human society. The monastic enclosure was strict, severe, rigorous. But this very rigor was a sort of critique of the surrounding world of the decadent capitalist trade market and so on. It was a reaction to the decline of the golden age of the Hispanic invasion of Latin America. The *Interior Castle* is delivered as a narrative to the world to show that such inner experience is possible. It is going between the interior and the exterior. I describe this as her being in an external inclusion or internal exclusion vis-à-vis the world. And she believed that what she was experiencing in her particular time and place was also true of the human condition. She was political as well as spiritual in her writing. She moves between the different worlds.

V.

RK: Another important question from the Boston College discussion concerns your analysis of Teresa's love. At some points (as Frances Restuccia notes) you detect elements of sado-masochism; at other points you have the narrator of *Teresa My Love*, Sylvie Leclerc, declare something to the effect of: "I am out of love with love. Crazy love is a disease." Could you say more about this paradoxical, not to say contradictory, position?

JK: I do believe that Teresa passes through masochistic experiences of faith. In the beginning of her vocation as a nun, she was very unhappy and suffering a lot; she was very sick. When she represents some of her early visions, the vision is of a God with a severe face who condemns her and, close to this severe face she sees a cowl, something that I see as being connected to sex, but in a negative way as a disgusting, repulsive representation of sex. And what happened in that period, as far as we know from the biographies of nuns and monks, is that they were driven between two emotions—on the one hand, the purity of God, and on the other hand, as young ladies they had the right to have visitors, and there were some love affairs. But this excitation, physical excitation was present and refused. So in refusing this, she opted for suffering. There was an exaltation of the masochism in a sense. And this situation changed when she realized through her confession that God is love. God does not prevent her from excitation, but approves her if she can translate this physical attitude into a more sublimated, verbal, transmissible movement. And she began to write about it. This is very interesting as a shift from masochism to the right to have pleasure—with restrictions, of course, but not with condemnation. And I think here Teresa triumphs at the very point where Freud's famous patient, President Schreber, failed. Why? Because Schreber was very excited on different occasions, but he thought that God would condemn him and cut him into pieces. And this notion of the fierce God is something that fuels masochism. Teresa changes this idea of the God that is closer to the Old Testament—the God that condemns us, the God of judgment—into the loving father. This shifting, which reduces without abandoning a certain severity, makes her more at ease with her conception of love. She continued in her life and writing to broaden her comprehension of the love experience—without masochism.

RK: So the temptation to identify with a so-called masochistic, sacrificial Christ was to be overcome?

JK: Yes, it was to be overcome, and in her epileptic fits, she shared also the suffering because when she describes what happens, there is a very interesting representation of hell. For her hell is not as we find it in the pictures—devils with different forms of torture that are very much eroticized in Western pictorial art. She thinks that this is something that is very superficial; this is not hell for her. Hell is the narrow place where the body itself cannot stay. It is the repression or regression of the body—there is no body at all, and there is no possibility to represent it. So the way to bypass hell is to restore the body and the capacity of representation, thus giving the body the possibility to find its language is resurrection, and hell is the impossibility to speak about the body. So we could say that Teresa is really a therapist of herself, but very much helped by this invitation that her confessors gave to her to speak and write.

RK: This raises the big question: are you reducing Teresa to psychoanalysis, or are you raising psychoanalysis to religion? Some commentators, like Dennis Taylor, think you are doing the latter and that this is what gives a singular energy to your work on Catholic mysticism. As Taylor put it in his question after your talk, "Is this something inside Catholicism, is it something outside Catholicism or is it Catholicism?"

JK: I think that psychoanalysis is, for today, the last daughter of Catholicism—because Freud was very attentive to Judaism and to Christianity, and he did what he could to show this heritage but at the same time to distance himself from it. I do not, I repeat, want to reduce Teresa to psychoanalysis. I think only that from the human sciences and the social sciences, the only rational approaches to human beings, psychoanalysis could come closest to her experience and to the experience of faith—particularly to the Christian faith because it is given in language. Teresa's Catholic experience of language, like that of psychoanalysis, witnesses to this coincidence, or this neighborhood, between excitation and verbalization. My problem is not to reduce her experience to what I say or what we can say from the psychoanalytic point of view. I do not think that psychoanalysis can analyze God, but it can analyze the *experience* of God. So it cannot become a theology; but it can say something about how people live their faith.

RK: I would like to press you again here on the relationship between Teresa and atheism. For me, Teresa is—like certain other mystics from Eckhart to Hillesum—an anatheist. But I would like to hear your own view of what Teresa can teach us about the intimate rapport between mysticism and the critical faith options of theism, atheism, and anatheism. Derrida notes that mysticism is often accused of being a-theistic, as was the case with several condemned heretics and even Leibniz. As you know, I myself prefer the term ana-theist in the sense of critically revisiting a genuine sense of the sacred after the death of God (understood in the metaphysical concept of a Supreme Being or Cause).

JK: I am happy to come back to this point. When Teresa was submitted to the Inquisition, it was not only because she was eccentric and an intrepid business woman—she describes herself as a business woman, *une femme d'affaires*—but also because in the *Interior Castle*, when you go to the seventh stage, you find Christ as "white light." Here, there is something that is sensorial but not really visible. It is something unvisible, nonvisible yet felt through the body. It is more in the sense of the purity of her Catholic faith, but she finds Christ in herself. So the Inquisition said, God is in you, you are God; this is blasphemy and we can burn you! Someone who understood this very well and transformed it into a philosophical experience, was, as you say, Leibniz. He wrote a letter to a friend saying that in his mathematical thinking about the monads—each subject enclosing the infinite—he discovered that there is no identity without being able to grasp infinity in itself. If you don't possess infinity, you don't have identity. You are a sort of a nonspeaking animal, without psychological awareness of what you are. It is a part of being an actor in the world. Leibnitz said, there was a woman, a nun, who experienced what I am doing in mathematics, because she considered that there is only God and her in this world, and God is in her. I think that this is the Christian notion of incarnation experienced, in a paroxystic way, by Teresa. So is this a denial of Christianity? Is this atheism? Some people from the Inquisition thought it was. I personally think that this is a step toward humanism, a new humanism worthy of its name—something close to what you call anatheism. But are we in a position to practice such a new humanism today if are losing the notion of the infinite? What is the notion of the infinite? Is it God? We can sustain this in order to explain maybe what we understand by God. But I will say in my agnostic way, it is the infinite chain of human beings who have been before us and will come after us. It is the infinite chain of the human mind, as far as it is able to analyze what is the big bang, what is before the big bang and after the big bang—this capacity of the human being to embrace being. It is a sort of dance around the Heideggerian notion of being that I propose. In the case of Teresa—she found this in herself. This appropriation of the infinite by humanity. In a sense, you can say that this was a sort of atheism, but informed by religion. And let me add this: When I interpret from a psychoanalytic point of view such mystical experiences, I do not seek to justify them or propose them as a model of behavior or of therapy for traumatic experience. Teresa was very eccentric but also very rational and very faithful to certain forms of institutional rules and authorities. She had no wish to disturb in a perverted way the canon of the church in order to demonstrate the extreme aspects of her love for God. She was quite moderate, finally. But even in the case of pathological experiences of psychotic or perverted excess, I think that scientific curiosity must never abandon the hope to understand such experiences, to follow them, and to help. The danger is for certain psychotic visionaries and leaders of sects to exploit such experiences in order to become "masters of the world."

RK: This raises questions of authentic mysticism as opposed to pseudomysticism. And I think this may be a good point to return to the critical relationship between faith and fiction. In the Christian tradition, faith has often been seen as a form of existential consolation—a matter of hope in things to come, as Augustine put it. Ernst Bloch explores this kind of faith as a desire for utopia, an imaginative faith in the dream of the not-yet. Fiction seems to be a way of consoling ourselves in the realm of the imaginary, the virtual, and the oneiric. But surely Teresa believed that her faith was more than a fiction. And surely this mattered to her, and to those who believed in her belief.

JK: Let me try and answer this personally. When I began to write novels, it was, for me, inevitable. It's something that was a reality that was imposed from without, and that I could not resist. So it was a sort of faith, yes, even a necessity to give words to certain traumatic events and to find a certain consolation by doing so, by the simple fact of addressing the pain in language, expressing what I was feeling by transposing it onto an empty page, voiding it into a form of writing which others might also like to read. This experience of sharing the traumatic experience is something that I cannot do with concepts. It is something other than theoretical writing: it is not only explanation. It is a sort of delivering, of freeing myself, with the conviction that it will be accepted. Even if it is for a small group of people, that's enough. There is a specific kind of faith in the writing of fiction—when I write fiction, it is a construction. It is something that I decide to do. If it is not an illusion, it is nevertheless an ephemeral act that can be analyzed. It can have one sense today and another sense tomorrow. I can also give some sense to this. One part of me is in need, entirely, and there is another part of me that is free of it, that can take some distance from it. I think that in our writings today and other aesthetic experiences, we have both of these attitudes: of engulfing ourselves in them and of being withdrawn from them. The second part is even more important sometimes than the first. This is the difference between what happens in the experience of mystical faith with and without writing. In mystical experience, it seems that the mystic liberates him- or herself from the control of the ego and superego—that is from the critical vigilance of thought, by way of rejoining primary regressive states in a state of complete sensorial abandon. Writing the abandon is never total, and the importance of reasoning along with the rhetorical formulation in concurrence with the literary and aesthetic memory of a civilization, remains constantly present and protects or "saves" the mystical writer, or the artist, from complete abandon. In my book on Teresa, I point out that the experience of the mystics that has survived is one that is written and even reflected on, which leads me to say that many mystics reached a certain distance from the pathological destructuration of abandon and, like Teresa herself, can be considered as authors of a universal message. I find most of the great mystics have these two movements. Think of the well-known anatheist sentence of Meister Eckhart: "I ask God to make me free from God." Teresa has something like this too. She was a great player of chess. She would say to her sisters things like, "you know it is forbidden to play in monasteries, but I allow you to play. You can play chess. Why? Because you may checkmate God, our Master, Notre Seigneur. And do not think that I am blaspheming by saying this, because there was someone who already checkmated him, it is our Mother, the Virgin Mary who took a child from him." Teresa has faith and she writes; she makes fiction and humor and she plays with God. She has a distance. It doesn't mean that she abolishes God. This distance is a freedom that I think is most possible in Catholicism.

RK: But not everyone can return to mystical experiences of Teresian Catholicism or medieval faith. How can one hope, if at all, to recuperate such moments of confession and conversion, to rehabilitate that lost sense of ecstasy and incorporation of the infinite? In today's society of consumerism and spectacle, which you so trenchantly diagnose in your recent works, what it to be done? My question is a practical one.

JK: Why I try to rehabilitate this through fiction, and not only through Heideggerian reading—we are not obliged to go from Heidegger to St. Teresa, though some people may be attracted by this—is because I have the impression that the world was created in order to end up as a book. Here I cite Mallarmé, to whom I dedicated my doctoral thesis, *La Revolution du*

Langage Poétique. Now, while I am in America—it happens in Europe too, but here it is even stronger—I get the impression that the world has been created in order to end in a market, and the book is condemned. It still exists; it will last in, or be transformed into, the internet. And why not? There are privileged innovations that come with the internet—rapidity, flexibility, the capacity to make linkages between very diverse people on some level. But what happens is that "inner experience" disappears in this rapidity of communication in the market. Market communications, visual communication, the society of spectacle and simulation—all of those modern trends (of which I would not want to deny the advantages) go in the direction of erasing the depth of the human psyche. The return of Augustine into the soul, the unconscious analysis of Freud, and other forms of interiority appear to be increasingly limited to privileged elites, rather than being available to contemporary society at large. I think that it can last for a while and that it is important for those who have access to this inner experience to try to rehabilitate it, because there is no other way to resist the other tendency. The other tendency will continue, and it also represents "progress" in a sense. We cannot deny it or destroy it, but we can still complement it with something else. I think it is not impossible to rebuild this deep, internal life. It may not be possible for everyone. It may be that the democratic utopia—where everyone could have this psychic depth, this capacity to read Plato or Teresa or Joyce—is a utopia. But it is important to maintain this horizon and to try to develop it as far as possible for those who participate in the open, globalized market.

VI

RK: I would like to return finally to the matter of hope—Teresa's hope. This is a question posed to you by William Richardson, the Jesuit philosopher, Heidegger scholar, and psychoanalyst. He argues that your writing on Teresa is richly literary and very profound psychoanalytically, but that it remains at the level of an anthropocentric analysis of a classic mystic. What is there in your understanding of her experience that makes hope necessary? What does her faith hope for? Your description in literary-psychoanalytic terms is a description of the *anthropos*, but it remains that. So the question remains, if the mystical experience of God or the Father as you describe it, does not imply something *more* than that? A transcendence as well as an immanence? In other words, where is the experience of *otherness* in all this, which enables her to have hope, faith, and wonder in the first place?

JK: Thank you for pursuing this and pushing me to be more precise. The otherness is in us. The transcendence is within. The speaking being is the one who has the transcendence in herself, and that is what Teresa finds in the seventh stage of her castle. This otherness is our capacity to love. If you have this desire to love, which is dependent on the need to believe in the other and in the otherness in oneself, it means that you are capable of infinite transcendence of yourself. And this transcendence of the self is what we call in psychoanalysis the subject capable of different creations and links. This is what makes the meaning that is outside of us also something that is fulfilled by us. Teresa's position, if I can summarize it, is that transcendence is what makes us go beyond our limits and the limits of every social framework. But this transcendence is incarnated in my capacity as a human being to speak and love. This capacity of speaking as loving is transcendence. And this, I believe, is very Christian. It is Christian in the sense of what you say God is. When you say that God is love, I suppose it doesn't mean that in the sky there is something waiting for me, to love me. It means that the anthropological condition is possible only if we consider that it is inhabited by the emotion of love and the capacity to sublimate it in different ways. That could be science, music, or art, and it could be some kind of generous politics—why not?—but this capacity of infinite loving sublimation is what transcends the biological being, what enables being to become being. This is outside of my capacity; it escapes me, but it is rooted in me. This is one of the manifestations of transcendence. So this, I would say, is Teresa's hope. Hope as the ability to transcend. I consider singularity, the capacity to be unique, and to transcend in a unique way, to be the greatest value of humans. Perhaps I should not use the word *value* since it is so related to the market, but it is the great particularity of human beings. It means that it is the only hope. It is so tremendous, positive, and encouraging, when you consider that every one of us—be it the genius or the disabled—is capable of this transcendence. This transcendence is not outside; it is here, it is in you and me, and it is on this table. But people have to make an effort to do it, to become transcending subjects rather than reduce themselves to passive and possessive objects. And here I return to the question of the infinite. We are finite beings as Heidegger and Freud remind us, yes, but there is no finitude for the word. There is finitude for the human body, the physical body, for physics, but my words will be sustained forever where human beings exist. The infinite is the word. This is a contradiction of finitude that makes us tragic, but this is precisely what pushes us to invest words, to move toward creation, toward the possibility to transcend our limits, into something that will speak to and for others, not only close to me today but in future generations when I will no longer be. The word is the hope and faith in transmission through creation, through the chains of writings in the infinity of time. And here we rejoin perhaps a dialogue with contemporary astrophysicists who are thinking about time and infinity. Is the world that we can know infinite, or can it stop—and if it stops, what will happen? The notion of the limit (*peras, finis, limen*) and the infinite is something very important for our ways of thinking. We can imagine an extra transcendental instance that we call God, and it will be an infinite itself. Or we can imagine the evolution of the existing world, as permanent construction and deconstruction, the big bang and then the big crunch, and it all beginning over again. But it does not concern the limit of the human being. It is may be a great pretension to imagine that the human being can be eternal, when what is eternal is our thinking about the evolution of being itself.

JULIA KRISTEVA is a psychoanalyst, critic, novelist, and educator, best known for her writings in structuralist linguistics, psychoanalysis, semiotics, and philosophical feminism. Her sizable body of work includes books and essays that address intertextuality, the semiotic, and abjection in the fields of linguistics, literary theory and criticism, psychoanalysis, biography and autobiography, political and cultural analysis, and art and art history. She is currently a professor at the University Paris Diderot.

Notes

1. Cf. my quotation of Husserl in "The Passion According to Teresa of Avila," in *Carnal Hermeneutics*, 259.

4 An Anatheist Exchange: Returning to the Body after the Flesh

Emmanuel Falque and Richard Kearney

I

EF: I recently read *Anatheism*. I find your idea of returning to God after God very interesting. What fascinates me is your suggestion that it is better for the theist not to reject but to listen to what it means to be a man-without-God. I come to a similar conclusion in the third chapter of my book *The Metamorphosis of Finitude* titled "Is There a Drama of Atheist Humanism?" There I observe that we are no longer in the situation of the 1950s, no longer in the context of Henri de Lubac. In his work *The Drama of Atheist Humanism*, de Lubac examines the positivism of Comte, the materialism of Marx, and the nihilism of Nietzsche, in order first to understand them and then to reject them. In other words, de Lubac's attitude is a good one in the sense that he wants to understand before condemning, and that was absolutely new when Christianity was confronted in France with seemingly "virulent" forms of atheism. But today, the conflict between theism and atheism has lost its drama. Atheism is no longer seen as virulent (as in the 1970s), but as coherent. We all have friends and family members who do not believe in God. We don't have to condemn them, even if we are believers and they are not. We simply have to understand that their conceptions are different from ours. If my brother, my son, my sister, or my friend does not share my Christian views, it does not mean that their lives lack meaning just because their meaning is not my meaning. On the contrary, I have to accept that it is possible to find meaning in life outside of my own meaning, even if God is the meaning of my life. We have to recognize that we can be transformed by this other—and not just try to convert him. One can be "without God" without being "against God," as the theologian Eberhardt Jüngel said. One of the greatest problems confronting Christianity today is to decide if there can still be sense and meaning outside of Christianity. It is exactly the question raised by Merleau-Ponty in his essay *In Praise of Philosophy*, without explicitly speaking of de Lubac. He asks, *Why do you say that every nontheism is an a-theism or an anti-theism? Why do you think that not speaking about God means that one is against God?* Merleau-Ponty recognized—and I think it is all the more evident today—that the historical situation has changed. The either-or of dogmatism or atheism is no longer sufficient. It hasn't been for some time. So for me, the question that must be asked is, "Should we search for a third path?" This, I think, is the question of *Anatheism*.

RK: Yes, it is. But the matter is complex. The third path, as you call it, is not some Hegelian mediation of theism and atheism leading to a higher synthesis of "absolute knowledge." There is no guarantee of dialectical progress. On the contrary, anatheism is a wager and a risk, an adventure and a drama. If it is a "third," it is a kind of excluded middle—what is forgotten or omitted in the adversarial binarism of theism-versus-atheism. I prefer to see the anatheist moment not as a telos but as a "possibility," a "promise," a "call"—a *dis-position* that bypasses the mutually exclusive "positions" of theistic or atheistic belief (namely, the propositional claim that God exists or does not exist). Anatheism is an invitation to think otherwise. Another kind of faith in the call of "Perhaps." That is why I wrote a book called *The God Who May Be* (2009) and why my first book was called *Poétique du Possible* (1984).

EF: But perhaps we differ in this: I am skeptical of this search for a third way whereas you embrace it. I would rather ask: "how can I be transformed by the atheist who lives without God but who is not against God?" It is for me a consequence of the Incarnation (our incarnation and Incarnation of God) that we have to think of this man without God but not against God. It is a paradox. But it means something like *Gaudium et spes* explains in § 22: it is because God became human that we understand what becoming human as such means. So my position is that, after the Incarnation, the word "atheism" is no longer adequate. I am not at all a defeatist with regard to the actual world—I often think of Kant who said in the beginning of his *Religion Beyond the Limits of Reason Alone* that each epoch believes itself to be worse than the preceding one according to a gradual decadence. What I explore in *The Metamorphosis of Finitude* is in a sense a fidelity to the spirit of Thomas Aquinas, who in the opening words of the *Summa Contra Gentiles* explains that he was obliged to seek refuge in Natural Reason, because he had no other means. For me, the Natural Reason of Thomas, the Natural Light of Reason, is nothing but the quest for a common name. Common for all people. Instead of saying "you need reason in order to be able to ascend to God," he says: "with the Jews I have the Old Testament in common, with the heretics I have the New Testament in common, but with the pagans I have nothing in common so I need to find this 'common' thing

I call 'reason.'" My hypothesis, then, is this: one does not have to follow Thomas Aquinas to the letter, but one should be true to his spirit.

RK: What would you say is the "spirit" of St. Thomas today? Would you equate it with an appeal to the natural light of reason? A sort of reprise of natural theology?

EF: I understand it as an openness to the novelty of one's time (for Thomas that was the introduction of Aristotle), transforming it in the light of Christianity. In *The Metamorphosis of Finitude*, I make the case that what we have in common today is no longer reason as it was for Aquinas. We think after Nietzsche, after Freud, so what we have in common is *finitude*, the consciousness and horizon of death, and thereby the necessity to ask the question of meaning from this perspective. If it is finitude that we all—believers and nonbelievers, Christians and pagan alike—have in common, then it is about finitude that we should first talk. This means that we have to speak primarily about the possibility of posing the question of meaning.

RK: So for you, the Christian is the one who lets him or herself be transformed by the one who does not believe. And at the same time, nonbelievers can let themselves be transformed by believers? I agree. Anatheism as I understand it is a crossing of belief and nonbelief. The holding open of a space and time where both can converse. In that sense it may be thought of as a double condition of hospitality to both faith and questioning—they need each other.

EF: The paradigm is dialogical, I agree, not as a paradigm of saturation but as a paradigm of transformation. How can the other who is without God but not against God teach me to be without God in my turn as well? So you see, I agree with your anatheist diagnostics. But I do have some hesitations about the idea of a third way, if the third way is only a manner of overcoming the opposition between theism and atheism. I worry that the third way—but you are very prudent on this point—might become a higher dialectical solution that reintroduces the question of God without us being transformed by the other who says that he does need God.

RK: I appreciate your reservations, but let me repeat: the *ana* of anatheism does not just come *after* theism and atheism, as some kind of speculative synthesis, but is a manner of being openly predisposed to the adventure of belief and nonbelief, of darkness and light. As when Dostoyevsky says that "true faith comes forth from the crucible of doubt," or John of the Cross and G. M. Hopkins testify that epiphany comes from the dark night of the soul. In a sense, the *ana*-turn is a return to the condition of the possibility of faith and nonfaith. It is what I call, following Keats, "negative capability":

namely, a disposition to receive what comes without *knowing* the answer in advance. Pure attention. Vigilance. Receptivity. What Rilke calls "the open." The *ana-* is a letting go of something, of all that you think you know, in order to open yourself to the possibility of something novel and strange (which sometimes can be the oldest thing in the book). And, from a philosophical point of view, one can see analogies in the repeated attempts of thinkers from time immemorial to get back to first beginnings in order to question and wonder at what is—the Socratic method of not-knowing, Cusa's *docta ignorantia*, Husserl's phenomenological epoche (suspension of the natural attitude of prejudice and presupposition) so as to open one's mind to the evidence, to the giving of givenness [*Gegebenheit/Es Gibt*], to the "things themselves" (which, for Husserl, are gifted as possibility and actuality). An openness to the call of the possible. A primary ontological attention to the primal ontological question: why is there something rather than nothing? Anatheism asks: Why is there God rather than no-God? It is a return to conditions of possibility, but deeper than Kant, because it is existential before it is theoretical. That is why the anatheist moment can be one of anxiety and crisis—experiencing one's finitude and limit—as well as of wonder and surprise. That moment is often best captured in imagination—art, myth, metaphor, story, testimony—before it ever becomes a speculative or conceptual theory. Which is why I give such attention to writers, artists, and poets in *Anatheism*. They are privileged witnesses to wonder and epiphany, to a nondogmatic sense of the sacred that, I firmly believe, every genuine religion needs to be nourished by.

EF: Please, say more about this. I agree, of course, that the sacred is a dimension of the human being. But is the sacred exactly an experience of God? What does that mean to speak about the presence of God without God? Why do we have to oppose speculative theory or dogma on the one hand, and literature and art on the other? What is the use of culture, and even of Christianity, in that sense?

RK: Stories are more open than doctrines. As Ricoeur rightly says, *l'imagination ne connait pas de censure*. Which does not mean it is mere fiction—or if it is, it is a fiction that speaks truth: an *as-if* that tells it *as* it is. Every tradition has its own unique set of narratives and testimonies and I do not want to attribute any triumphal superiority to those of my own Catholic Christianity—though of course they have priority for me as my personal faith heritage and primary belonging. I realize I have much to learn from the stories of others. I believe that narrative faith traditions have an *equal* right to be heard and read—which does not mean for one moment that they are the same. This for me this a crucial aspect of anatheism. It signals its essential *inter-religiosity.* A readiness to provisionally suspend one's own inherited beliefs in order to listen to another's faith narratives in a way that allows for a more liberating, pluralist, and amplified appreciation of one's own. This detour of self-through-other permits one to return to one's own God anew. (Or maybe not, one may well embrace another spiritual path). Again, it is a risk and a wager, but a journey worth taking. A journey of exodus and possible return. That is why ana-theism is a movement of God-after-God. And narrativity is indispensable here. Without stories—our stories and the stories of others—we do not go beyond our enclosed selves; or if we do, we are left with an existential experience that we cannot communicate; or that is betrayed by being reduced too quickly to the rigid conceptual doctrines of our own tradition. Divinity is too big for one mansion. That is why God has many mansions. And many voices. And insists on revealing the divine in scriptures and stories—for example in the Abrahamic tradition, we might cite the narratives of Genesis, Exodus, and Kings down to the four gospels and the hadiths.

II

EF: How does this apply to your reading of your own narrative tradition? Is there something specific for you in the epiphany of God in Christianity?

RK: What interests me about Christ is that he came on earth to heal and tell stories. I see Judeo-Christianity as marking a mutation from one kind of God to another. From God as superintendent of the universe to God as suffering servant. That was the message of Isaiah. And it was Christ's too when he exclaimed "My God, my God, why have you forsaken me?" In that moment of atheism, he let go of the God of theodicy, the God of expiatory sacrifice, of substitutional atonement, of Patriarchal Power and Might—the magic Nobodaddy—and out of that moment of suspension and kenosis came the opening to another kind of God (after God)—to which Christ then consents: "Unto thee I commend my spirit." It is the same for Judaism (I am against supercessionism). Abraham on Mount Moria let go of the God of blood sacrifice: he ultimately moved beyond Elohim's command to sacrifice his son Isaac by embracing a God of Mercy, Yahweh, who says "Do not kill your son." Likewise, at Mamre, Abraham forwent his tribal God in order to welcome the three strangers from the desert—who are subsequently revealed as the God of hospitality and natality (the strangers at Mamre announce the birth of an impossible child, Isaac, prefiguring Gabriel's annunciation of another child, Jesus, in Nazareth). The annunciations of Mamre and Nazareth are two pages from the same book. Indeed, I often imagine that what Mary is reading in all those classic religious paintings of the Annunciation—there is always a page open at a lectern—is precisely the scene of the strangers announcing the birth of Isaac to Sarah and Abraham! In the hosting of strangers from nowhere, the impossible is made possible, hostility becomes hospitality. Abraham's old God is suspended [*epoche*] so that a new God can appear. There is a constant repetition of God-after-God-after-God. So I would say there are two ways of reading *Anatheism*. The first is the historical and sociological—as a phenomenon of contemporary faith after Freud, Marx, and Nietzsche, after the secular enlightenment and modern democratic revolutions—and the second is the existential, ontological, eschatological. The first is culturally and contextually specific; the second is trans-cultural, universal, timeless. Both are relevant.

EF: We should perhaps say that the drama of atheist humanism—or the return of anatheism—is not merely a question of time, history, culture. It is really an ontological question to be asked on a theological level. If we do not, we are simply thinkers of our time.

RK: Yes. But we need to think *both* our particular time and the quasi-universal condition of possibility of hospitality to the stranger, which I see as the inaugural "anatheist" moment of all wisdom traditions.

EF: But in order to transpose the question onto a theological level, you have to ask it in terms of human experience. Starting from myself, I can never affirm that *after* mankind there is something. It is God who says that there is something after me. That is the sense of Golgotha and of Christ on the cross. The theological question is to know what is meant by *Eli, Eli, lam sabachtani*. We know the famous phrase of Moltmann that God has been abandoned by God. With many others, Balthasar among them, I have criticized this thesis because the proper quality of God on the cross is that he continues to address himself to the father. That is, for me, the sense of the death of the son: that in his dying, he remains open to alterity. It is the father who opens this alterity. Or take the example of the disciples at Emmaus. It is not sufficient to remark that they only recognized Christ at the moment he disappeared. You have to interpret the text not from its end but from its beginning—"Weren't our hearts burning in us when we walked with him?" At this point, we cannot stay with hermeneutics. It is an affair of *pathos*, of a *divine empathy*—the kind that exists between two men who meet each other in their sorrow. The disciples recognize Christ because they have *already* experienced the feeling of recognizing him without recognizing who he is. This is the power of Christianity, but also its greatest difficulty: only through man can we see God.

RK: That sounds like apologetics or Christocentrism. Are you saying everyone is a Christian, even if they don't know it? Are you espousing a version of Rahner's "anonymous Christians"?

EF: No, they are not anonymous Christians. They have to be baptized, even secretly in their hearts. The question is not a question of identity (to be Christian or not) but of community (what do I have in common with the others who are not thinking and speaking like me?). Even if we are believers, we still have something in common with our "human brothers," as Bernanos says. It is what I call *l'homme tout court*, the human as such, in the sense of our finitude: birth, anguish before death, suffering, joy, body, eros, and so on. Our community of humanity is the basis from which our differences can emerge. That is why I want to avoid any form of apologetics. My aim is not to convert anybody; I simply want to develop a *credible* Christianity, which is not only *believable*. It is God's business to know if people convert, not mine. I only want to furnish words—in the line of Vatican II, starting from contemporary culture, in the words of actuality, words about finitude, and so forth—to say that Christianity can be credible. Instead of apologetics, I want to know and to make known *where we are as human beings*. But that does not mean that we have to stop at the cross—not because we don't support the anguish of death, but because it is the choice of the father to make us pass from the corruptible to the incorruptible in his son. The *Metamorphosis of Finitude* is not just the title of a book, but the act by which the son carries the weight of the world and passes it to his father to transform it in the force of the Holy Spirit.

RK: Is it philosophy or theology you're talking now?

EF: It is theology. But it is precisely because it is now theology that I can say that it was first philosophy. We don't always suspect that someone who is speaking theologically is a philosopher and vice-versa. But I say that you have to cross the Rubicon. It is only when I am on the side of the resurrection that I can say, "truly I have been on the side of finitude." Only when I am speaking theologically can I recognize myself as a philosopher.

RK: But could an atheist philosopher say that?

EF: He can't assume to be a theologian, of course. But he can and must understand that I am a true philosopher when I am speaking about finitude at the beginning. I am against crypto-theology in philosophy, and I don't want to live in what Paul Ricoeur called a "controlled schizophrenia" regarding the distinction between philosophy and theology. Today, as far as I can tell, we have two models: the model of separation and the model of crossing. The first seeks to establish "true discourse" by doing away with tradition. Contemporary philosophy of God is searching for a pure discourse: it may be the discourse of charity (Jean-Luc Marion), of the face (Emmanuel Levinas), of prayer (Jean-Louis Chrétien), of the flesh as pure Christian experience (Michel Henry), and so forth. What we observe with these representatives of the "French theological turn" is that they are thinkers of rupture. The three orders of Pascal are always interpreted as separation and not figuration (which is my own interpretation, because Pascalian thought is first rooted in the link between the two testaments). The second model of crossing is closer to the chiasmus of Merleau-Ponty than to the overcoming of metaphysics in Heidegger: it tries to show the inverse, that there is something in common in all humanity and that the order of believers is not necessarily better or superior than the others. The paradox is the fact that Catholic thinkers in France seems to be completely Protestant when they claim this model of rupture that is as sort of translation of the doctrine of pure grace in theology into philosophy. As long as Martin Heidegger remains the key source, French phenomenology will always stay in this model of rupture, which is the opposite to the model of continuity, as in Thomas Aquinas for example.

RK: I think you could also add the deconstructive model of radical alterity to your list of Jewish/Protestant rupture. Though it is curious how most of the French phenomenologists of the theological turn you just listed are of Catholic formation (who is more Catholic than Marion?). Ricoeur, a Protestant, seems to be closer to your second model of crossing and mediation! So let me try to understand your position better. For you, it seems, Catholicism is a theology of mixture, mediation, and *métissage*. And you oppose this to the current French phenomenology of separation and rupture, which is contextually and historically linked to the critical influence of Heidegger who, after 1917 and his turn to Lutheranism, had a position much closer to Protestantism than to Catholicism.

EF: Indeed. And that French Heideggerian movement could be said to mark a conversion of theology by philosophy. But on the other hand, we have what I call the act of "crossing of the Rubicon." It is not enough to convert or to translate theology into philosophy—with Heidegger—we have to also convert philosophy into theology. The conversion of philosophy by theology means that the link between philosophy and theology is two-way. I argue that this second option evolves in three phases in the history of Christian philosophy. The first phase refers to Duns Scotus, who wanted to liberate God and thereby—let's say accidently, because it was not his aim—provoked contingency. He says that contingent being is positive being. And this is precisely the first moment: I do not have an experience of God other than through the human being. The second phase is that of Thomas Aquinas. He says that one can understand certain aspects of God—for instance, existence, unity, or infinity. But other aspects, he argues, cannot be accessed without revelation—that is that God is a trinity, that his only son became incarnate, that he suffered, died, and rose again. But what else does he say? He adds that human beings can grasp everything thanks to revelation. I do not have to reason my way to the understanding that God exists. I know it from scripture: "I am who I am" (Exodus 3:16). The third phase is Bonaventure. He introduces the idea that everything is contained in God. Nothing happens to men that does not happen first in God, that is, in the trinity. For me, God becomes the author of transformation in the world. If there is anxiety in me, this anxiety is experienced in the relation between the father and son and is thereby transformed. For example, if a couple receives the Christian sacrament of marriage, the erotic love of a man for his wife and vice-versa, is transformed in the trinity. In my eyes, there is no equivocity (Nygren) and no univocity (Marion) between eros and agape, but rather a sort of metamorphosis of eros in agape. The trinity is the author of this transformation and conversion. In that way, love or eros is not first an ideal of charity, but the meeting of two persons in their own chaos in the attempt to share it together and eventually to convert it into God. We must renounce the ideal of transparency or the transcendent view from above, as Merleau-Ponty said.

RK: Merleau-Ponty is not a thinker of rupture but a "continuist," as Sartre observed. My own understanding of God-after-God is very informed by Merleau-Ponty as I try to show in the fourth chapter of *Anatheism*, entitled "In the Flesh: Sacramental Imagination."

EF: Absolutely, even if the term "continuist" is not exactly the same as the term "chiasm" or "crossing" used by Merleau-Ponty, or as the term of "tiling between philosophy and theology" I use in *Crossing the Rubicon*. It is astonishing that neither Ricoeur, Henry, Chrétien, Marion nor Lacoste ever cite Merleau-Ponty. But today, for my generation, Merleau-Ponty is the philosopher *par excellence*, and I know he is also a key reference for you in *Anatheism*. My job is to show that we can think differently about philosophy and theology without contradicting the above-mentioned philosophers. That is also, for me, the reason for debating with Derrida and Marion in *Le combat amoureux* (*The Loving Struggle*), for example. Derrida has his *chora*, but Marion rejects it. Why? Because *chora* is a place of resistance and not of a transcendence (or of a gift) first given. In the words of Derrida, *chora* is the place of an irreducible darkness. Marion only seeks the darkness of bliss that is coming from Denys the Areopogite:

being blinded by too much light. On this point Janicaud offers a compelling critique, which is addressed to all French phenomenology: can we found a phenomenology on the basis of a phenomenality that is not immanent? And his response is an emphatic no. That is why I think the proper sense of Christianity is to take seriously immanence and incarnation, which makes it all the more astonishing that contemporary French phenomenology is rather a phenomenology of transcendence and of the absolute.

RK: The anatheist embrace of immanence—or, more exactly, of transcendence-in-immanence—is also a responsive openness to *chora*. Christian incarnation is not dualist or gnostic. It starts with *chora*. The questions of God and chora need to be asked together.

EF: Yes, I would speak rather of a *circumscription of chora*. That is why I have developed the concept of a *limited phenomenon* instead of a *saturated phenomenon*—not against it, but only because there are two different ways in philosophy as in theology. In philosophy, it means that the beginning is not first revelation but finitude, not first the gift but the resistance of the world, the consistence of the body and the anxiety of death. It is another point of departure. And in theology, it means that God articulates himself and is namable, only within limits. God has chosen to be inscribed in limits because of his incarnation. It is the debate between Balthasar and Rahner on the anthropological reduction. For me, it is not enough to say with Balthasar that Rahner's "anthropological reduction," by means of the concept *kenosis*, has reduced God to humanity. Rahner simply accepts the fact that God transformed himself into a man. We don't have to choose between Balthasar and Rahner; but we have to understand that we can't speak only about the excess of God in the Dionysian way or about the absolute freedom of God in the manner of Duns Scotus. There is also the possibility of speaking about the humility or poverty of God in the manner of Bonaventure or about man created first in his own limits, as Thomas Aquinas implies.

III

RK: Some thoughts come to mind as you speak of revelation and the debate between von Balthazar and Rahner. The first is baptism. What does it mean? How does it begin? Is there a natural baptism of desire—as when Christ speaks of those "baptized in fire and spirit" (Matthew 3:11)—or does one need the official ritual of the church? I believe there is a baptism of desire that everybody shares. An "ecclesiastical" baptism may come later from a priest for Christians, as a supplementary seconding in the doctrinal language of the church. Otherwise, one has that crazy (now-suspended) Catholic doctrine of Limbo—as a place where babies go who don't get dipped in a baptismal font! Ridiculous. Creation and kenosis and incarnation and salvation all come *before* the sacrament of baptism. Christ was begotten and made flesh and conceived and born before he was dunked by John the Baptist in the Jordan. Christianity as human incarnation comes before the sacrament of baptism. The sacrament of baptism simply confirms something that is already going on as promise, call, desire. Would you agree with this idea of natural baptism of fire or desire? A baptism that is ontological before it is theological?

EF: That is a difficult question, indeed. Yes, we could speak of a baptism of desire that is—if I understand you—a personal experience. But a baptism of desire presupposes desire. For me, however, the first experience is not the desire for God. The first experience for human being is the experience of death and finitude. In our culture, and even in our experience, it is no more possible to presuppose the existence of God or the aspiration to God. God is only a revelation or a manifestation given in the heart of finitude, in our limits. He is not first the accomplishment of our own desire to find something else, which is always a manner to run away from our living conditions. We have to speak after Nietzsche and the rejection of the "*arrières mondes*." I can't stand Irenic Christianity with its romantic groveling before the newborn child. From Freud, after Nietzsche, we learn that birth is a rupture—that life is tragic. There is no surpassing my human condition by means of some form of pious desire. A nonbeliever is before death and not beyond it. A medical doctor, for example, knows that he is going to die like all his patients in the hospital. But he does not need to believe in the afterlife to give a sense to his own life. Perhaps it is, inversely, because he is not a believer that he tries to find sense in this life, by serving other people and so on. It is always a defect of believers to believe that there is no meaning to life independently of their belief. That's why philosophy is always for me first.

RK: It sounds like Dr. Rieux in Camus's *The Plague*.

EF: Exactly. He has given a meaning to his life, and he doesn't need something that comes after, so desire is not the foundation of reality. To talk about the baptism of desire, we must acknowledge a desire that God has placed in each of us. But it is not a desire that we know from the start.

RK: I actually mean desire as a primordial ontological hunger, not some romantic fantasy. Eros as a primal drive for connection and love, already present, as Klein and Freud realized, from the moment we are born. I think even Plato might agree (at least in the *Symposium*). So what I wanted to express is that, for me, the sacramental—whether it concern the first rites of baptism or the last rites of extreme unction—starts already with birth. And therefore, the first *kenosis* for each human being is birth. I think here also of the Orthodox Christians who hold that the first *kenosis* of God is the moment of incarnation (with its attendant acceptance of limit, finitude, humanity as earth-bound or *humus*). The second is the baptismal drowning in the Jordan. The third is the crucifixion, the letting go of the Alpha-God in order to become fully human and therefore fully God. And each time, eros is accompanied by a certain thanatos, living with a certain dying (to oneself), ascent with descent. There is nothing Irenic or sentimental about it. So, I like to think that there is a baptism at birth, which is what you might call a moment of death, of separation, of loss, and trauma. Even Levinas speaks of an "original trauma." There is, from the start, already a radical experience of finitude and kenosis. I would thus link *eros* and *kenosis* as coterminous from that moment onward. Maybe it is proto-eros and proto-kenosis together making up a proto-baptism. One does not need to be baptized in a church to be saved, according to the old Catholic doctrine *extra ecclesia nulla salus*. I think that the emphasis you and I are putting on Merleau-Ponty and the flesh, even all the way down to the animal—certainly the animal in us—reveals that there is nothing that cannot be sanctified. Joyce insisted on that too as a good anatheist "Catholic." It is in that sense of potential inclusivism that I want to say that the ecclesial sacrament of baptism expresses an ontological predisposition. Anatheism is not saying something like: you are born a pagan nobody, then you are instituted into the church, then you lose that faith and then you discover God anew. No, anatheist eros is there *from the beginning*. The *ana* is not just what comes afterward, but, equiprimordially, what goes back to the very start. In that sense, anatheist knowledge (*connaissance*) starts with birth (*naissance*). Eros is what Christians have in common with the Greeks, the atheists, and so-called pagans. A sort of erotic *lumière naturelle*.

EF: This reminds me of Nicodemus's question in the gospels. How can a man reenter the womb of his mother and be born again? Indeed, you have to develop a phenomenology of natality in order to be able to develop a phenomenology of resurrection. It is very interesting what you are suggesting, that birth is already a kenosis. I completely agree with you. But we are not obliged, in a first step, to speak about birth in terms of kenosis or about eros in term of agape. Our first experience is only a human one because God became human. So, there is no way to speak about God outside of our humanity.

RK: I agree with your last sentence, but would add that precisely as human, the first cry of the child is the cry of abandonment and loss, of kenotic emptying and exposure (Nancy's ex-peau-sure): a primal natal cry which finds its Christian culmination in "my God, my God, why have you abandoned me!" Which reminds me of Joyce's line in *Ulysses* "What's God? A cry in the street."

EF: How true.

IV

RK: Let's turn to another question central to anatheism and your own work—the role of the body and animality in all of this.

EF: This point is important and more difficult. In *The Metamorphosis of Finitude* I developed the hypothesis that the resurrection of the flesh is the resurrection of life, of the experience of the flesh. But it was not enough, and that is why I then wrote *The Wedding Feast of the Lamb* about the Eucharist and the organic body. Of course, it is not so easy to defend today the idea that we will be resurrected with our organs without using them. This is what Thomas says in the last part of his *Summa Contra Gentiles* after Augustine in his *City of God*. But we have lost the sense of the organic body, even in phenomenology, by talking too much about the "lived body." If Augustine or Thomas Aquinas supported the idea that we have to be resurrected with our organic bodies, it doesn't mean, of course, that we will use our stomachs or sexual organs in eternity. But they wanted to affirm that nothing is lost in the act of resurrection. Everything is assumed and saved by God, as Gregory of Nyssa said. So we have to link resurrection and Eucharist in theology as we have to link the lived body and the organic body in phenomenology—even if French phenomenology has always favored the lived body over the organic body, because of a certain interpretation of Husserl.

RK: Husserl, as you note, says that we are not only objective *Körper* but also subjective *Leib*. That raises the important question of animality. You have previously written about the priority of the flesh over the body, the priority of the *experience* of the flesh. Phenomenology has traditionally given priority to sense over nonsense. But now you seem to be going in the opposite direction by raising the issue of organic matter?

EF: Here we have to pass from *The Metamorphosis of Finitude: Birth and Resurrection* to *The Wedding Feast of the Lamb: Eros, Body and Eucharist*. In a course given on Nietzsche and chaos by Heidegger in 1936 in Freiburg, he asks of Kant, what happens if matter can't be subsumed under a concept? One option is the intuition of the sublime, of saturation. The other possibility is that this experience is *unassignable*. It cannot even be constructed. The sublime is always already constructed—the saturated phenomenon of Marion surpasses me because of its excess of sense. It is not the absence of sense, or the outside of sense. But what if we find ourselves confronted with the radical *impossibility* of meaning, what Kant is calling in his *Critic of Pure Reason* the "mass of sensation"? Following this path, Merleau-Ponty asks the very same question. He speaks of brute nature (*nature brute*) of the wild world (*monde sauvage*), echoing Husserl who, in *Cartesian Meditations* §16, mentions the first, pure, silent experience, still waiting to arrive at its proper sense. But the difference between Husserl and Merleau-Ponty is the fact that for the latter, the silent experience is not necessarily waiting for sense. So, the question becomes: what if sense does not arrive? Should we believe that passions, desires always find their meaning? In this respect, I criticize the priority of sense over nonsense.

RK: This reminds me of Jean Vanier when he talks of the disabled as wounded beings who have a lot to offer us and teach us, outside our habitual understanding of mental normality or conceptual sense. A sense before sense as it were.

EF: Indeed. I would like to add a third prioritization often claimed in phenomenology—after the priority of flesh over body, and the priority of sense over nonsense—namely, the priority of passivity over activity. In reality, we see that the moment we speak of phenomenology, what really counts is passivity. The passive synthesis in Husserl and so forth. And when there is some activity in phenomenology—for instance the authentic *Dasein*—all French phenomenology rejects it as being an idolatry of the subject. But in prioritizing passivity over activity, we have lost, in my eyes, the sense of a phenomenology of power. Not that I dismiss the importance of talking about vulnerability, the face, hospitality toward the other. But I think we forget the sense of the struggle in life—not only the vulnerability or the welcome of the other but also the necessity to offer a true resistance, because of our irreducible differences. It is like the combat of Jacob with the angel in Genesis. Jacob needs the combat to test himself, to know who he is. That's why he asks to continue the combat. There are some "good combats"—the "combats to achieve victory" as St. Paul said.

RK: Who understood the fact that life is a struggle better than Levinas? Not the struggle *for* life, as Darwin would have it; but a struggle *inside* of life. Existence is agonistic, a wrestle, violence. *In the accusative I exist*, says Beckett. Levinas might well have added, "In the dative, in the persecuted, in the solicited I exist." And, of course, we also have Marion's notion of the *adonné* (the gifted or addicted recipient of saturation). All of the above link struggle with radical passivity.

EF: Yes, but there is a difference between being responsible for the other (Levinas) or being an *adonné* (Marion), and being in a true combat. Phenomenology doesn't deny a certain sense of force or strength, but it always prefers passivity to activity, weakness to force. We have to retrieve a philosophy of force, and a theology of force, that is of the Holy Spirit.

RK: So it seems you are proposing a theological reinterpretation of power in a positive fashion. Do you mean the power of the powerless as a call for action? A bit like what Dorothy Day did with the Catholic worker movement in the United States, opening hospitality houses to those down and out in the city centers of America? Or, like Vanier and Teresa of Calcutta when they speak of vulnerability and build shelters for the poor and disabled—empowering others to do likewise?

EF: Jean Vanier is not at all supine or Irenic—neither is Levinas. He starts *Totality and Infinity* with war! But we have a tendency to sentimentalize their vision. The question is not Levinas himself or Jean Vanier himself, but the use of their work today in theology, medical care, education, and so forth. In fact, there is, in my eyes, a profound difference between the first Levinas of *De l'existence à l'existant* or *Le temps et l'autre*, during and after the war, and the later Levinas of *Totality and Infinity*. The primacy of the face of the other in *Totality and Infinity* has led to us forgetting the importance of the "*Il y a*" or of the "hypermateriality of the body" in *Le temps et l'autre*. The experience of insomnia is absolutely foundational for Levinas, because the experience of the other—in this case myself—is the one I never welcome. I am encumbered by my own body. I am an object to myself.

RK: Ricoeur understood this with his key notion of the "conflict of interpretations." He spoke of democracy as a debating place for multiply competing interests. *Un combat amoureux*. I think we find this view strongly expressed in his reading of the "tragic" in his sketch of a "little ethics" in *Oneself as Another*.

EF: Yes, I use the same term—*Le combat amoureux*—as title for my book on French phenomenologists from Merleau-Ponty and Derrida to Jean-Luc Marion and Jean-Louis Chretien. Ricoeur is probably one of the only French philosophers who never abandoned this dimension of conflict and struggle in his work.

RK: In interreligious dialogue there is also a *combat amoureux*. It is not just about agreeing with one another. I am struck by your acknowledgment of specific hermeneutic differences and *différends* in the opening section of *Crossing the Rubicon*. You speak of Ricoeur's Protestant hermeneutic, Levinas's Jewish hermeneutic, and your own Catholic hermeneutic. It is very unusual to see that kind of admission in contemporary phenomenology and hermeneutics.

EF: Yes, but I never wanted to open a war of religion or confession by this type of argument. It is just to say that nobody can think and speak outside of his or her own experience. Catholicism is not for me an identity against Protestantism or Orthodoxy—and the context is, on this point, completely different in France than in the United States. Christianity is no longer considered to be against Judaism or Islam. I am not first a Catholic because I want to defend a position, or out of a dogmatic conviction, but because it is where I am spiritually rooted, as Levinas is rooted in Judaism and Ricoeur in Protestantism. We can learn more from our differences. And my astonishment is that the Catholic tradition, at least in France, always needs the Jewish (Levinas) or the Protestant (Ricoeur) to define itself. About those differences, for instance, as a Catholic, I both admire and disagree with Levinas, a Jew, and with Ricoeur, a Protestant. There is no incarnation in Levinas. How could there be? And how could we not disagree on such a fundamental issue? Ricoeur offers a hermeneutic of the text. Catholicism does not primarily rely on the text, but on body and world (the "book of the world" rather than the book of scripture). Ricoeur says, "Enough of this referring back to sources. What counts is that the text can transform us." If the critical-literary method has worked on the letter of the text, Ricoeur's hermeneutics has specifically developed the moral sense of the text: the transformation of the reader. But I emphasize the allegorical or anagogical sense of the text. What counts is not that the text talks to me, but that it does not talk to me. The text speaks of Christ and for that reason it remains a stranger. I think it is important for Catholicism to develop a phenomenology on the basis of its tradition, a phenomenology of the body and the voice. Why the voice? Because the voice is not the text. A text exists independently of its author. That is what allows Ricoeur to talk about "distanciation." The voice never exists without a body. Even if you don't see the body, you need a body to hear a voice (behind the door for example, or on the phone). The voice of the word is for us today what the flesh was for Christ's disciples as magnificently observed by Hughes of Saint-Victor in his essay, *The Word of God* (*Verbum Dei*). That's why we have to develop a "hermeneutic of the body and the voice" in the Catholic tradition that is not the same as the "hermeneutic of the sense of the text" in the Protestant one (Ricoeur) and of "the body of the text" in the Jewish one (Levinas). And that is why in Catholicism the liturgy of the Word (voice) is born in the liturgy of the Eucharist (body).

RK: So you want to reintroduce the force in activity, the nonsense in phenomenality, the body in the flesh. On the latter point, do you want to challenge the traditional phenomenological prioritizing of *Leib* over *Körper*, as Derrida does in *Le Toucher* and Nancy in *Corpus?*

EF: Let me put it like this. Just as Descartes thought that the soul was easier to know than the body, I would say that the *Leib* is easier to know than the *Körper.* The experience of the flesh is relatively simple and direct. I talk from within my experience as flesh. So the real problem today is not the flesh but the body. In *Ideas II*, Husserl is faced with the problem of the body. But when he writes *Cartesian Meditations*, he uses the word *Leib* in the fifth meditation, the second reduction. Levinas translates this as *corps organique.* He doesn't say *flesh* [*chair*]. Why? Because he translates *Leib* as we always do in French. For instance: Nietzsche's *der Leib philosophiert*, we had never thought of translating it with *chair.* Afterward, Ricoeur writes his commentary on the fifth meditation and he speaks about *chair.* Merleau-Ponty, in the *Phenomenology of Perception*, speaks constantly about *Leib* as *chair.* Since then, all French philosophers say that the central problem is the *experience* of the body as flesh [*chair/Leib*]. But I would ask, what do we do with the natality of the body? That is a philosophical question. It is also a theological one. It is what I call the *backlash.* Why? Because this is the problem of Michel Henry. I asked in my book *Le combat amoureux*, "Is there flesh without body?" When Henry interprets the fathers of the church—in particular Ireneus and Tertullian—on the subject of the Incarnation, he makes Tertullian into something that Tertullian is not. He is looking for the flesh experience in Tertullian. But what does Tertullian say in the passage about the incarnation? He says, "Christ is not an angel"—this is against Valentinus—"He has had a body like us, bones likes us, hair like us, a stomach like us." So, because of the backlash of theology against phenomenology, we cannot remain at the level of the flesh as lived-body [*Leib*] unless we root it in a material or organic body [*Körper*]. Christ, in his incarnation, assumed a true body, an organic objective body and not only an experience of his body as a subjective *chair.* To avoid gnosticism, we have to challenge and critique the primacy of the flesh over the body in phenomenology.

V

RK: Does Tertullian talk about the sex of Christ? I found during a recent visit to Rome artistic representations in which the adults around the infant Christ are inspecting and touching his sex. It is to show that he is fully human. They are all looking at his genital organs. He is not an angel.

EF: It is an interesting example. There are, in fact, many things to say about the humanity of Christ or about the recognition of Christ as a human being because of his body. The first is that Christ is real matter. Christianity is about matter. That is why we can't develop a phenomenology of the flesh without the body. That is one of my critiques, as I said, of Michel Henry. If we consider Husserl's writing in *Ideas II*, we see that he presupposes the problem of the status of a body without flesh. What is that? It is, for me, a limited experience that consists in observing your body as if it was not yours. Husserl knows the experience. He gives the example of cutting your finger: you see that it is your finger that is cut. This is the case of the foolish people Descartes talks about. Descartes asks if we could imagine that this body here is not mine. It would make me crazy. The crazy man is he who doesn't recognize his body as his own. It is a body without flesh.

RK: In the *Myth of Sisyphus*, Camus writes about experiencing your own body as a stranger to yourself. And he talks about the body of the other that doesn't respond because it is dead or seeing someone on the telephone without hearing what she says—experiences of the strangeness, the absurdity of the body. Or the uncanny feeling of suddenly not recognizing your wife or your friend, or even yourself, when subjective flesh becomes objective or alien body. A body that resists intentionality, experience, appropriation, humanization. Camus speaks of this alien body as "absurd."

EF: My search for something between an objective body and a subjective body goes beyond a phenomenology of *Leib/chair/flesh*. The problem of *Körper* invites us to develop a new concept that I call the "spread body" (*le corps épandu*). It is, for me, a zone at the limit, a border zone between the *corps étendu* of Descartes and the *corps vécu* of Husserl. I am preparing a new book that is called the *Spread Body*. It is a purely philosophical work. A spread body is a body that is organic, thus an animal body. The animality in us is, first of all, corporeal. I have assisted at the autopsy of a pig with medical doctors and after that witnessed the same procedure done on human bodies. It is exactly the same. I said to myself, I have some pig stuff in me! But that is not the philosopher who says, "I suffer" and "I am my body" instead of "I have a body." The spread body is, in the first place, a human body. When we see a human body suffering, sick, we do not approach it as an animal body. A doctor does not approach a human body in the same way as he approaches a pig's body. The spread body is a biological, human body, made—as Nietzsche would say—of passions, instincts, dissections, respirations, of all the unconscious, organic functions at life's service. But this body is approached, by me or by another, as being human. Instead of saying that it is an experienced body (*corps vécu*)—that there is someone who has had the experience of being that body—I can only say that I see it as a human body. The same thing happens when we observe another person sleeping, as Proust magnificently describes Albertine sleeping in *La prisonnière*. Where is the other? He or she has gone. But where? The body is there—"as a plant or flower that would have been deposited there," writes Proust.

RK: Your emphasis on the corporal body resonates with me. The anatheist sense of the stranger is also deeply rooted in carnal hermeneutics—that is a sensing of the other through our primary sensations, taste, touch, and smell. Sense as sensibility. This is witnessed not just in our existential and phenomenological experience of others as both flesh (*chair*) and body (*corps*), but also in the primal scenes of most wisdom traditions—Abraham and Sarah sense the divine strangers at Mamre in the sharing of food, Baucis and Philemon sense the disguised Hermes and Zeus in the tasting of herbs, the disciples recognize the risen Christ in the sharing of bread (Emmaus) and fish (Galilee). Jacob encounters God in the body-to-body wrestling with the stranger at night—that is, by touch. And this is replicated in many other spiritual traditions. The radical alterity of the other is revealed not first as text or thought, as idea or concept, or as doctrine or dogma, but as carnal sensation, in corporeal experience. Eros also combines the physical and metaphysical in its reaching out toward the other, in its hunger for connection and bonding, for new life (as Freud also recognizes in *Beyond the Pleasure Principle*). How does the notion of the sensing and desiring body relate to your idea of the "spread body" (*le corps épandu*)?

EF: Michel Henry speaks of *eros* as the fact that I feel what the other feels, just as Merleau-Ponty speaks of the *touchant touché*. But I think that *eros* is also on the side of the organic, and not only of the "lived experienced" of myself or of the other. *Jouissance* is psychic and organic, not only psychic. It is a resistance of bodies, as we spoke before about a "good combat" or a "good struggle." That's why eros is never fusion, but always opposition or differentiation, hand to hand, body to body. This common experience of eros is one of the reasons I tried to invent an intermediary concept between Descartes's *corps étendu* and Husserl's *corps vécu*. Once we accept this, we must leave behind the angelic sphere of phenomenology, the gnosticism of theological phenomenology. To come back to the question of animality, the question is not just to speak about animals but to reach a part of myself that is precisely prior to any verbal formulation. As the angel is a limit hypothesis of "a consciousness without body," the animal is a limit hypothesis of "a body without consciousness." So animality is everything in us that is of the order of passions, impulses, digestions. It is through the "organic" that we are in the world. But the problem is that we do not have access to this organic realm because we always already give sense to everything. That's why we have to first recognize this part of animality in us. This is also, theologically, the sense of the Eucharist. The formula "this is my body" has first to designate a true body, or a body that is truly human, even though it is not a form of cannibalism. The Eucharist is not only the passage from humanity to divinity, but also the passage from animality to humanity. Christ came to inhabit our chaos of passions and drives, to remain in them, and to convert them in him.

RK: So in a way, you are bringing back the theme of hospitality into your reflection, precisely the primal experience that for me is fundamental to anatheism—and indeed a hospitality that is not some sort of conscious decision about the stranger but a willingness to transform and be transformed. This is what we are trying to do in the Guestbook Project, "Hosting the Stranger." For you, the "animal" is a word for the "stranger" in all of us, no? But if that is the case, why then has animality not received more attention in theology?

EF: I think it is because we need a concept to distinguish between animality and bestiality. The essential point is that there are two motives for the Incarnation. The motive of solidarity—Jesus died with and for all humanity—and the motive of redemption—Jesus died to save us from our sins. The first has to do with animality, which is good in itself. So Christ, by assuming humanity and thus animality, has become an animal himself. Don't forget that the first representations of Christ are images of animals: the lamb, the lion, the fish. Somewhere along the way, the animal as representative of Christ was lost (except, perhaps, in the Franciscan tradition). To be able to retrieve this tradition, it is necessary to distinguish animality from bestiality. What is bestiality? It is the unique possibility of humans to fall beneath the level of their animality. The word *bête* in French can be applied to human beings. You say, for instance, *sale bête*. Man is a beast in so far as he does not accept the animal in him. Sin is not the fall from humanity into animality, but the fall from animality into bestiality. Bestial behavior, pornography, or torture, for example, is something only humans are capable of. But Christ takes residence in our animality, and he rescues us from bestiality. Salvation is not Christ's attempt to bring order into disorder. Salvation is Christ being present with me in my disorder. Salvation is the fact that it is no longer me who lives but Christ who lives in me. It is Christ's inhabitation of who and what I am. As Pascal says, nobody knows himself except through Jesus Christ. He knows my animality better than I do.

VI

RK: That brings me to the next point: resurrection. You seem to want to exclude animality or corporality from the resurrected self, but isn't that a tacit return to some kind of neo-Platonism, even gnosticism—the very move you critique in Marion and Henry? Why shouldn't resurrected bodies use their digestive and sexual organs? Eat and have carnal pleasure?

EF: The question of the status of the organic body in the resurrection is a very complicated one, not only for me, but for all believers and for Christianity in general. I have just published a paper entitled "The Three Bodies or the Unity of the Philosophical Triduum." I tried to understand the unity of the three corpses in the resurrection. Everything–singularity and alterity—will be resurrected. The problem for Thomas is the organic. Today, we have a completely different image and experience of the body. My proposal is to reintegrate *Körper* into *Leib*. The resurrection of the flesh is the resurrection of the body. The body is, however, the *pathos*-bound experience of my organs. Because I am recognized by my organic body today, I have to think about the status of my organic body at the end of time. "Returning to the body after the flesh" must be a central concern for the resurrection. But what exactly is the sense or the consistency of this organic body in resurrection? We have to think it, but it is not easy to imagine.

RK: Why not? Why shouldn't all our organs and carnal capacities be resurrected? Agamben has a great essay, "The Glorious Body," about the risible attempt by certain theologians to exclude certain bodily and genital functions from the risen body—of Christ and of the rest of us. I believe there is nothing genuinely carnal that escapes the resurrection. It is the integration, the recapitulation of everything—what Greek fathers like Irenaeus called *anakaphalaousis*. (Again, the *ana* of anatheism). It is what Thomas also suggests: you can't have the resurrection of *form* alone. It also involves matter. The corporal particularity and singularity of each material self is equally resurrected. The unique *thisness* of each person, their materiality (Thomas), their haeceity (Scotus). Nothing human—or "humanimal"—is ineligible for the divine. That is the basic message of the ancient notion of theopoiesis: the becoming human of the divine and the becoming divine of the human. Theopoiesis is recapitulation of every body, and every part of every body without remainder. Theopoiesis promises the resurrection of everything good in creation—or it is not worthy of the name. Nothing is lost in the kingdom, neither word nor flesh. Neither body nor soul.

EMMANUEL FALQUE is Honorary Dean of Philosophy at the Catholic University of Paris, where he teaches Medieval Philosophy, Phenomenology, and Philosophy of Religion. He occupied the Tipton Chair at the University of California Santa Barbara from 2015–2016, and the Gadamer Chair at Boston College from 2016–2017. His recent work includes *The Metamorphosis of Finitude; God, the Flesh and the Other; Crossing the Rubicon*; and *The Weeding Feast of the Lamb.*

Part II: At the Limits of Theology

5 The Anatheistic Wager: faith after Faith

Brian Treanor

I

There are myriad perspectives on religion and faith. Nevertheless, there are certain positions with which almost everyone is familiar, at least in the Western philosophical and religious traditions. First, there are various forms of dogmatic theism, often supported by philosophical or theological argumentation. Opposing these theistic rationalists, we will find militant atheists, most of whom deny the existence of God based on the lack of available evidence—consciously or unconsciously basing their denial on some variation of Ockham's Razor. The most common position between these opposed camps is to remain agnostic, suspending judgment about the existence or nonexistence of God because there is insufficient evidence to decide the case. Note that each of these three positions plants its standard in the soil of evidence or rationality, asserting either that there is sufficient evidence to rationally affirm the existence of God or that the lack of evidence leads to the rational conclusion that there is no God or that insufficient evidence demands that we suspend or delay judgment.

Distinct from these positions, and familiar to people who follow both academic and nonacademic religious debates, are various forms of fideism (which may or may not be militant or dogmatic) that affirm the theistic thesis on the basis of a "leap of faith" instead of on the basis of available evidence. I believe that a clearer understanding of the latter two categories—agnosticism and fideism—will help us to appreciate several important aspects of what Richard Kearney calls the "anatheistic wager." However, in order to explain how anatheism differs from agnosticism and fideism, we will have to begin with their definitions, especially because Kearney is using several key terms—among them "wager" and "leap"—in a specific way.

In previous work, I argued that postmodern philosophy is in need of a way to distinguish faith from belief, just as it has distinguished belief from knowledge.[1] The latter distinction is much discussed because postmodernity has been engaged with a turn away from what it takes to be the hubristic confidence in reason that characterized the Enlightenment. Take, for example, John D. Caputo's excellent book *The Prayers and Tears of Jacques Derrida*. Caputo tell us that deconstruction alerts us to the undecidability of otherness, which leaves us unable to say what is an example, what is a translation, and so on. Contrary to appearances, however, undecidability is not "the apathy of indecision but the passion of faith."[2] *Faith* is required when we do not *know* and, nevertheless, must make a decision. For deconstruction, "*everything* begins and ends in faith."[3] However, although highlighting the undecidability of choice seems—following Kant—to make room for faith by denying knowledge, on further consideration it makes sense to ask whether all undecidable choices merit the designation of "faith," or if we might be well served by distinguishing between belief and faith just as we distinguish between belief and knowledge.[4]

In the aforementioned article, I argued, "Faith is more than hedging your bets. A leap of faith requires something else in order to earn the name 'faith' rather than 'belief,' 'guess,' 'opinion,' or 'wager.'"[5] The difference between belief and knowledge is epistemic and has to do with how certain we are about a given proposition, while the difference between belief and faith is existential. To use Kearney nomenclature here, it has to do with our commitment to live in light of a certain proposition.

> Knowledge requires verification. Belief is assent to something that is not verified. Faith is a particular kind of belief that entails a leap with *commitment.* At the limit, such a leap constitutes an "irrevocable" wager on which "everything" is staked. Faith differs from knowledge in what I can verify of the proposition (i.e., in terms of certainty) while faith differs from belief in what I give to the proposition (i.e., commitment). Thus, faith can be roughly demarcated by three claims: (1) faith is not knowledge (uncertainty); (2) faith is not mere belief (commitment); and (3) faith need not be fanaticism (humility).[6]

Thus, I characterized wagers as more or less trivial sorts of belief on which not much is staked, while I thought of faith as a kind of leap on which a great deal—one's very identity—is staked. Kearney, however, uses a somewhat different terminology, distinguishing between a reckless leap and a wise or considered wager. The former is blind and characteristic of fideism.[7] The latter is made with humility in the context of careful discernment and is characterized by fidelity rather than fideism, emphasizing, I would argue, its existential character over its epistemic character. There is good reason to retain Kearney's use of the terms, which preserve the familiar notion that wagers are made because of reasons (good odds, some particular skill or knowledge, and so on), while leaps suggest an approach that is a bit more reckless. To avoid confusion, when I use the term "wager" in this essay, I will retain Kearney's usage of the term, which overlaps my own previous characterization of "faith," and which is circumscribed by the five aspects of imagination, humor, commitment, discernment, and hospitality.

II

Kearney's work has unfolded as a series of wagers—wagers about identity, nationality, ethics, divinity, and so on. However, while these wagers all share important characteristics—influenced as they are by Kearney's deep hermeneutic commitments and his own unique history—each is distinct. If the provisional and qualified nature of the anatheistic claim, qua wager, is familiar, the terms in which it is fleshed out is refreshingly new, even for those of us familiar with Kearney's work.

The anatheistic wager is unpacked in ways that distinguish it from other contemporary wagers—hermeneutic and deconstructive—about religion. The "ana" of anatheism seems to suggest a return of some sort, perhaps along the lines of Plato's *anamnesis*; but Kearney distances the anatheistic return from Plato in favor of Kierkegaard, a repetition forward rather than a recollection backward. Anatheism is "a movement of return," a return to the "primordial wager . . . at the root of belief" (A, 7). This return to the primordial wager distinguishes anatheism from many other postmodern philosophies of religion, including Kearney's own *The God Who May Be*.[8] There are innumerable books that grapple with the aftermath of the "death of God"; but *Anatheism* is less about who or what God is after the death of God and more about what it means to have faith after the death of Faith. This account is more narrative than ontological; it is for this reason that Kearney assures us that anatheism is "not an end, but a way" (A, 166) and that we might be well served by thinking of it as an adjective, describing a way to *have* faith, rather than a noun, naming *a* faith (A, 184). It is as much an account of how to wager—a wager about wagering, if you will, as it is an account of the object of the wager: the wager about who or what "God" is. Indeed, the subtitle of the book, "returning to God after God" could just as easily, and perhaps more appropriately, have been "recovering faith after Faith."[9] The lowercase "faith" is, we will see, an important distinction from the capitalized "Faith" that follows it, for anatheism is "lowercase from beginning to end."[10]

How shall we understand this wager? Kearney describes it as both philosophical and existential. He does this not to suggest that there are two wagers, but rather to describe the rich complexity of the wager. Although the hermeneutic arc of the wager should, I believe, be capable of accounting for the development or evolution toward the moment of choice, the wager itself—philosophical *and* existential—is made "in an instant," the instant in which we choose hospitality or hostility, trust or suspicion, hope or despair, or resignation (A, 40).

The philosophical wager "regarding the interpretation of diverse voices, texts and theories about the meaning of the sacred in our time" is that "interpretation goes all the way down. Nothing is exempt. There is no God's eye view available from nowhere" (A, xvii; xv, 46). We cannot know with clarity or certainty the fullness of the truth; we see, at best, "through a glass darkly" (1 Corinthians 13:12). Because of this, divinity is unknowable in any absolute sense and, therefore, "humanity must imagine it in many ways" (A, xiv). This philosophical wager is primarily epistemological and hermeneutic in nature and has a strong family resemblance to other postmodern religious wagers.

However, crucially, the anatheist wager is also existential—a lived orientation or disposition. More than an esoteric, academic question of epistemic uncertainty and fallibility made by some disembodied rational mind, the anatheist wager is made by a complete (carnal, emotional, psychological) living subject. It is not the exclusive province of *sadhus* and saints, priests and professors, or bishops and Brahmins; it is "central to *everyday* movements of belief and disbelief, of uncertainty and wonder" (A, xvii, emphasis mine): "The moment of not-knowing which initiates the anatheist turn is not just epistemological. Nor is it a prerogative of elite intellectuals. The anatheist moment is one available to anyone who experiences instants of deep disorientation, doubt or dread, when we are no longer sure exactly who we are or where we are going… Anatheist moments are experienced in our bones—moods, affects, senses, emotions—before they are theoretically interrogated by our minds. And they are, I would insist, as familiar to believers as to nonbelievers. No human can be absolutely sure about absolutes" (A, 5).

Although we can distinguish these two aspects of the anatheistic wager for the purposes of analysis, doing so is an abstraction. The "philosophical" aspect and the "existential" aspect of anatheism are two facets of the same wager. What we know, believe, and think is not only a matter of our epistemic-hermeneutic wager, our cultural and linguistic traditions, or our individual answers to Ricoeur's question: *d'où parlez-vous*? What we know, believe, and think is ultimately and intimately connected to an existential-carnal wager about the kind of beings that we are and the ways in which we inhabit the world. When Kearney says hermeneutics goes all the way down, he means *all* the way down: "it begins in our nerve endings, organs, and sensations" (A, 46).

How do these two aspects of the anatheist wager—philosophical and existential—interact with each other? The first epistemic aspect of the wager has to do with what we can—or, more properly, cannot—know about God. As such, the philosophical aspect of the anatheistic wager about God has much in common with other philosophical wagers made by Pascal, Kierkegaard, Ricoeur, Derrida, and Caputo, among others. It is a wager not just about *what* we will believe (God, the *Übermensch*, and so on) but even more essentially about *how* we will believe it (hermeneutically open-ended or humbly, for example). However, the second, existential aspect of the wager is at tension with the first insofar as it is as concerned with doing as it is with knowing and believing. "Such narrative wagers—following Ricoeur and Taylor—differ from Pascalian wagers in that they are more about imagination and hospitality than calculation and blind leaps. They solicit fidelity not fideism" (A, xvii).[11] So, while anatheism is concerned with the question of what we can know, it is also—and perhaps more intimately—concerned with where we stand. The first aspect of the wager is calculative, having to do with what we can and cannot *know*; the second aspect of the wager is imaginative and embodied, having to do with what we *do* about what we know or believe. The latter is clearly inseparably tied to the former; nevertheless, there is a fundamental concern with commitment as opposed to conviction. And while the philosophical mode of the wager is essential, it seems to me that the existential aspect of the anatheist wager is—to use a word that is becoming crucial to Kearney's thought—at the heart of this new work on religion.

The tension between these two aspects of the anatheist wager—one epistemological and the other existential, one calculative and the other ingenuous—induces a sort of "grounding" effect (which, paradoxically, returns us to the experience of being unhinged), reconnecting (*not* returning) us to the primordial experience at the origin of faith, the "enduring promise of a sacred stranger, an absolute Other who comes as gift, call, summons, as invitation to hospitality and justice."[12] This disorientation is essential to any reorientation and to the realized "second innocence" (not ignorance) of anatheistic faith (A, 7–8).[13] "The *ana* signals a movement of return to what I call a 'primordial wager,' to an inaugural instant of reckoning at the root of belief . . . an invitation to revisit what might be termed a 'primary scene' of religion: the encounter with a radical Stranger who we choose, or don't choose, to call God." (A, 7)

The anatheistic wager reconnects us with the experience of "the strangeness of things"—a voice in the wilderness, a stranger in the night, impossible forgiveness somehow made possible, or the simple wonder that there is something rather than nothing, reconnecting with the wager at the heart of all faith is unnerving. When we are reminded that our comfortable certainties and assumptions are *wagers* at root, and therefore not so certain at all, "all bets are off." Or, put another way, "all bets are yet to be made," for as Kierkegaard points out, we wager anew in every moment.

This wager—and the doubt, uncertainty, disorientation, or dark night that it entails—involves a certain degree of risk: "The double 'a' of anatheism holds out the promise but not the necessity of a second affirmation once the 'death of God' has done its work."[14] It may be that it ends in a more mature faith—a wiser, humbler, more ecumenical commitment. However, it could just as well end in atheism or, more likely, agnosticism. "Emancipating the audience from the ideologies and mythologies of first belief, the aesthetic space liberates each spectator into possibilities of nonbelief or second belief. No longer a given, faith becomes a choice, a matter of interpretation" (A, 11); we have the option to believe or not to believe in God, differently or otherwise. Returning to the wager at the root of faith may end in placing one's bet elsewhere—either in atheism, in a different theism—or in an unwillingness to wager at all (agnosticism). But atheism and agnosticism are still risks one must run as part of the anatheist wager.

Assuming one is a more-or-less committed theist (or atheist), why run this risk? Why embrace the nature of faith as a wager when it could result in the loss of one's faith? First, because as Kearney points out, none of us are really absolutists about our absolutes; second, because wagering one way or the other is ultimately necessary.

Any mature faith must come to terms with its nature as wager. As Kearney notes, Dostoevsky claimed that true faith "bursts forth from the crucible of doubt" (A, 8). Just as "childlike" faith in an anthropomorphic God should eventually cede to a more mature faith that appreciates the role of indirect poetic communication in accounts of the divine, naïvely accepted faith unaware of its own contingency should eventually—after a passage through doubt or unbelief brought about by awareness of contingency—undergo a metamorphosis into a second innocence that is unlike the first because it is chosen rather than (merely) received. In our postmodern, globalized world, we are—or ought to be—acutely aware of the contingency of our traditions. If a committed Catholic had been born otherwise (elsewhere or elsewhen), she would likely inhabit some other narrative—Muslim, Hindu, secular humanist, or atheist—perhaps with equal conviction. The Catholicism of a "cradle Catholic" is an accident of birth until she returns to the moment of religious choice and chooses it (that is, *wagers*) again.

Indeed, some thinkers suggest that mature belief must do more than play with the idea of atheism; it must run the gauntlet of atheism, struggle with it in a "dark night of the soul," giving it its due and actually considering its possibilities. In this vein, Kearney cites W. H. Auden: "every Christian has to make the transition from the child's 'we believe still' to the adult's 'I believe *again*.' This cannot have been easy to make at any time and in our age it is rarely made, it would seem, without a hiatus of unbelief" (A, 15). The dawn of reawakened wonder must be preceded by the night of loss. The anatheistic return to the wager is necessary if our faith is to become something more than an accident of our birth.

III

If anatheism frees us from the limitations of a first naiveté regarding our faith in order to deliver us to, or make possible, a liberating second innocence, what is the nature of the second innocence? It seems to me that contrasting anatheism with agnosticism will shed some light on this second innocence and the role played by the epistemological and existential wagers in it.

I noted at the outset that the most well-known way to inhabit the space between the "yes" of absolutist belief and the "no" of absolutist unbelief is the "perhaps" of agnosticism. Agnosticism, generally speaking, is an attempt to withhold judgment due to insufficient evidence. I have no proof God exists, so I will not affirm that he does exist. On the other hand, I have no proof God does not exist, so I will not affirm that God does not exist. Returning to the image of the wager, it might appear that the agnostic, perhaps wisely, refrains from placing a bet at all, waiting on the sideline until she gets some inside information that will make the odds a bit clearer.

However, while it might appear that the agnostic refrains from betting—indeed, this is the very claim that defines agnosticism—this is not the case. The agnostic, as James and others have pointed out, may claim to withhold judgment (the philosophical-hermeneutic wager); however, in reality, this usually means that the agnostic lives and acts like an atheist (the existential wager). Perhaps the agnostic is not like a dogmatic and absolutist atheist but an atheist nonetheless:

> We cannot escape [the issue of belief] by remaining skeptical and waiting for more light, because, although we do avoid error in that way *if religion be untrue*, we lose the good, *if it be true*, just as certainly as if we positively chose to disbelieve. . . . Skepticism, then, is not the avoidance of option; it is option of a certain particular kind of risk. *Better risk loss of truth than chance of error*—that is your [agnostic's] exact position. He is actively playing his stake as much as the believer is; he is backing the field against the religious hypothesis.[15]

So while the agnostic claims to be standing outside the religious choice—belief or unbelief—the way in which she does so amounts to a wager for atheism. She may succeed in maintaining epistemological neutrality, but her existential wager is on atheism.

What about the anatheistic wager? Where does it stand in the picture with respect to the epistemic wager regarding God's existence and nature, and to the existential wager regarding what one should do about it and how one should live?

Here it may be useful to think of anatheism as a sort of distant relation to agnosticism. Like agnosticism, anatheism acknowledges the uncertainty of our assertions about God (for example, that God exists or that "Jesus" or "Shiva" or "Yahweh" communicates something important about the divine). Both of these middle positions reject the claims of certainty associated with absolutist versions of theism and atheism. In other words, agnosticism and anatheism share a sort of epistemological humility. However, while this is an important similarity, it is overshadowed by the significant differences between agnosticism and anatheism. Philosophically, these differences revolve around the quest for certainty; existentially, these differences have to do with where one places one's wager.

While agnosticism and anatheism both acknowledge the uncertainty associated with questions about the divine, agnosticism views this as a liability and anatheism views it as an asset. The agnostic, presumably, wants to overcome her epistemic uncertainty so that she can affirm—the more certainty the better—the existence or nonexistence of God. That is why she is waiting for "more evidence" or "better arguments." However, clearly the anatheist does not see the diversity of religious claims—including the atheist claim—as an *aporia* to be overcome but as an *aporia* to be embraced, even celebrated, as the source of enriched understanding. For anatheism, it is precisely the hermeneutic gap between the sacred and our interpretations of and orientations toward it that allows for diverse, mutually enriching, open-ended engagements with it. Agnosticism's humility is the result of *insufficient evidence*; but anatheism's humility is the result of the *surplus of meaning* that signals the possibility of the "impossible made possible" (A, 183). The former is the result of a limitation that frustrates knowledge; the latter is liberating, and it facilitates and enriches interpretation and understanding.

Although Kearney insists "one can be an *anatheistic* theist or an *anatheistic* atheist" and that he suspects "many of us are often one and the other by turns," it seems to me that anatheism, like Ricoeur's second naïveté, does more than hold out the option of a second affirmation.[16] It holds out the promise of the possibility, and even, I think, the hope for such an affirmation. Existentially, agnosticism wagers on atheism (despite its claims of abstention), while anatheism, I believe, wagers on theism.[17] It is true that the wager of anatheism runs the real risk of atheism and that it must do so—and even does so gladly; but qua wager, it remains an affirmation, or the hope for an affirmation, of theism. It is possible that the awareness of contingency that initiates the anatheist wager might be terminated in atheism; however, the hope is that the potential anatheist will traverse the dark night of the soul, reconnect existentially with the primordial wellsprings of faith, and emerge enriched by the experience. This return to God is evident not only in the term itself (*ana-theism*), but also in Kearney's assertion that the "fictive *as if*" of poetic release is not the same as the "anatheist *as*," a commitment and wagered belief in the divine.

IV

Our understanding of the unique contribution of this wager can be fleshed out with a final, if brief, analysis of the "fivefold motion" that helps to circumscribe the delicate and daring "faith" that Kearney envisions: imagination, humor, commitment, discernment, and hospitality.

In terms of religion, imagination is necessary to faith as faith. "One cannot wager unless one has options to choose from. Such choice, to be free, presupposes our ability to imagine different possibilities in the same person, to see the Other before us *as* a stranger to be welcomed or rejected" (A, 40). If one cannot genuinely choose between options, one's decision is not free. Walker Percy's answer to the question "why are you a Catholic?" was "what else is there?" A witty retort to be sure. However, if there are no other possibilities—Protestant, Jewish, Muslim, Hindu, Buddhist, atheist—then the "choice" to be Catholic is not particularly meaningful, is it?

The gap between the transcendence of the other, human or divine, and my perception of the other solicits and requires an imaginative response. And the recognition that imagination is our only response to this gap means that the wager must be characterized by a deep humility that acknowledges our finitude and our limitations, our "earthly and earthy limits" (A, 42). Guarding against dogmatism, humor reminds us that even when dealing with the most serious of issues, we cannot take ourselves too seriously, helping us to remember—through "the ability to encounter and compose opposites"—that, in spite of how things seem to us, they might be different.

However, we wager in the face of our finitude and limitations, and, as we have seen, that wager can be characterized by a deep commitment and fidelity. The key point here is the role played by the will in wagering. Surprisingly, perhaps, it turns out that our willingness to make the wager, to commit to the leap, has a salutary effect on the leap itself. We can help to make the truth—*facere veritatem*—and to live this truth as troth. For example, Ricoeur acknowledges that his own Christianity was a chance, an accident of birth in a certain time, place, and tradition. Nevertheless, the contingent nature of that accident does nothing to belittle or denigrate the depth of his conviction, summed up in his beautiful claim that the chance or accident of his Christianity was "transformed into a destiny by continuous choice."[18] Our commitment bears witness to the truth to which we are committed, not as an epistemological gamble, but as an existential, lived wager. This is significant because, as William James points out in *The Will to Believe*, the irresolute leap (in the sense we have been using "wager") is doomed to failure:

> Suppose, for instance, that you are climbing a mountain, and have worked yourself into a position from which the only escape is by a terrible leap. Have faith that you can successfully make it, and your feet are nerved to its accomplishment. But mistrust yourself, and think of all the sweet things you have heard the scientists say of *maybes*, and you will hesitate so long that, at last, all unstrung and trembling, and launching yourself in a moment of despair, you roll into the abyss. In such a case (and it belongs to an enormous class) . . . refuse to believe and you will be right, for you shall irretrievably perish.[19]

Religiously, an irresolute leap will not make one a theist (or an ana-theist), much less a Christian, Muslim, Jew, Hindu, or Buddhist. Ethically, it poisons fidelity and hospitality, and forecloses the possibility of impossible love, hospitality, or forgiveness. Politically, it insures, to take just one example, that Israelis and Palestinians will never overcome the weight of history to arrive at some sort of agreement allowing them to live side by side. Each of these "leaps" or "wagers" must be made with commitment, "as if" success is assured, or at the very least *possible*, otherwise the leap will fail and the wager is lost. If one is resolute, the leap may fail—after all, it remains a wager—but if the leap is irresolute, the leap is doomed to fail.

But Kearney is quick to remind us that there is a difference between a blind leap and a wise and considered wager—and it's a good thing, too, given that the existential component of the wager in question means that one bets one's life. Although we cannot escape the hermeneutic circle—interpretation goes all the way down—not all wagers are equal. Since we cannot know in advance which wagers are worthwhile, we must get by with discernment—otherwise a wager would not be necessary; the choice would be, as Caputo points out, "programmable." There are no sure bets, but there are certainly better and worse bets. While discernment is not foreknowledge, neither is it blind. We see—or, better, interpret—through a glass darkly. "The drama of discernment involves an intense act of attention starting at the most basic carnal level and accompanying the reflective movements of imagination, commitment and humility" (A, 47).

However, if discernment is integral to the anatheist wager, this does not mean that knowledge trumps love. At best, says Kearney, love of the stranger is a form of "faith seeking knowledge." Hospitality suggests that we should strive to begin with the presumption of love rather than fear, welcome rather than refusal. Although ultimately, discernment will play a role in determining who we allow into our homes and communities—though God can be unconditionally hospitable, as finite beings, we cannot—we should begin with love as our "default attitude," so to speak. Anatheism, like any wager, entails risk; and here is another one. We might open our arms, our homes, or our communities to someone we should have avoided. "But such risk is not groundless. Love—as compassion and justice—is the watermark. There is a discernible difference between one who gives water to the thirsty and one who does not, between one who heals and one who maims, between one who hosts and one who shuts the door" (A, 47).

To sum it up: (a) imagination makes the wager or leap possible by opening up alternative ways of seeing; (b) humility flows from recognizing the necessity of imagination, and reminds us that traditions and beliefs about God are interpretations rather than empirical facts. Taken together, humility and imagination remind us that there are always other translations and interpretations of the "deep ground" that is the source of religious expression (A, 179). This keeps our faith from becoming dogmatic or closed-minded. Nevertheless, despite the epistemic humility and uncertainty, there is (c) a commitment in the anatheistic wager that safeguards it from indecision or infidelity, insuring its lived, existential significance. In the course of making wagers that are both uncertain and deeply significant by their very nature (d) discernment regulates imagination by reminding us that not all possibilities are equal, and moderates commitment by reminding us that some wagers are ill-advised. Finally, (e) hospitality conditions discernment in order to insure that it is as just and loving as possible, even believing in the possibility of the impossible, so that discernment does not become unjust prejudgment; and it challenges commitment and imagination to remain open to the advent of the other so that they begin with the presumption of openness and welcome in the face of our natural tendency to fear and exclude the stranger.

Taken together, these five aspects both support and delimit each other, describing the kind of wager Kearney has in mind and circumscribing the kind of faith—the *form* of that faith, not the *content* of that faith—properly called anatheistic. Anatheism is open rather than closed, humble rather than triumphal, imaginative rather than literal, engaged rather than passive, and exploratory rather than parochial. The hermeneutics of suspicion leads us to abandon the innocence of absolute and certain faith. In so doing, we run the gauntlet of atheism. However, the hope is that by returning to the deep ground that necessitates the wager, we can recover faith, "returning" to a second innocence, one still open to the surplus of meaning found at the wellsprings of faith but without the ignorance of the first.

BRIAN TREANOR is Charles S. Casassa Chair and Professor of Philosophy at Loyola Marymount University. He has published widely on topics in environmental philosophy, ethics, and philosophy of religion. His recent works include *Emplotting Virtue* and, with Richard Kearney, *Carnal Hermeneutics*.

Notes

1. See Treanor, "Blessed Are Those Who Have Not Seen and Yet Believe."
2. Caputo, *The Prayers and Tears of Jacques Derrida*, 338.
3. Caputo, "What Do I Love," 296. (Emphasis mine).
4. Kant, *Critique of Pure Reason*, 29.
5. Treanor, "Blessed Are Those Who Have Not Seen and Yet Believe," 10.
6. Ibid, 17.
7. However, Alvin Plantinga offers a useful working definition for our purposes: a fideist "urges reliance on faith rather than reason," and further "*may* go on to disparage and denigrate reason" (emphasis is mine). Using this definition, not all fideism would be based on a blind leap. Rather, some kinds of fideism—those that emphasize faith but do *not* disparage reason—could reasonably rely on some form of discernment, imagination, or even forms of rationality to support the leap or wager.
8. Although the God of *posse* described in *The God Who May Be* is certainly consonant with anatheism, Kearney's former work was more engaged in questions about the nature of God (as activity or passivity). In contrast, *Anatheism* is much more focused on the *how* of belief rather than the *what* of belief, which I contend is one of its most significant contributions.
9. Kearney seems to suggest as much when he notes that anatheism includes a "return (*ana*) to second kind of faith" (A, 9). I'd add that the idea of a "recovery" of faith is a useful image not only for the meanings of "recovery" as "get back" and "find again," but also as a "return to health."
10. Kearney, "Returning to God after God: An Anatheist Attempt to Re-Imagine God."
11. See note 8 regarding a broader definition of fideism.
12. Kearney, "Returning to God after God: An Anatheist Attempt to Re-Imagine God."

13. Or again, "For, as Hölderlin shows, unless we first experience a uncanny sense of homelessness (*Unheimlichkeit*) we cannot begin the journey of homecoming (*Heimkommen*), a journey which is never a return to a fixed origin (*Heimat*) but a turn toward a home always still to come (*Heimkunft* as *Ankunft*)" (A, 13).

14. Kearney, "Returning to God after God: An Anatheist Attempt to Re-Imagine God."

15. James, *The Will to Believe*, 26. I would, however, not push this distinction too far in today's postmodern climate. There are some agnostics who no doubt live lives that are externally (i.e., in terms of their actions, their commitment to justice, and so on) not so different from others who consider themselves "spiritual but not religious," or even those who think of their religiosity along the lines of something like anatheism. The agnostic wager for atheism is not necessarily a casting of one's lot with militant atheism. Nevertheless, even where the existential wagers of an enlightened agnosticism approaches something like anatheism, I would maintain that there is a significant difference that, while it could be unpacked at length in a paper of its own, could be summed up as the hope for and faith in the "possibility of the impossible."

16. Kearney, "Returning to God After God: An Anatheist Attempt to Re-Imagine God."

17. Thus, Jacques Derrida "quite rightly [passed] for an atheist" while Kearney quite rightly "passes for a theist." See Kavanagh, "An Interview with Richard Kearney 'Facing God.'"

18. Ricoeur, *Living Up to Death*, 62.

19. James, *The Will to Believe*, 59.

6 Kin and Stranger: Kearney and Desmond on God

Richard J. Colledge

Over the past couple of decades, Richard Kearney and William Desmond have developed kindred but strikingly different philosophical theologies that draw on distinct, if at times overlapping, traditions within the history of philosophy and contemporary Continental philosophy. The relationship between their respective bodies of thought is both fascinating and important, and their dialogue—largely implicit, though with a number of direct engagements now available in print—is, I suggest, one of the richest in contemporary Continental philosophy of religion. This essay looks to provide a necessarily cursory interpretation of their relationship. There is both an extensive kinship between their respective bodies of work and an equally deep rift between them concerning the relative priority accorded to the archaeological "is" and the eschatological "may be." Given the limitations of space, my focus will be more on the former than the latter, for I suspect that their differences may be more appreciated than their striking similarities. Further, insofar as differences are addressed, I will focus largely on suggestions concerning the potential for each approach to helpfully challenge the other.

Kearney and Desmond share much in common in terms of their cultural formation. Both are Corkmen who completed their undergraduate work in Ireland in the early to mid-1970s, before traveling to North America and Europe for their graduate work. This common heritage is evident, even given the different directions their work was to take: Desmond tackled metaphysics largely via the Germanic tradition; and Kearney immersed himself in the world of French phenomenology and hermeneutics. Notwithstanding these very important differences, I suggest that the deep affinities between their bodies of work can be understood in terms of the series of senses in which Desmond is himself an anatheist, as much as Kearney is a metaxologist. In the first two sections that follow, I take each of these in turn. In the third section, I discuss what I consider to be the core point of difference in their thought before then turning (in the fourth and final sections) to senses in which their respective approaches might be seen to positively push or challenge the other.

I

Kearney's *Anatheism* brings into sharp relief a number of key themes in his thought that are highly significant for understanding his intellectual kinship with William Desmond. Unlike Kearney's *The God Who May Be*—to which Desmond wrote a friendly but quite forceful response—the methodological motif at the heart of Kearney's *Anatheism* fits strikingly well with Desmond's own thought. In this section, I suggest several broad senses in which Desmond himself can be legitimately regarded as an anatheist in just the sense that Kearney describes.

First, Desmond's work echoes the strongly *existential* and *hermeneutic* flavor of the anatheistic spirit that is deeply suspicious of abstract theoretical claims to absolute knowing.[1] This concern underlies Desmond's oft-voiced Pascalian distinction between the *esprit géométrique* and the preferred *esprit de finesse*.[2] It also drives many of his voluminous engagements with Hegel.[3] If, as Kearney puts it, anatheism (and hence also theism and atheism) is a kind of existential "wager," if "interpretation goes all the way down," then the question of God cannot be settled in any final or absolute sense (A, xv). To the extent that we see, it is always only ever as beings in the midst of the light and shadow of our existence as it is lived; it is only ever "as through a glass darkly." Seen through this prism (and as I argue below), Desmond's patient attentiveness to the "showings" of the between involves a genuine hermeneutical sophistication.

Further, for Desmond and Kearney alike (and in a way that runs utterly counter to so much contemporary analytic philosophy of religion), the question of God as such is ultimately an existential, not a narrowly epistemic one. Anatheism, according to Kearney, is not an intellectual position, a belief *that* God exists or does not exist—or *that* God exists in this way and not some other way. It is much more about the *how* of faith than the *what* of faith. As he points out, anatheism "is not an end, but a way," and in this sense, it "might be said to serve more often as an adjective (or adverb) than a noun" (A, 166, 184). Of course, both Kearney and Desmond actually have a lot to say about the "what" of faith as well (on which, more later), and indeed there is a sense in which these two questions (the what and the how of faith) are ultimately inseparable. Nonetheless, the way of viewing faith as an existential wager (and not primarily as a matter of propositional assent) changes everything. If Kearney speaks of faith as a wager, for Desmond, it is a question of existential trust—a "decision to curse or bless" that can only be taken in the context of living in an ethically, aesthetically, and metaphysically complex chiaroscuro where the answers are never cut and dried.

Another dimension of this existential nature of anatheism seen in Desmond as well as in Kearney, concerns the way in which the question of God is confronted by the whole person and not simply by the rational mind. The anatheistic wager is an unfolding. It is experienced by an embodied, rational, emotional, instinctual, psychologically complex subject. As Kearney puts it: "[a]natheistic moments are experienced in our bones—moods, affects, senses, emotions—before they are theoretically interrogated by our minds" (A, xvii). Indeed, the very names of Kearney's chapters in *Anatheism* enact this embodied existential sense: "In the Flesh"; "In the Text" (with its focus on narrative and character); "In the World"; and "In the Act." Similarly, for Desmond, the question of faith is not something that can be divorced from the carnality of human beings. He writes, for example, of "[t]he aesthetics of creation" that "both delights and disgusts us, resonates with us and repulses us, sweetens us and nauseates us.... There is singing, there is howling."[4] As such, the question of God is inextricably intertwined with the visceral sensuality of human experience.

Second, the motif of struggle, decision, and the lack of any bedrock of certainty is one that is found often in Kearney's account of the anatheistic wager as well as in Desmond's account of metaxological mindfulness. Kearney puts it this way: "It is often through a moment of breakdown, loss and nothingness—the kenotic moment of abandonment—that we find ourselves returning to God after God" (A, 159).[5] Or again: "The anatheist moment is one available to anyone who experiences instants of deep disorientation, doubt, or dread, when we are no longer sure exactly who we are or where we are going. Such moments may visit us in the middle of the night, in the void of boredom or melancholy, in the pain of loss or depression. Or simply in the 'holy security' of radical openness to the strange. Far from being the preserve of hypercognitive cogitos, the event of radical dispossession is felt by any human being who is deeply bewildered by what existence means" (A, 5).

A similar motif of struggle with deeply held uncertainty is found very often in Desmond's texts, especially in the form of a recurring account of what might be called four "moments" of dwelling in the worldly "between." The first moment involves initial wonder, or first innocence: the joy of the first love of being, especially as experienced idiotically (the self in its immediacy) and aesthetically (the beauty of the world in which one finds oneself). There is then invariably an account of the fading of this wonder, a kind of fall from this first innocence through which the ethos is reconfigured in determinate forms where the initial elemental love of being is lost. *Conatus* takes over, and with this comes the eclipse of the *passio essendi*.[6] Third comes existential despair, "the return to zero." Life inevitably disappoints, and death and destruction come. Despair, he says at one point, "is love of God frustrated."[7] In time, this can lead to bitterness or even to a redoubled and defiant *causa sui* project. Unfulfilled *conatus* can even bring on a sense of the worthlessness of being. Finally, there is the possibility of rebirth: the gift of a renewed sense of wonder and astonishment at being ("agapeic rebirth," as he calls it) in which a chastened but deepened sense of the goodness of being—the *passio essendi*—emerges, and the void is transfigured.[8] This new primal "yes," by which a reclaimed "ontological trust" emerges, involves various dimensions: "idiotic rebirth," "aesthetic recharging," authentic "erotic outreach," "agapeic resurrection."

For the time being, I put to one side the powerful archaeological sense in Desmond's thought that this cycle enacts and the contrast with Kearney on this score; at this point I highlight simply the motif of existential struggle before the profound abyss of being and meaning as such. Importantly, for neither Kearney nor Desmond does this struggle ever end in a moment of final triumph; rather, it is the very stuff of the human condition. The question of God—to those for whom it is a real and live question—is always a dynamic one. "The choice of faith," Kearney emphasizes (in a moment of strong solidarity with Kierkegaard's notion of "repetition forward"), "is never taken once and for all. It needs to be repeated again and again" (A, 17). So too for Desmond. His motif of the existential moments (or "stages of faith," if it might be so-called) is not to be read as an account of ultimate triumph in the return to a (dialectically higher) Eden, but rather as a new preparedness for on-going "intermediation" of the never finally reducible equivocity of living in the chiaroscuro of being.[9] While there is clearly a kind of simple life chronology embedded in the motif, his point is that despair, redoubled willing, and agapeic rebirth can "pass into each other, appear and recede, interrupt and continue, diminish and augment each other" at various moments of life.[10]

Third: In most respects, Desmond echoes the anti-dialectical and anti-teleological sense of Kearney's anatheism. For his part, Kearney's own antiteleological sense and its centrality for anatheism could not be clearer: "Anatheism is not a hypothetical synthesis, in a dialectic moving from theism through atheism to a final telos. Anatheism does not subscribe to a Master Narrative about the maturation of humanity from primitive religion through secular critique to a new spirituality for the third millennium (i.e., some postmodern faith composed of the 'best' ingredients of all wisdom traditions).... There is no Theology of Fulfilment here. Anatheism is not supersessionism" (A, 6).

As will be seen in a moment in relation to Kearney's own metaxological mindedness, anatheism involves a dynamic openness to both theism and atheism and a serious relationship to both. This is why it is not synonymous with a stance *about* God, but is rather an account of the structure of faith as such. Faith requires this openness: a continual "reopening of that space where we are free to choose between faith or non-faith." As such, it is simply "a new name for something very old" (A, 7) by which genuine faith is continually purified. On this, Kearney cites W. H. Auden's comment that "every Christian has to make the transition from the child's 'we believe still' to the adult's 'I believe again'" (A, 15). In this way, "anatheistic suspensions of theistic certainties allow for a return (*ana*) to a second kind of faith," (A, 9) for "the Absolute requires pluralism to avoid absolutism" (A, xiv).

Desmond's movement from dialectical mediation to metaxological "intermediation" is a powerful expression of this very archetypal anatheistic movement.

As such, he rejects both world-historical master narratives that look to neatly resolve infinitely complex realities in teleological crescendos as well as expectations concerning final resolutions to the individual struggle to reconcile the equivocities of being. Of the former, he rejects "theological determinism," such as he detects in all "Gods of geometry" that emerge from thinkers like Descartes, Spinoza, and Leibniz,[11] and, of course, Hegel.[12] Of the latter, his antiteleological approach is closely related to his existentialist and hermeneutic sense (noted above), but is seen more specifically in his reflections on the individual responses to evil and suffering (to which I now turn).

Fourth, Kearney and Desmond are both clear that horrendous suffering and evil play strongly into the question of God and thus into what Kearney calls the anatheistic wager. "After the terror of Verdun," Kearney writes, "after the traumas of the Holocaust, Hiroshima, and the gulags, to speak of God is an insult unless we speak in a new way" (A, xvi). Accordingly, he takes aim relentlessly against what he calls "the God of metaphysics and theodicy" (A, 59). As will be seen, Desmond would not wish to abandon metaphysics in quite this sense or to simply lay the failures of mechanistic theodicy at its door without careful qualification. But with this caveat in place, it seems to me that he would largely echo Kearney's approach to the matter. A key theme in Desmond's thought is precisely the need to confront—in brutally honest ways—the realities of evil and suffering. As such, he stands resolutely against any attempt to rationalize evil away, be it the evil committed by human beings or "evil relative to creation."[13] His presentation particularly of the latter is, at times, shockingly frank, and as such he does not flinch in his admission that it challenges the very heart of his keynote claim concerning the goodness of "to be." If God is known through creation, then the perversity of nature presents us with a deeply equivocal view of God's goodness. The flood that brings life-giving water can also wash away homes, livelihoods, and children.[14] Like Job, we can know "in the flesh the shudder of God's power: incomprehensible power that exceeds our measure of justice," power that is "inexplicably permissive" of suffering and apparently arbitrary injustices, power "as violent as the killer whale battering in joy the helpless seal squealing on the shore's edge."[15] The deep equivocity, the capriciousness, of nature—the experience of "a pre-determinate promiscuity of good and evil" by which evil "somehow haunts the good"[16]—can shake us to the core, liquefying our "ontological trust" and our "immediate rapport with the goodness of being."[17]

There is a palpable anatheistic sense here in Desmond's wrestling with the mystery of evil that is closely tied to his refusal of easy teleological resolutions. It is also essentially related to his emphasis on existential concerns noted above. A good case in point is his account of the response of the individual to suffering and the decision, in its wake, to curse or bless a world within which this can happen.[18] In such instances, there is no calculus to help provide the answer: one simply must choose to consent or refuse, to give a "yes" to being, or to withhold one's assent.[19] This betweenness of curse and blessing is a kind of "Gethsemane."[20] The context for this decision is a profoundly hermeneutical one that comes down to one's idiotic (as much as rational) reading of the between within which we dwell. Even a renewed "yes" is still rife with equivocity.[21] The grounds of the "yes" are not logically demonstrable: the "yes" cannot be proven or universalized, since it is a movement of freedom rooted in the idiocy of the self. Consequently, there is no guarantee that any particular individual will side with consent. The experience of radical evil can "assault . . . and crush . . . our trust in the goodness of life."[22] The outcome "is shaped by who we are, how we have lived, how we responded to what we were given. . . . How we come out of it, no one can say in advance. . . . Some come out broken, some transfigured, many more come out with a germ of battered hope, still seeking to be rooted again and to sprout." [23]

II

In outlining a few senses in which Desmond enacts much that is at the heart of Kearney's anatheism, I have already said a great deal about Kearney as metaxologist.[24] After all, anatheism is, in many respects, precisely a matter of mindfully dwelling in the between, as Desmond might put it, and thus being open to a plurivocity of indications that require considered interpretation and mediation.

It is therefore unsurprising that at the outset of his *The God Who May Be*, Kearney includes the term "metaxology" (explicitly borrowed from Desmond) among the series of ways of naming (or "pseudonym[s] for") the kind of philosophy of God he is looking to develop in the book albeit with the immediate disclaimer that he doesn't share Desmond's use of the term by which he "re-thinks transcendence in largely Platonic-Augustinian terms" (GWMB, 6–7).[25] This is a shorthand way of steering clear of a number of senses that Desmond would see as central to his conception of the metaxological, which go to the heart of their very different directions. According to Kearney, what they share in common (and that which justifies the borrowing of Desmond's term), is "a common determination to choose a middle way (Greek *metaxy*) between the extremes of absolutism and relativism" (GWMB, 6).[26] This is a relatively thin basis for making use of Desmond's term, and there is much in *The God Who May Be* that would place the viability of doing so in question. Nonetheless, with the publication of *Anatheism* seven years later, significant dimensions of their community of thinking emerged more clearly, and in this way Kearney's allusion is shown to be very pertinent. Here, briefly, are some of those dimensions, as I read them.

First, if faith, for Kearney, is a wager, then it is a commitment that goes out on a limb. As such, faith inhabits the middle ground between certainty and ignorance. It is no random event that emerges merely through chance; rather one takes a position and is prepared to risk much in the belief that one has understood something vital. Faith involves commitment. But at the same time, faith is always existentially rooted, and can never involve demonstrative certainty if it is to remain true to its nature. Importantly, I think, in using the language of the "wager," Kearney chooses to avoid the notion of faith as a "leap," a description that is perhaps redolent more of *fideism* than the anatheistic sense of faith he has in mind. Perhaps a wager does involve a kind of leap, but however these terms are understood in their connotations, anatheistic faith is in no sense to be construed as an act of irrationalism or unthinking submission. But neither is it a matter of rationally sizing up the options in the manner of an intellectual wager where one plays the odds on the basis of a quasi-statistical calculation (à la Pascal's famous thought experiment).

It is difficult to think of a position on the question of faith that is more compatible with Desmond's. For him, all thought—and thus any movement of ultimate trust—involves an interpretation of the *metaxu*: the "between" or the middle condition within which we live and move and have our being. Like Eros in Diotima's myth in the *Symposium*, in our efforts to understand, we humans are always between poverty and wealth, ignorance and knowledge: we are always *on the way* to wisdom.[27] It is only through our efforts to mediate the diverse aspects of our condition—not through taking flight from that condition in a kind of pure theoretical bubble, nor through the contrary move of abdicating the vocation of authentic thought—that wisdom of sorts is possible. Metaxological mindfulness, then, is an intrinsically hermeneutical exercise in the fullest sense of that term.

Kearney's wager of faith is deeply metaxological in conception in just this way, just as Desmond's faith qua "hyperbolic trust" is in this sense deeply anatheistic. "The most important thing I learned from hermeneutic philosophy," Kearney insists, "is that interpretation goes all the way down. Nothing is exempt.... There is no God's eye view available to us" (A, xv). For Desmond, too, there is no "prepackaged foundationalism."[28] We work with traces and intimations—powerful ones, to be sure, but not conceptual blocks that can simply be pushed into place to reveal pure knowing. We are, irreducibly, creatures of the between.

Second, anatheism dwells programmatically and dynamically in the space *between* theism and atheism, or it involves a constant movement between the two. As Kearney puts it: "anatheism ... marks that middle space where theism dialogues freely with atheism.... It is a wagering between belief and unbelief... moving intrepidly between engagement and critique, recovery and loss, sadness and joy" (A, 184). Desmond's metaxological mindedness is, in some senses, precisely a call to find what Kearney calls "that middle space where theism dialogues freely with atheism," which is an always dynamic mindfulness that resists any return to a new "static position that risks dogmatism in turn" (A, 184); for anatheism "presupposes this a-theistic moment as antidote to dogmatic theism" (A, 186). There is a telling parallel here in the movement of Desmond's metaxology as it progresses through and retains aspects of the univocal, equivocal, and dialectical, even in transcending all three. Further, his search for hermeneutical "finesse" is always a search for a nuanced account that rejects the absolutism of certainty with its counterfeit "yes." Kearney, like Desmond, dwells often on the moment of *not* knowing, at the edge between belief and rejection, while always appealing for a rebirthed recognition of the divine.[29] Even if the conceptions of the divine to which Kearney and Desmond give voice are strikingly different, the structure of continual and hard-won return (*ana*) to theism is common to them both. If it is to be genuine, faith cannot stand still: it is, as Kearney puts it, "a movement—not a state" (A, 16).

Third, Kearney, like Desmond, freely moves between—and often occupies the space between—philosophy and religion, and anatheism occupies the middle ground between the two. Both assume an intimate commerce between the two realms of thought. Desmond speaks of a "porosity between religion and philosophy" by which "communications can be carried or received from both sides."[30] For Kearney, "Athens and Jerusalem are both guests and hosts to one another" (A, 9). Of course, these metaphors still assume a boundary between the two, albeit a permeable one. Porosity does not indicate an indiscriminate flowing together in which one is indistinguishable from the other except at the margins; and guests must cross the threshold into the domain of the host in order to *be* a guest.[31] For both thinkers, "philosophy of religion" is not simply a sub-specialization within a wholly theoretical field. Religious thought is parodied when it is considered only within the confines of formal propositions. Philosophy, says Desmond, "requires more than system: it asks for the finesse of religious poetics."[32] In order to open itself to the phenomenon in a serious way, philosophy must be—to use Desmondian language—genuinely receptive to its religious "other" in an *open* mediation in which one does not try to reduce the other to its own terms. Or, to use Kearney's image, if philosophy is to understand religion, it must allow religious thought to be a guest within its house, and such hosting requires that the otherness of the guest be respected and engaged. Here again, Desmond and Kearney are methodologically at one.

Fourth, and even more broadly, Kearney, like Desmond, is a thinker of the scholarly between. While drawing richly on the western philosophical tradition, both work frequently with religious, literary, and artistic texts and figures. This dwelling with and between many ways of being "mindful" is programmatically announced in Desmond's *Philosophy and Its Others*, where he looks to make a case both for philosophy enacting Aristotle's *noēsis noēseōs* ("thought thinking itself," philosophical self-mediation) as well as the complementary goal of "thought thinking its other" (intermediation between philosophical thought and what is other to it).[33] While retaining a keen sense of the integrity of philosophy as an ancient tradition of inquiry in its own right, he stands unequivocally opposed to "those who think of philosophy as a specialized technical activity, essentially insulated from, or to be insulated from, any contaminating otherness."[34] Indeed, in some senses, narrative has a unique capacity to reveal elemental truths in their experiential urgency and immediacy. Again, Desmond the hermeneutist comes to the fore.

Kearney is a thinker of this interdisciplinary between *par excellence*. In his extraordinary *Strangers, Gods and Monsters*, he "interpret[s] otherness" in a double sense, exploring the profoundly formative role of alterity in the formation of identities through close attention to diverse forms of mythological discourse and representation that are sharply other to sanitized forms of philosophy and canonical monotheism (SGM). In *Anatheism*, we see a thinker who is at home in the interdisciplinary between as he moves almost seamlessly from Ricoeur to Proust; the Song of Songs to Joyce; Homer to Hopkins; Derrida to the Hadith. It is partly due to this proclivity for rhapsodic movement across all kinds of texts that Desmond classifies Kearney as more of a "lover" than a "theorist": that is, one who is open to understanding religion more from the inside, hermeneutically, by entering into its texts—both sacred texts and secular texts that open into moments of spiritual insight—than by pretending to stand in some position of objectivity on the outside.[35] Of course, similar things might be said of Desmond. Both are deeply hermeneutical thinkers, searching to interpret the traces of the divine in the commonplace. Neither are "theorists" in the narrow sense of being purveyors of concepts that are moved around the philosophical chessboard in search of a logical eureka moment when God will be established (or banished) beyond all rational and empirical doubt.

A good deal more could be said concerning the intellectual kinship between Kearney and Desmond both on these and other matters. One might, for example, focus on the trajectory in both to move from inner struggle to outward action: Kearney's emphasis on the imperative towards hospitality as an expression of "ethical and spiritual praxis" (A, xix), an "ethics of kenosis" (A, 133); Desmond's toward what he calls the "community of agapeic service."[36] However the foregoing survey of the community between anatheism and metaxology must suffice for now as I turn to consider some key points of difference and, more specifically, how each challenges the other.

III

If the community of thought between Kearney and Desmond is to be sought mainly in the *how* of faith and in the parameters for thought on this theme, a very significant rift opens when one considers their perspectives on the *what* of faith. It is to this issue of stark difference—the implications of which are diverse and profound—that I turn, all too briefly, in this present section. In the short sections that follow, I will conclude with a number of suggestions about ways in which one approach challenges the other in productive ways.

If, as suggested above, Kearney and Desmond are *both* more "lovers" than "theorists," they are in many senses different *kinds* of lovers. Here, the contested status of the eschatological and the archaeological comes to the fore.[37] Kearney's love is consummated in an eschatological vision centered on the possibility of being and on the God who may be. In contrast, Desmond privileges an archaeological strategy that searches among the "hyperboles of being" for the ubiquitous intimations of the (divine) agapeic origin. Kearney's position is perhaps best summed up by the opening words of *The God Who May Be*: "God neither is, nor is not, but may be . . . God, who is traditionally thought of as act or actuality, might better be thought of as possibility" (GWMB, 1). To think of God in terms of acts and of the world in terms of divine action, is to delve into the discredited ideology of onto-theology. The way forward is to dispense with the onto-theological and to reorient toward the eschatological. On this approach, God is thought not as the actual but as the possible; and Divine action is no longer thought in terms of cause and effect (Divine omnipotence acting on a passive world), but as God "possibiliz[ing] our world from out of the future, from the hoped-for eschaton" (GWMB, 1). This is the divine *posse* of which he writes (sometimes with direct allusion to Cusanus's *posset*[38]). To stay with Desmond's characterizations of "lovers" and "theorists" for a moment, I would suggest that Kearney's love is the love of one who pines—like the Shulamite woman in the Song of Songs—after a loved one who resides always just over the horizon; who is always in the process of coming into presence, but whose full presence is always deferred, always tantalizingly out of reach. His is the love of one who loves in deep and patient hope that human goodness, courage and commitment will mean that the loved one will be brought into our midst, albeit in the most unexpected ways and at the most unexpected time.

For Desmond, to think of God simply in terms of eschatological possibility is to overlook the superabundant traces of transcendence that are *already* discernible in the between. This is not a pure presence—there is no "direct and univocal pathway" to divine actuality—but there are, if we are attentive to them, hyperbolic intimations sewn into the fabric of being. "Beings are showings of excess," he writes, for the "rich particularity in the between, show[s] forth the ontological foison of finitude."[39] This "foison" names the fecundity of being, of which beings are a plentiful outpouring. So much of Desmond's work may be understood, then, as attempts to give voice to the showings of this excess. He writes, for example, of the "hyperboles of being"[40]: elemental wonder at the sheer givenness of being in its profusion, experiences of beauty and the sublime in nature, and the majesty of selfhood and the erotics of desire and will (including the various forms of ethical selving[41]). Desmond too, then, is a lover—though his love is expressed more in the mode of a patient attentiveness to the traces of the loved one that in a hyperbolic sense are *already* present and everywhere, so much so that the world itself is hauntingly bathed in the loved one's presence, albeit in the most over-determined, surplus sense. One pines not for the coming of the loved one who is not present, but rather to understand the strange, overabundant presence of the loved one whose presence is nonetheless laced with absence and shadow.

For all their significant intellectual kinship, each approach is oddly foreign to the other. How then might their mutual porosity be rediscovered? How might each become guest to the other? I conclude with some suggestions as to ways that each might be understood to challenge the other in the hope that the continuation of the dialogue will open new perspectives. In what senses might the nascent archaeological be identified in Kearney's oeuvre and the eschatological in Desmond's?

IV

First, I turn to Kearney's critique of the archaeological, at the heart of which is a sharp disjunction between the onto-theological (aligned with the archaeological and the teleological) and the eschatological. For Kearney, the God of onto-theology is "the old notion of God as disembodied cause, devoid of dynamism and desire" (GWMB, 3). However, if such a characterization might name something important about, say, Aristotle's unmoving and unmoved God, it hardly does justice to the kind of God (qua "agapeic origin") that emerges through Desmond's metaxological attentiveness to the hyperboles of being that involves a rejection of univocal accounts of origin and the teleology of speculative dialectical accounts alike. I would suspect that Kearney would concur with this assessment, yet the appraisal concerning the failures of all kinds of onto-theology remains.

There are two aspects of Kearney's approach to the archaeological that might be profitably challenged. In the first place, Kearney tends to think of *archē* as referring to the past, and even the static past. He writes, for example, of "[t]he preferential option for hospitality over sovereignty . . . [that] privileges the maybe of the eschaton over the has-been of accomplished history" (A, 54). However, Desmond's *archē* is not simply reducible to the past any more than an eschatological view is fixated on the far, distant future. The latter is a point that has already been broached in their public exchanges, with Kearney "tak[ing] Desmond's point about the temptation to think of divine *posse* exclusively in terms of the future": that is, the eschatological encompasses an attentiveness to past and present as well.[42] In a similar way, I would suggest that Desmond's archaeological orientation should be seen in its full sweep, including its focus on the hyperbolic traces of the *archē* in the between in present tense, not to mention the implications of the always present *archē* into the future.

Similarly, Kearney's tendency to conflate *archē* with actuality might be challenged, for *archē* would seem to be both the radical condition of possibility of both actuality and possibility. It is the fecund source that makes both actuality and possibility possible. Desmond makes this point in arguing for "a stronger archaeology of possibility" that he sees is called for by the question: "What makes possibility itself possible?"[43] Or again, "we cannot think last things without first thinking first things, there being no re-creation and eschatology without first creation."[44] On the basis of the preceding point, I do not believe Desmond is saying that creation happened first and therefore has fixed priority (i.e., a temporal claim), but rather that an archaeological view provides a sense of the character of being on which an eschatology can take shape and direction. In one of Desmond's clearest expressions of the transtemporal priority, he gives to the archaeological over the eschatological. He comments, "Eschatological desire waits in hope on that hyperbolic origin that is neither in the beginning nor in the end, but gives the beginning and the end. We human beings are in the middle of that hopeful gift—never quite univocally sure of what God might be—or might not be."[45]

Kearney's acknowledgement of the challenge posed by Desmond's claims concerning the priority of *archē* leads him into a discussion of the impossibility of speaking of God in Godself, meaning that we can only refer to God "in the limited phenomenological terms of time and history."[46] We can only speak of the God who may or may not be manifested in history through the human "yes."[47] This is the second main point of challenge that I would like to raise. Kearney's point would seem to be that, since Desmond insists on an archaeological framework, he must be claiming knowledge of God in Godself, who brought the world into being "in the beginning." It is true that Desmond writes chapters on "Origin" and "Creation" in his *Being and the Between*.[48] However, far from holding forth concerning the inner life of God the creator, these chapters are reflections on the experience of the radical contingency of being, thereby evoking a sense of astonishment at the richness of what is, as a springboard to contemplation (via metaphor and hyperbole), about origins. Desmond's discretion in speaking directly of "God beyond the between" (God in Godself) is highlighted in his tentative "adventure in speculative metaxology" in which he cautions, "Everything I say above, I say under qualification: it is spoken from the between. It is a venture in hyperbolic thought, and as thinkers we know nothing of God, save what we glean from the ambiguities of being in the between."[49]

Desmond's discourse on God as "agapeic origin," then, is hermeneutically rooted and ventures forth only on the basis of "showings" in the between. To this extent, might it not be that Kearney overstates the gap between Desmond and himself on this matter? Speaking of what he sees as a basic difference between Desmond and himself, Kearney has written of a mismatch between "the metaphysical and phenomenological approaches to 'being,'" seeing this as lying "at the root of [their] disagreement."[50] However, this neat demarcation between Desmond the metaphysician and Kearney the phenomenological, hermeneutical thinker is already undercut by the observation made earlier concerning the intrinsically hermeneutical nature of metaxological mindfulness. But one might go further. Without making any claims of his own in this regard, Desmond's work sometimes shows a nascent, phenomenological finesse in his description of metaxological attentiveness. Consider, for example, the exemplary phenomenological (almost Husserlian) sense glimpsed in Desmond's description of what he calls the "aesthetics of happening" (his second hyperbole of being): "By 'happening' I mean not only the idiocy of givenness, but the fact that this givenness shines forth with its own intimate radiance, coming to manifest its own marvelous intricacy of order ... By 'aesthetic,' I mean the sensuous showing that ... shines from itself in the happening of being."[51]

My suggestion is not that Desmond is a closet Husserlian, but rather that his metaxological method perhaps provides more of an opening to an historical orientation than Kearney recognizes. After all, Desmond's thinking of the divine is programmatically read off a thinking of the between: the middle state of human dwelling in the world. It is, by definition, a "bottom up" exercise—a reading of the world.

One is therefore led to wonder what might be lost or betrayed if Kearney was to venture some "speculative metaxology" of his own within the context of his own onto-eschatological framework. Must the two be so radically opposed? Must any such venturing be understood as a capitulation to onto-theology and thus a betrayal of his keynote focus on the "may be" of the human response to the divine in history?

V

I conclude with some complementary thoughts about possible avenues by which Kearney's sharply eschatological approach might fill out Desmond's conceptions of agapeic community, as well as the yearning evident in Desmond's reflections on evil.

First, I indicated above that Desmond's archaeological orientation should not be understood as limited in scope to a focus on the past, for its implications extend profoundly into the present and beyond. However—analogous to Kearney's acceptance of his over privileging of the future in his onto-eschatology—one consequence that an enhanced eschatological focus in Desmond's work might have is a sharpened orientation toward future possibility. Such an admission would involve the recognition of the need to develop a stronger account of the possibilities for the unfolding of the *archē* in history. This is not to be confused with a teleological account of the inexorable realization of the historical trajectories implicit in the *archē*. The point rather concerns the development of a sharper focus on the centrality of *praxis* as the way individuals and communities respond in a spirit of hospitality to the gratuitous (and agapeic) gift of the between. It is not that such a focus is absent from Desmond's work, as seen perhaps most strongly in his *Ethics and the Between*.[52] It is rather that the focus here tends to be on close readings of the intimate showings of the between rather than on the open possibilities that are authentic responses to such experiences. Might not a sharpened attentiveness to the demands of hospitality or the courage of social action release new energies in such a direction within the scope of his account of the "community of agapeic service"? In doing so, Desmond need not accept the terms of Kearney's "bringing God into being" through our actions, for there are many quite traditional ways of speaking of God's becoming present and tangible through the action of good people in the world.

Second, Desmond's many striking reflections on evil provide a powerful context for reflecting on how an enhanced eschatological urgency might complement his keynote focus on being as good. At times Desmond stretches the bounds of his metaxological hermeneutic to speak in quasi-theological terms about "the agapeic origin" as the "absolutely patient good, willing and waiting for the promise of its gift to be renewed again and again, despite its being betrayed again and again," working "incognito with the evil to turn around what is still promising in the corruption."[53] This talk of divine agency, however subtle, would not likely meet with Kearney's approval, but it does speak of a relatively undeveloped eschatology in Desmond's thought. Most often, however, Desmond provides his reader only with an honest and profound silence in the face of the shadow side of being's goodness (the "ominousness of divine reserve," as he calls it), and indeed a kind of offence at the hyperbolic patience of the agapeic origin that lets creation be itself and doesn't intervene. Yet there is strength in this reserve that bespeaks of a fidelity to the limitations of a hermeneutics of the between. Take his reflection on the dead bird:

> Why [a] desire to speak of the goodness of creation? I came upon a dead small bird on the causeway near Inchydoney. Still whole. I picked it up. Blood in its eye. Delicate beauty. So perfect. Its life gone. Never again. Cold and perfect still. I looked up at the estuary, tide ebbed. Other birds, so various, oyster catchers, herons, gannets, gulls.... The quiet stunning beauty of the world. The world is perfect. Yet there is death. Blood in the eye of beauty. I turned to the grey darkening clouds over the hills. And the beauty of the world was menacing, menaced.[54]

It is only subsequently that Desmond makes some halting moves in the direction of a response. He speaks of the agapeic origin and metaxological community as holding in balance the universal/whole and the individual/singular, and he even alludes to Jesus's words on God's tender care for each individual being.[55] There is a profound and unresolved tension here as Desmond stretches the bounds of his hermeneutical metaxology, and it is one that Kearney does not face given his bracketing of God in Godself. It is a tension that is nonetheless unavoidable for Desmond's onto-archaeology of the good.

RICHARD J. COLLEDGE is Senior Lecturer and Head of the School of Philosophy at Australian Catholic University. His research focuses on phenomenology, metaphysics, the philosophy of religion, and philosophical psychology. He has published articles in a range of international journals and edited collections, and is currently working on a monograph dealing with the topic of Heidegger and the real.

Notes

1. In one place, Desmond explains this as an influence of the ancients, "for instance, the Socratic practice of starting from where we find ourselves in the midst of things, and then working out from there in a variety of more complicated intellectual moves." Such moves need to "be brought back to the concreteness of the human condition," lest they be untrue to "the practice of philosophy." See Kearney, "Two Thinks at a Distance," 240.
2. Desmond, *God and the Between*, 4.
3. For Desmond, it is not that Hegel misses the existentialist sense of the human condition, but that he betrays it through the intellectualism of his dialectic: "The space between the abyss of nothing and the excess of infinitude becomes the medium in which the finite self as speculative philosopher mediates the extremes as merely two sides of a total process of self-mediation." See Desmond, *Is There a Sabbath for Thought?: Between Religion and Philosophy*, 91.
4. Desmond, *God and the Between*, 39.
5. Cf: the themes of "breakdown" and "breakthrough" in Desmond's *Philosophy and its Others*, chapters 5–6 (209–311) and *passim*.
6. In Desmond's thought, erotic sovereignty—with its emphasis on *conatus essendi*—is associated with dialectical thinking.
7. Desmond, *Ethics and the Between*, 219.
8. For Desmond, this renewed wonder—with its emphasis on *passio essendi*—is associated with metaxological (open-dialectical) thinking.
9. See Desmond, *Being and the Between*, 182, and *Perplexity and Ultimacy*, 14–15.
10. Desmond, *God and the Between*, 122.
11. Ibid., 64–68.
12. Desmond, *Hegel's God: A Counterfeit Double?*
13. Desmond, *God and the Between*, 257.
14. Ibid., 76.
15. Ibid., 82. See also Desmond's reflection on the small dead bird in *Perplexity and Ultimacy*, 164 (quoted below).
16. Desmond, *God and the Between*, 81.
17. Ibid., 77.
18. Desmond, *Perplexity and Ultimacy*, 257.
19. Ibid., 164.
20. Desmond, *God and the Between*, 85ff.
21. Ibid., 121.
22. Desmond, *Ethics and the Between*, 378.
23. Desmond, *God and the Between*, 121.

24. In preferring this formulation to the equally possible "metaxologian," I am perhaps alluding to the essentially methodological sense of Desmond's philosophy of the between, as opposed to any doctrinal sense of a supposed "metaxology."

25. Further, in his response to Desmond's critical engagement with that work, Kearney acknowledges that it is "deeply indebted to Desmond's notion of *metaxu* and metaxology." See Kearney, "Maybe Not, Maybe," 191.

26. Note, however, the telling example Kearney gives here. Rather than give the example of finding a middle way between overly kataphatic and overly apophatic ways of naming the divine, Kearney in fact names as his "two polar opposites in contemporary thinking about God" two kinds of apophaticism: viz, the hyper-transcendentism of the Gods of Levinas and Derrida that defy hermeneutical appropriation at all, and the hyper-immanentism of the Gods of Zizek, Lyotard, Kristeva, and Caputo, that are likewise inaccessible to thought in their "slipping *beneath* the grid of symbolic and imaginary expression, into some primordial zero-point of unnameability" (GWMB, 7). The kataphatic is essentially off the radar.

27. Desmond, *Being and the Between*, xi.

28. Desmond, *Perplexity and Ultimacy*, 257–258.

29. At times one senses in Kearney a greater degree of equanimity toward atheism per se—so long as it is an "agnostic" rather than a "militant" atheism (A, 16)—than one senses in Desmond's more characteristically relentless appeal for the *recognition* of the traces of transcendence.

30. Desmond, *Being and the Between*, xii.

31. Interestingly, in the opening paragraphs of *God and the Between*, Desmond himself notes that "[t]o be a philosopher at all is to invite the atheist to take up lodging in one's soul" and to dialogue with this lodger (xi).

32. Ibid., 137.

33. Desmond, *Philosophy and its Others*, 6ff, chapter 5, 209–311.

34. Ibid., 1.

35. Desmond, "Maybe, Maybe Not," 100.

36. Desmond, *Ethics and the Between*, chapter 16, 483–514.

37. Given the limits of space, I put to one side the equally contested and pertinent contrast between the "erotic" and the "agapeic," noting Kearney's thought-provoking response to Desmond on this score, according to which he suggests "a very specific modality of eros, agapeic eros, that would be suitable to God." Kearney, "Maybe Not, Maybe," 195.

38. See GWMB, 2–5, 110–111. There is a great deal that might be said on the vast complexities around Cusanus's various divine names (*non aliud, possest, posse ipsum*) and how this plays into both Kearney's and Desmond's projects respectively. As Desmond has himself indicated, the conversation is likely to be at least as productive vis-à-vis Desmond as for Kearney (see Desmond, "Maybe, Maybe Not," 106–107). Unfortunately, this is a topic for another time.

39. Desmond, *Being and the Between*, 182, 229.

40. See Desmond, *God and the Between*, chapter 7, 159–169. Elsewhere, Desmond indicates that these hyperboles are concerned with "happenings of immanence that exceed the terms of immanence and bring us to the boundary where finitude becomes porous to what exceeds it. Kearney, "Two Thinks at a Distance", 239.

41. See Desmond, *Ethics and the Between*, Part III.

42. Kearney, "Maybe Not, Maybe," 197.

43. Desmond, "Maybe, Maybe Not," 108.

44. Ibid., 100. See also, "Contingency s not self-produced or self-explaining; it is given to be, and as given in being, points to its being given from an origin that is other to it." Desmond, *Being and the Between*, 229.

45. Desmond, "Maybe, Maybe Not," 118.

46. Kearney, "Maybe Not, Maybe," 192.

47. There is an interesting parallel between Kearney's phenomenological bracketing of the whole matter of God in Godself and the Whiteheadian notion of God's dipolarity. In the latter case, the "primordial nature" of God is acknowledged, but only in the most formal of ways, leaving all the focus on God's "consequential nature." Significantly, Kearney approvingly references Whitehead in GWMB, 123, 151, though he expresses some concerns over the potential teleological tendencies of Whitehead's disciple, Charles Hartshorne (GWMB, 46).

48. Desmond, *Being and the Between*, chapter 6 and 7, 225–297.

49. Desmond, *God and the Between*, 164–165.

50. Kearney, *Maybe Not, Maybe*, 195.

51. Desmond, *God and the Between*, 134. It is noteworthy that in a published conversation Kearney himself makes allusion to Desmond's "existential, almost phenomenological … description of experience." Kearney, "Two Thinks at a Distance," 239.

52. See Desmond, *Ethics and the Between*, chapter 5, 163–220 and chapter16, 483–514; and also the fourth hyperbole in chapter 6 of his *God and the Between*, 150–158.

53. Desmond, *Being and the Between*, 523.

54. Desmond, *Perplexity and Ultimacy*, 164.

55. Ibid., 238–239.

7 Is it Possible to Be a Reformed Anatheist?

Helgard Pretorius

THIS ESSAY EXPLORES the significance of Richard Kearney's anatheist wager for the life, witness, and thought of a particular faith tradition, namely the Reformed Christian tradition.[1] It poses the problem of what the anatheist wager is in fact wagering. Does the wager imply the loss of a confessional tradition or community, or does the *return* to God *after* God refer to a reimagining of one's confessional tradition? And, if this is the case, is there room for something like ana-*theology*?

As Kearney never fails to remind us, such interpretive endeavors always speak from somewhere. I speak from the perspective of a theologian and pastor in the Reformed family of churches, living in South Africa, yet I convey these labels with great hesitation. South Africa is a place of highly contested and sometimes conflicting perspectives and the story of the Reformed church, globally, but also on this southernmost tip of Africa, is equally complex and contested. It is, as Dirkie Smit puts it, "a story of many stories."[2] Thus my attempt to explore the significance of the anatheist wager is limited and may prove to be inadequate. Nevertheless, it is my hope that this essay may spark a discussion about anatheism's broader reception as others respond to the anatheist wager from their own perspectives and traditions.

I

Richard Kearney begins with the question, "why anatheism, and why now?" (A, xi). His initial response is a personal narrative, which stresses that the wager to "return to God after God" can hardly be avoided in light of the brokenness of our global society. *Anatheism* is a response to deeply challenging and pressing issues, with global ramifications, including the often disastrous "return of the religious" to contemporary world politics, the disturbing rise of hostility toward the other—in both its fanatical and liberal democratic forms—and the desperate need for a reimagined sense of the sacred in cultures rife with despair, apathy, and nihilism. The anatheist wager, as the gravity of these challenges suggests, emerges within contexts of great *risk*, but not without *promise*.

Kearney finds inspiration in his Catholic upbringing, marked by the Benedictine monks of Glenstal Abbey, whose hospitality gave tangible witness to the possibilities of ecumenical reconciliation, interreligious understanding, and a faith beyond (and within?) the great atheist critiques. But his sources of inspiration are as broad as they are deep: the sacred texts of the three great monotheist faiths illustrate the encounter with the sacred stranger; the diverse critical voices of Ricoeur, Bonhoeffer, Levinas, Derrida, Kristeva, and others facilitate difficult and important dialogues; the modern poetics of Woolf, Proust, and Joyce provide what Charles Taylor has called the "subtler languages" so necessary for describing new forms of "sacred secularity"; and the exemplary lives of Dorothy Day, Jean Vanier, and Mahatma Gandhi give incarnate expression to the call of "the God who may be."[3] From this richly diverse and fertile ground, the anatheist wager daringly takes up the call to reimagine the sacred, choosing to do so with ears pricked in hermeneutical vigilance rather than retreating into either reductive secularism or an uncritical embrace of the return of the gods. It is not a blind leap into the absolute, but an open-ended hermeneutic questing and questioning after what we are doing when we speak and act in the name of God or reverently decline to do so.[4]

For Kearney, the anatheist wager involves both philosophical and existential aspects (although I am wondering whether we could add a third theological aspect). As a philosophical wager, Kearney is particularly concerned with the hermeneutic and epistemological questions that emerge as one reflects on "the meaning of the sacred in our time" (A, xvii). Instead of clamouring for epistemological certainty, the anatheist wager—in the diverse tradition of Socrates, Augustine, Cusanus, Kierkegaard, and Husserl—chooses to embrace the holy insecurity of *not* knowing. "My wager throughout this volume is that it is only if one concedes that one knows virtually nothing about God that one can begin to recover the presence of holiness in the flesh of ordinary existence" (A, 5). Here anatheism stands in a formidable theological and philosophical tradition of *docta ignorantia*, posing a welcome challenge to the stifling confessionalism, epistemological arrogance, and self-righteous pietism that has become such a big part of the Christian story.

While acknowledging the above, some of Kearney's theological interlocutors have nevertheless raised concerns about what anatheism envisions for the credibility of ecclesial creedal testimonies and the dogmatic traditions that seek critical expositions of such symbols of faith.[5] They lament his rhetorical use of false antitheses, arguing that it fails to accurately "translate" the important nuances and paradoxes constituting theological concepts.[6] What is implied, for example, when robust and diverse intellectual traditions are together assigned to the sweeping category of "dogmatic theism"? And what role, if any, may dogmatic or systematic theology hope to play after having to perform the part of polar extreme at the opposite end of "militant atheism"?

These critiques are valid and raise awareness of how significantly Kearney's own project is informed by authentic engagement with confessional theological traditions. It is striking to observe how Kearney's Socratic style of conversation leads him, at times, to defend particular theological positions, only to question and challenge theological points of view from philosophical and ethical perspectives when the conversation requires it. While this in no way exempts anatheism from theological critique, too strong evaluations of particular theological *positions* may miss the point of the unique and daring interdisciplinary *disposition* it seeks to evoke across disciplinary divides. By taking the risk of entering this interanimating space, Christian believers may find themselves addressed with an invitation to wager on their own "return to God after God"—that is, after claiming to love God, know God, and side with God.

Before making this theological wager more explicit, it is first necessary to view anatheism as an existential wager. Unlike agnosticism, which is ultimately still driven by a desire for the securities offered by epistemological certainty, anatheism's apophatic moment is simply the recognition of that existential mood "available to anyone who experiences instants of deep disorientation, doubt, or dread, when we are no longer sure exactly who we are or where we are going" (A, 5). From this precarious and embodied starting point, Kearney helps us to reinscribe faith as a recovered disposition rather than a well-prepared deposition, a matter of lived, committed reorientation instead of cool cerebral certainty.

As with Pascal, we are reminded that reason inevitably lags behind the call to faith, making faith "not a thing like a theory but a thing like a love-affair," to cite G. K. Chesterton's famous description of St. Francis of Assisi.[7] Like Christ's commandment to love one's enemies, faith cannot be reduced to the rational outcome of a prefabricated methodology. However, unlike popular caricatures of Pascal that want to see him bolstering his naked wager with a thin theory of probability, the anatheist wager is sustained by the thickness of narrative imagination, soliciting, says Kearney, "fidelity not fideism" (A, xvii).

It is important to note that in seeking to inspire a new type of fidelity, Kearney is not advocating a new super-religion or imposing a supersessionist social imaginary onto current trends. Anatheism is not to become another -*ism* or to be understood as a Hegelian synthesis, resolving yesteryear's tensions between atheism and theism. The emphasis falls not on the suffix, but on the prefix (*ana-*), signifying that the anatheist wager is "nothing particularly new," but a "new name for something very old." It *returns* (*ana-*) to an "inaugural instant of reckoning at the root of belief" to re-consider "the *option* of retrieved belief." But *ana-* also signals *repetition*, suggesting that the anatheist moment is "constantly recurring in both the history of humankind and of each life" (A, 7).

It is in this light that Kearney's disclaimer against his lack of theological expertise should be understood. Here, he is emulating Ricoeur's quest for a post-religious faith by situating his own philosophical work on anatheism as a "preparatory discourse," seeking merely to clear a space in which "a retrieval of a liberated faith within the great religious traditions" may take place (A, 74). Like Ricoeur, Kearney is convinced that the philosopher may only "imagine such a faith," but that it remains "the business of postreligious believers to realize it" (A, 74). This is why, after explicating his own intellectual, confessional, and ethical commitments, Kearney invites readers of the book "to situate their own perspectives and presuppositions" (A, xv). Rather than abstracting from the particularities of confessional communities and practices, I would argue, the anatheist wager triggers a third theological wager within actual faith traditions, inviting proponents of those traditions to repeat the "primordial wager" *forward.*

For this reason, understanding the text *Anatheism* merely as a work of apologetics, leaving only atheists and sceptics with the task of "returning to God," would be a serious misreading. As I understand the anatheist wager, it also calls proponents of confessional faith traditions to a moment of *metanoia*, a call to return to God *after* God. Speaking from a Reformed perspective, such a return is best understood as a *gift.* And yet, as Kearney reminds us, it is certainly not a *given*: "if anatheism signals the possibility of God after God, it is because it allows for the alternative option of its impossibility" (A, xiv). Like true moments of conversion, the anatheist wager allows for the possibility of not being found awake, of declining the offer, or of bowing before an idol instead of the living God.

II

In response to this invitation to "repeat the wager forward," I feel compelled to situate my own Reformed theological heritage. After all, shouldn't the wager on a return to God be accompanied by something like ana-*theology*? Alongside the philosophical and existential issues already mentioned, can we not recognize serious theological questions? What, or rather, who is the God that comes after "God"? Does this God deserve our adoration and service? What does returning to God mean? And for whom? Do we return as individuals or persons in community? And how will a return be taken up in practice? At the outset, both the Reformed and the anatheist may perceive the other as an uninvited guest. But who, in this encounter, is the guest and who is the host? Whose house is this anyway?

As a meeting of strangers at the threshold, the Reformed and anatheist wagers have more in common than first impressions allow. Would it be a mistake, on second reflection, to recognise a deeply anatheist logic in the Reformed faith's *repetitive* (*ana-*) *return* (*ana-*) back to the sources (*ad fontes*), to the word made flesh, to the living God, and therefore always in an open-ended quest, an endless reformation in life and witness of a church and society *always to be reformed* (*semper reformanda*)? Not to mention that the Protestant Reformers, like Kearney, always claimed that they were doing "nothing particularly new"!

In fact, points of resonance between anatheist and Reformed wagers abound. In affirming the authority of the Bible, for instance, what distinguishes Reformed hermeneutics is its stress on the whole of scripture, emphasising its pluriform and complex detail and thereby committing communities of interpretation to the ongoing task of listening for God's voice in and through "a bewildering variety of voices."[8] In this regard, the Reformed tradition shares anatheism's critical hermeneutic commitment to the open-ended spiral of interpreting "diverse voices, texts and theories about the meaning of the sacred in our time" (A, xvii).

Or consider Kearney's claim that "moments of epiphany are always embedded in the conditions of culture and always require representation and reading" (A, 7). It portrays a hermeneutical and historical consciousness similar to that found in the characteristic Reformed understanding of *confessions*. Considered to be a *confessional* tradition (in the narrower meaning of the word), the Reformed faith has always known a plurality of confessions and is marked by a readiness to wager on new confessional moments (*status confessionis*) emerging in new contexts and situations. In this tradition, grateful reception of the confessional past is accompanied by an equal amount of freedom, emphasising the *relativity* (always deferring authority to God's Word, of which there can be no final interpretation), *historicity* (deeply sensitive to the vicissitudes of text and context), and *finitude* (profoundly conscious of human fallibility) of these expressions and, in that light, knowing them to be always open to revision, adaptation, or rejection.[9]

One may almost begin to wonder how it is possible for a Reformed believer *not* to be an anatheist. However, recognizing these and other characteristics of Reformed faith does not imply that these are always practiced and embodied. As Dirkie Smit notes, for instance, regarding the above mentioned historical sensitivity: "Whenever this was ignored, it led to positions and practices that contradicted and even betrayed fundamental Reformed convictions—truth easily became the accuracy of propositions; faith became intellectual obedience to authoritative documents, meetings, decisions or figures, the knowledge of faith became intellectual information about historical facts and correct formulations, certainty became rational conclusions based on irrefutable axioms, authority became primarily institutional and legal, Reformed confessions themselves became systems of thought to be used to discipline people who do not adhere to their precise expressions and formulations."[10]

It is because such betrayals of the Reformed spirit are so pervasive, that the anatheist wager is indeed a guest to be welcomed.

Thus, to better understand what the Reformed tradition could learn from the anatheist wager, it may be instructive to consider Kearney's distinction between the three "hermeneutic arcs" within the "grammar of *ana*," namely: protest, prophecy, and sacrament. The first of these, also known as the *iconoclastic* arc, entails the movement towards un-knowing. It refers to the profound wisdom that allows one's first naivety to be cleared by a hermeneutic of suspicion so that a second faith becomes a possibility. Exemplified by Ricoeur's famous maxim that it is only after the idols have been smashed that the symbols may speak anew, anatheism embraces atheist critiques of religion as a purging of religion that makes way for a postreligious faith. "[Anatheism] is a movement—not a state—that refuses all absolute talk about the absolute, negative or positive; for it acknowledges that the absolute can never be understood *absolutely* by any single person or religion" (A, 16). This Protestant movement to resist all absolutist positions—theistic or atheistic—regarding the absolute reminds us of a recurring theme in the Reformed tradition. It amounts to what Paul Tillich has called the "Protestant principle," variously defined as the conviction that the Unconditional cannot be bound to any manifestation of itself in the conditional, or that "no one can grasp that by which he [*sic*] is grasped."[11] The latter suggests that, at least for the Reformed wager, this deeply challenging deconstructive arc is both demanded and sustained by its faith in the unconditional grace of God, making it a task always to be taken up again.

"The rebel," however, Kearney notes, "falls short of the prophet" (A, 73). The moment of protest needs to be followed by a *prophetic* wager on the impossible possibility of speaking (again, anew) before the inexpressible word. For anatheism and Reformed Christianity alike, protest and prophecy, while remaining distinct, always go hand in hand, for they recognize "that the moment of not-knowing that initiates the anatheist turn is not just epistemological" (A, 5). What the moment of protest rises against is idolatry, which the Reformed humanist John de Gruchy defines as "the tyranny of human power acting as though it is divine."[12] Within the anatheist wager therefore, the movement of deconstruction isn't an end in itself but must be followed by the prophetic wager of restoring proper worship of the living God. Therefore, Kearney supplements the Jewish iconoclastic purging of religion (Levinas, Derrida) with the two prophetic voices of Bonhoeffer and Ricoeur.

It is conceivable that such a shift from protest to prophecy requires the nurturing of something like a *prophetic imagination*. But how can this be achieved without the support of long and accessible institutions of memory, practices of attentive listening and hopeful action, mutually accountable communities of interpretation, and community life that embodies empathetic solidarity with the suffering? These needs fall outside *Anatheism*'s scope in the narrower sense of a philosophical exercise, suggesting that confessional traditions with their intellectual goods, institutional bodies, communal practices, and ecumenical commitments may be called on to step into the gap. In a cultural milieu that so easily succumbs to the tyranny of the present, the immediate and the parochial, to wager on these fragile gifts, so central to the life's work of both Ricoeur and Bonhoeffer, is particularly needed.[13]

The anatheist wager would, however, be incomplete if it did not also reckon with what Kearney calls "the recovery of the *sacramental* in the lived world of suffering and action" (A, 153). Less concerned with endless interconfessional debates about the sacraments or the narrow meaning of the sacraments in their cultic setting, the anatheist wager tries to understand the sacramental in post-religious terms. The emphasis here falls on the need for the word to be made flesh, for faith to be incarnated in acts of love and peace, and for eschatological proclamation to be embodied, however tentatively and precariously, "in the lived world of suffering and action" (A, 153). The sacramental arc of the anatheist wager is twofold, combining the sacramental *vision* of imagination and aesthetics (chapters 4 and 5), with a Eucharistic *ethics* of the everyday and the secular (chapters 6 and 7). In Kearney's words: "The sacramental moment of anatheism is when we finally restore the hyphen between the sacred and the secular. It is also the moment we return from text to action, from the realm of critical interpretation to the world of quotidian praxis and transformation. This ultimate transition from word to flesh is witnessed daily wherever someone gives a cup of cold water to a thirsting stranger. For in such moments one's faith in God as stranger is not a matter of theories or ideas but of living witness to the word made flesh" (A, 153).

It is here, with the sacramental, that the Reformed wager is found to be most vulnerable. For all its protestant daring and prophetic imagination, a shadow falls on the Reformed tradition's carnal call to be a priestly presence in the world. Not that this clichéd Reformed weakness has gone unnoticed within the tradition itself. We are reminded of Tillich's observation that the "Protestant Principle" must be supplemented by what he called the "Catholic Substance." We could also point to Ricoeur's theological dialectic of *manifestation* and *proclamation*—not to mention Calvin's own deeply sacramental theology, which supplemented his prosaic commitments to social justice with an equally sophisticated theological poetics of the Eucharist, in contrast to the excarnating thrust of later polemics, orthodoxies, and cultural concessions within the Reformed world.

Echoing these Reformed voices, Kearney reminds us that sacred strangers, if and when they appear, do so in flesh and blood, here and now, calling for both a prophetic proclamation of justice and "a sacramental return to epiphanies of the everyday"; both being hosted by the God who may be and "a hosting of the transcendent in the immanence of the present"; both critical vigilance against idolatry and "a special attentiveness to infinity embodying itself in daily acts of Eucharistic love and sharing" (A, 85–86).

From a South African Reformed perspective, it is most significant that ethics and the Eucharist are brought into dialogue in this way. One could say that the story of apartheid started when the Lord's Supper was first celebrated in separation from people of different races. By deforming the sacrament through which union with Christ and communion with one's fellows is established, church and society were irrevocably marred. And in what stark contrast to Calvin's deeply sacramental theology and ethics in which the Lord's Supper took center stage:

> We shall have profited admirably in the sacrament, if the thought shall have been impressed and engraved on our minds, that none of our brethren is hurt, despised, rejected, injured, or in any way offended, without our, at the same time, hurting, despising, and injuring Christ; that we cannot have dissension with our brethren, without at the same time dissenting from Christ; that we cannot love Christ without loving our brethren; that the same care we take of our own body we ought to take of that of our brethren, who are members of our body; that as no part of our body suffers pain without extending to the other parts, so every evil which our brothers and sisters suffer ought to excite our compassion.[14]

Calvin's sacramental theology exhibits an interplay between the sacrament as both divine gift and all-encompassing divine claim within the embodied context of secular life, reaching towards what Kearney calls "sacred secularity."

In light of the above, it may help to recall that the Reformed tradition has always been critical of attempts to divide life into distinct "sacred" and "secular" spheres.[15] Like it's anatheist counterpart, the Reformed wager need not be threatened by secular or postsecular contexts, but welcome the vocation of living *coram Deo* in and through secular institutions. Drawing on anatheism's nuanced vision for a recovery of the sacred within the secular, in which ethics and poetics meet, the Reformed wager is encouraged to challenge the hegemonic discourses of secularism while strongly rejecting, especially within its own ranks, the temptations of privatizing forms of self-secularization or retreats into self-indulgent fundamentalism (A, 139–142). In this way, the anatheist wager may help to recover the characteristically Reformed commitment to socio-political justice and humanization.

III

Of central concern to all three of these hermeneutic arcs—protest, prophecy, and sacrament—is the anatheist wager's preference for "the stranger" as a "primary scene of religion." *Anatheism* makes the compelling claim is that it is not only highly likely that the divine manifests in strangers, but that something of God's character and will becomes revealed in the insistence of the stranger (A, 7). This obviously has radical implications for both God and the stranger, but also for any authentic attempt to return to God after God.

If one asks how the Reformed faith has fared in its witness to the sacred stranger, an ambiguous history emerges in which the still, small voice of the stranger has often been stifled by louder ideological interests. In South Africa, for instance, Reformed Christianity became horribly complicit with histories of colonial violence and an oppressive system of apartheid, neither of which could add "hospitality to the stranger" to their résumé. And yet, the Reformed heritage was also an important site and inspiration for the struggle against apartheid, unmasking the apartheid ideology as heresy but also mobilizing liberation movements and nurturing a compassionate piety that offered solace and healing to the wounded.

This ambiguous story resonates with anatheism's sober vision of religion, which attests to an "inaugural ambivalence" towards the stranger at the heart of religion: "From its inception then, religion tells a double story of violence or compassion, of genocide or justice, of *thanatos* or *eros*. And often both at once." Both the Reformed and anatheist wagers begin with the recognition that "Western religion is the history of this either-or" between *hostility* and *hospitality* and that any wager on a return to God is called to operate within this inescapable drama (A, 38). The question is how does one deal with the paradox of a tradition that has the potential to be a liberating force while simultaneously displaying a tendency to oppress and exclude?[16] Can one enter this "battleground of interpretations" without being either desensitized or led to apathy? "The challenge," Kearney rightly notes, "is to struggle with angels of death and life, turning the pressures of night into the promise of natality" (A, 38).

An important place to pick up this challenge, I would argue, is where anatheism meets the quest for a responsible historical and theological hermeneutic.[17] By introducing the ana-theist yeast into its theological dough, the Reformed tradition would be challenged to draw critically and creatively from its ambiguous past in a way that nurtures hospitality in the present and future. In this light, the anatheist hermeneutic of the stranger would recall, for instance, that John Calvin lived most of his life as a stranger, fleeing for his life to Basel, Strasbourg, and later Genève, a city in which one third of the inhabitants were refugees.[18] Consider the following gloss by Calvin on the moral law, here on the inherent dignity of the other: "Humanity is both the image of God and our flesh. Wherefore, if we would violate the image of God, we must hold the human person sacred—if we would not divest ourselves of humanity, we must cherish our own flesh."[19] Calvin's grammar of the other, expressed in the cohabitation of the image of God and the flesh in the human person, strikes a middle way between the absolute transcendence of the other (image of God) and the immanent presence of another person in flesh and blood (our own flesh) that is similar to Kearney's hermeneutics of the stranger as "the one who is recognizable enough to appear but who nonetheless retains a distance."[20]

For Calvin the divine image in humanity was not restricted to interpersonal encounters, but proved to be influential for his broader socio-political thought in what Wolterstorff calls "Calvin's theology of the tears of the social victim."[21] The following quote is from one of Calvin's sermons on Galatians 6:9–11. It follows on Calvin providing a portrait of God looking on Godself in human beings as in a mirror: "As long as we are human, we cannot but behold our own face as it were in a glass in a person that is poor and despised, though they were the furthest strangers in the world. Let a Moor or a Barbarian come among us, and inasmuch as they are human, they bring with them the looking glass wherein we may see that they are our brothers and sisters and neighbors."[22]

With this realization, the command to love one's neighbor is extended to include "the most remote stranger." "Our savior having shown that the term neighbor comprehends the most remote stranger, there is no reason for limiting the precept of love to our own connections. The whole human race, without exception, are to be embraced with one feeling of charity: that here there is no distinction of Greek or Barbarian, worthy or unworthy, friend or foe, since all are to be viewed not in themselves, but in God."[23]

Here, Calvin articulates a call to show hospitality to the *sacred stranger*, not as someone who is "the same as me," but in typically anatheist fashion, as someone who, in their particularity and otherness, bears the image of God. Like Kearney's retrieval of Nicholas of Cusa, such anatheist readings brush against the grain of mainstream reception history and in this way serve to expose and dismantle positions that rely on monumental pasts to maintain the status quo. An anatheist reimagining of the Reformed ethos and pathos for the stranger should be read against all historical manifestations of Reformed faith that betray it.

IV

This tentative attempt to read the anatheist wager from a particular perspective of faith responds to an invitation that I believe is an inherent part of Richard Kearney's project. In taking up this invitation, I have not answered the question of whether it is possible to be Reformed and anatheist. Perhaps this is for the best. After all, it is a firm Reformed conviction that one should never aspire to be Reformed, but only human before the face of God. The same, I am sure, could be said of anatheism. I would therefore like to keep the question open and invite others to continue the anatheist conversation from other perspectives and traditions. For as Kearney says, "Wagering between belief and non-belief . . . never comes to a full stop. . . . Far from signalling a lukewarm zone of noncommitment, the anatheist wager is at all times dynamic and attentive, moving intrepidly between engagement and critique, recovery and loss, sadness and joy. Instead of *never* making up its mind, it is *always* making up its mind" (A, 184).

Words that would have warmed Calvin's anatheist heart.

HELGARD PRETORIUS is Junior Lecturer at Stellenbosch University (South Africa) and Doctoral Candidate in a joint-degree program at Stellenbosch University and Vrije Universiteit Amsterdam. His current research project on the intersection of theology and phenomenology is called "Being Human After the Ascension of Jesus Christ."

Notes

1. What makes Christian faith and spirituality "Reformed" is notoriously hard to define. Historically speaking, "Reformed" refers to the Protestant tradition that has its roots in the sixteenth-century European reformations and, more specifically, the heritage associated with John Calvin (Genève), Ulrich Zwingli (Zürich), and others. A sense of Reformed identity and vision will surely emerge as the essay progresses, although this will no doubt be a disputed one. This very confessional weakness, characterized by plurality, openness to (self-)critique and continued revision, may in be one of the Reformed confession's most distinctive characteristics.

2. Smit, "Reformed Theology in South Africa: A Story of Many Stories," in *Essays on Being Reformed: Collected Essays* 3, 201–16.

3. See Taylor, *A Secular Age*, 757.

4. Cf. "I like to think of this book as a small intellectual agora where theists and atheists might engage in reasonable debate, acknowledging the possibility of what I call an anatheist space where the free decision to believe or not believe is not just tolerated but cherished" (A, xiii–xiv).

5. See Kearney and Zimmermann, *Reimagining the Sacred: Richard Kearney Debates God*, 219–39.

6. Ibid., 234–236.

7. Chesterton, *St. Francis of Assisi*, 16.

8. Johnson, "Theology and the Church's Mission: Catholic, Orthodox, Evangelical, and Reformed," in *Reformed Theology: Identity and Ecumenicity*, eds. Alston and Welker, 80. It may be important to note that this Reformed *openness* to a plurality of voices isn't restricted to the Bible but extends in a significant way to all sources of truth and wisdom. See Gerrish, "Tradition in the Modern World: The Reformed Habit of Mind," in *Toward the Future of Reformed Theology: Tasks, Topics, Traditions*, eds. Willis and Welker, 16.

9. Smit, "Trends and Directions in Reformed Theology," 317–319.

10. Ibid., 318.

11. Tillich, *Systematic Theology* 3, 245.

12. de Gruchy, *Liberating Reformed Theology: A South African Contribution to an Ecumenical Debate*, 98.

13. See the fascinating and instructive conversation between Kearney and Simon Critchley in Kearney and Zimmermann, *Reimagining the Sacred: Richard Kearney Debates God*, 147–174.

14. See Calvin, *Institutes of the Christian Religion*, book I, chapter 17, section 40.

15. See Dalferth, "Post-Secular Society: Christianity and the Dialectics of the Secular," *Journal of the American Academy of Religion* 78, no. 2 (2010): 338–339: "In the Protestant understanding of Christian faith ... no area of thought is intrinsically more 'sacred' or 'religious' than any other. In each of them, humans can live in appropriate or inappropriate ways with respect to the creative presence of God's love, and how they live decides on the theological character of this area of their life.... Christian faith does not add a dispensable religious dimension to human life but rather transforms its existential mode from a self-centered to a God-open life that puts its ultimate trust not in any human institution, whether religious or non-religious, but in the creative presence of God's love. Seen from this perspective, Christian theology has no interest in defending or returning to a pre-modern society that is dependent on religion or religious institutions."

16. Consider the deliberately ambiguous title of John de Gruchy's *Liberating Reformed Theology*, in which he argues for the liberating potential of Reformed *and* the need for Reformed theology itself to be liberated. In a sense, my own argument is that anatheism is a suitable conversation partner for both of these tasks.

17. In this regard, Kearney's work on a hermeneutics of history and tradition that is self-critical, discerning and creative would be an immensely useful resource. See, among others, Kearney, *On Stories* and *On Paul Ricoeur: The Owl of Minerva*.

18. See Vosloo, "The Displaced Calvin: 'Refugee Reality' as a Lens to Re-Examine Calvin's Life, Theology and Legacy," *Religion & Theology* 16 (2009): 35–52. After showing how Calvin's complex theological thought emerged from the challenges of being a pastor for and with refugees, Vosloo concludes, "Amidst a world of growing migration, displacement and xenophobia, we may well discover that Calvin's life and theology, with all its limitations, may provide surprising insights that can aid in the reclaiming of a graceful theology of hospitality."

19. Calvin, J. *The Institutes of the Christian Tradition*, book II, chapter 8, section 40.

20. Kearney and Semonovitch, *Phenomenologies of the Stranger: Between Hostility and Hospitality*, 14.

21. See Wolterstorff, "The Wounds of God: Calvin's Theology of Social Justice," in *Hearing the Call: Liturgy, Justice, Church, and World*, 114–132.

22. Cited in Ibid., 123.

23. Calvin. *The Institutes of the Christian Tradition*, book II, chapter 8, section 55.

8 Anatheism and Inter-Religious Hospitality: Reflections from a Catholic Comparative Theologian

Marianne Moyaert

Richard Kearney is a philosopher of dialogue and negotiation, committed to freeing deadlocks and bridging apparent impasses. A hermeneutic determination to choose a middle way (Greek, *metaxy*) and negotiate between extreme positions marks his entire philosophical journey, and this determination is obvious in Kearney's book *Anatheism*. As is the case in all his works, Kearney develops his reflections in dialogue with philosophers (Derrida, Arendt, Benjamin) but also with novelists (Proust, Dostoyevsky, Joyce) and poets (Hopkins), as well as with religious figures (Gandhi, Dalai Lama) and texts from other wisdom traditions. Adopting a posture of benevolence, he looks for what is meaningful and valuable in the work of others who hold a differing viewpoint on certain issues. Kearney's commitment to dialogue is his response to conflict. He asks, how can we reconcile the irreconcilable? How can we bridge seemingly unbridgeable positions? How can we mediate between exclusive claims? As a thinker of the *possible*, Kearney always seeks to find a way out of deadlock, imagining novel readings of what, at first glance, seem to be opposing positions.

In the volume under discussion, Kearney returns to the God question. In his own words: "What do we mean when we speak in the name of God? Do we mean an omnipotent God who will solve our problems, save and scold, condemn and control? Or something different" (A, 57). In pursuing this question, Kearney mediates between two extremes: fundamentalist atheism and dogmatic theism. Beyond both rigid positions, he opens up a space in which God-talk *after the death of the metaphysical God* (contra dogmatic theism) becomes possible *again* (contra fundamentalist atheism). Kearney calls this fragile space *anatheism (ana-theos)*. Passing through the desert of criticism, anatheism seeks to open up new possibilities of returning to God with a more mature faith—a faith that has renounced the all-too-human desire for certainty and control.

What I find interesting is that interreligious hospitality is at the heart of anatheism (A, 48). Welcoming "strange gods" is one of the ways in which anatheism is put into praxis. In this chapter, I wish to further explore Kearney's philosophical understanding of interreligious hospitality. I am sympathetic to his approach to interreligious dialogue, yet I have some questions. These questions are connected to the location from which I speak.[1] Unlike Kearney, I am not a philosopher but a Catholic theologian. Even though I do not want to go too deeply into the discussion about the complex relation between philosophy and theology—and I do not think it is wise to draw to sharp boundaries between both disciplines—I do think our starting points differ.[2] As a theologian, I am engaged in reflection on and out of faith—a reflection that is kept alive in a particular religious community that revolves around an age-old tradition that privileges particular religious texts that claim revelatory status. This does not mean that I do not engage or study texts from other traditions. Quite the contrary. But it does mean that these texts do not have the same authority for me as the Bible, which I read through the lens of tradition. The tradition to which I belong also makes certain truth claims with regard to salvation and revelation (as do most religious traditions), one of which (probably its most central one) is that the Christ-event is the culmination of salvation and revelation history.

I share with Kearney the firm conviction that a spirit of interreligious hospitality has the potential to break through the spiral of tribal tendencies, but I do not share his negative stance on dogmatic traditions. I do not think dogmatic theism necessarily excludes welcoming strange gods; matters are more nuanced. I write this contribution as a Catholic theologian who belongs to a tradition in which doctrine plays a central role, and I will point to some of the Catholic theological resources for interreligious hospitality. It remains to be seen if these theological resources affirm or negate the anatheist wager.

I

In the volume under discussion, Kearney asks what comes after the onto-theological God of metaphysics. How can we speak about a God who has been removed from his sovereign throne and stripped of his power and presence?[3] What follows when we have to let go of the God of terror? In pursuing this question, Kearney explores the possibility of a third way moving beyond the extremes of "dogmatic theism and militant atheism." Lacking in symbolic imagination, both dogmatic theism and militant atheism paint a black-and-white picture unable to acknowledge the complexity of belief. Their stance on the God question is rigid and oversimplified. Deep down, the fundamentalist atheists and the fundamentalist theists are like minds looking for certainty, control, and mastership. Militant atheists (the position of what Kearney calls the anti-God squad figuring Dawkins, Dennet, and Hitchens) "invoke the certainties of science against the falsities of faith, not appreciating that genuine faith has never expressed itself with certainty, but always through a cloud of unknowing" (A, 168). Dogmatic theists (for example, fundamentalist Christians) are not all that different; they too are fixated on obtaining certain knowledge—in their case not by relying on scientific evidence, but rather on a quite literal reading of the Bible or by relying heavily on the authority of tradition. Moving beyond both extremes, Kearney explores the possibility of a third way, which he calls anatheism. As the etymological meaning of the prefix *ana* (back, again) suggests, anatheism is about repetition and return. To be more precise, anatheism is another word for returning to a God "beyond or beneath the God we thought to possess." It is not a new religion; it is rather a way of believing after letting go of any form of triumphalism. It is "another word for another way of seeking and sounding the things we consider sacred but can never really fathom or prove" (A, 3). How does Kearney envision this third way?

Anatheism begins with an act of protest, by saying "no" to any form of triumphalist theism. Kearney clearly states, "the concept of God as absolute Monarch of the Universe stems from a literalist reading of the Bible along with unfortunate misapplications of a metaphysics of causal omnipotence and self-sufficiency. This has led to the ruinously influential notion of theodicy, namely the belief that God as Sovereign *causa sui*, as immutable emperor of the world, exercises arbitrary and unlimited powers over his creatures. Everything—even the worst horrors—could thus be justified as part of some divine Will (the ultimate Will to Power)" (A, 53).

Moving beyond this "old God of sovereignty and theodicy," Kearney challenges us to accept and appropriate the ideology critique. He turns to those prophetic voices of post-Holocaust thinkers who have announced the death of the God who "orchestrates good and evil alike" (A, 58). He explores, among others, the works of Elie Wiesel, Dietrich Bonhoeffer, Etty Hillesum, and Jacques Derrida. However, Kearney's understanding of anatheism resonates especially with what his philosophy tutor Paul Ricoeur calls postreligious faith. In his hermeneutics of religion, Ricoeur reserves an important place for the so-called masters of suspicion: Freud, Marx, and Nietzsche. They have taught us to critically relate to our traditions and probe into the deeper, often unconscious, and problematic dynamics that motivate our traditional cultural attachments, which can be brought to light only by adopting a hermeneutical attitude of suspicion and scrutiny. Their atheism offers a critical instrument of demystification, bringing to light the deadly nature of the ontotheological god. In Ricoeur's understanding, atheism does not come to destroy religion as such; rather, it points in the liberating direction of what he calls a postreligious (i.e. purified) faith.[4] What springs forth from this exploration is the image—not of a powerful Sovereign God (*potestas*), but rather of a God whose power lies in his powerless invitation to love (*potential*), a God who depends on our response to his invitation. His invitation will remain powerless unless we respond.

Kearney not only draws inspiration from these post-holocaust prophets who protest against the image of an almighty God, but also to various mystical voices who point to the apophatic dimension of all God-talk. The abandonment of the old metaphysical God also implies a retrieval of the mystery of the divine, which cannot be captured, grasped, and thus controlled in human language (even though we have no other means to talk about "him"). To Kearney's mind, there is an unsaid in every religious tradition that precedes any God-talk—a source that cannot be mastered, a *foundation* that gives no foundation (anti-foundationalism). In his words, "at the root of each religion [is] a silent, speechless openness to a [w]ord that surpasses us." Here, too, Ricoeur is an important source of inspiration; he speaks of a *fonds sans fond*, a mystical ground.[5] The appeal to this mystical ground is another response to dogmatic theism that makes undue claims about the divine, even to the point of becoming violent. According to Kearney, "the best way to tackle this violent tendency.... is to go all the way down to the source that religion does not master and that refuses to be rendered into dogmatic formulae or ideological manifestos ... And it is in this hearkening back to a source that one does not possess or manipulate, that we may find new resources for nonviolent resistance and peace" (A, 179). Beyond the death of God (and the justified critique of atheism), anatheism returns to this deep ground in the name of which no violence, exclusion, or oppression can be justified.

II

Central to anatheism is the idea that the divine comes to us in the guise of an unforeseen stranger. As an unexpected visitor, the holy one interrupts our daily pursuits (life as it is) and (more or less banal) preoccupations and gives us a feeling of not-being-at-home [*unheimlich*]. As Ian Corbin explains, "for Kearney, God is a meek stranger who evades our comprehension and upsets our expectations, and no one could ever have truly received God without accepting her ignorance, and opening herself to the strangeness of God."[6] According to Kearney, this is not a novel (postmodern) philosophical insight. Rather, he points out that "most religions have acknowledged the inaugural moment of religion as an encounter with the stranger."[7] In the moment of divine visitation, we are presented with an ethical choice: *hospitality* or *hostility*? This choice is a wager: when faced with the stranger, what do we do? Do we open the door, or do we close it? Do we welcome the stranger in our midst or turn our back on him as if he were our enemy? The moment of being interrupted by the stranger is marked by ambivalence; the possibility of hospitality is always overshadowed by the twin of hostility.[8]

The association between the divine and the stranger is symbolically multilayered. First, it evokes the idea that the sacred is and remains *other*, in the sense of mysterious and irreducible to our human categories. Something of God's own strangeness breaks through in the strange other, that is his holiness, which cannot be exhausted by our categories but tunes the human being to the unexpected.[9] This association not only reaffirms the apophatic dimension of all God-talk; it also tallies with Kearney's earlier criticism of the sovereign master God. By associating the divine with the figure of the stranger, Kearney points to the kenotic structure of epiphanies: the divine is not all-powerful and self-sufficient, but rather vulnerable. In an outpouring of love, the divine asks our recognition and response knowing that he might be (and often is) rejected. He approaches us with vulnerability rather than power. What's more, the association between the divine and the stranger clearly points to the intertwinement between religion and ethics. If the image of the master God springs from and nourishes the all-too-human desire for power and control, the anatheistic logic of the divine stranger translates in a kenotic ethics of service and hospitality. Whoever welcomes the stranger in his midst welcomes the divine.

"This hospitality," Kearney continues, "applies not just within religions but also between religions" (A, 49). Indeed, interreligious hospitality follows almost naturally from anatheism. To acknowledge that the divine mystery of the truth is always greater than can be grasped in symbols and doctrines brings forth a certain humble openness to other traditions. All the themes from the book seem to culminate in this point. Let me quote Kearney at length:

> [Anatheism] is an effort to retrieve a unique hospitality toward the Stranger at the inaugural scene of each belief. In thus exposing ourselves to the Gods of other traditions we take the risk of dying unto our own. And in such instants of kenotic hospitality, where we exchange our God with others—sometimes not knowing for a moment which one is true—we open ourselves to the gracious possibility of receiving our own God back again; but this time as a gift from another, as a God of life beyond death. In losing our faith, we may gain it back again: first faith ceding to second faith in the name of the stranger. That is the wager of anatheism. And the risk. For in surrendering our own God to a stranger god no God may come back again. Or the God who comes back may come back in ways that surprise us (A, 181).

For Kearney, reading and comparing religious texts belonging to different traditions is at the heart of interreligious hospitality. At stake is a practice of cross-reading.[10] Kearney asks:

> What happens, for instance, if we read the text about Shiva's pillars of fire alongside biblical passages on the Burning Bush or the Christian account of Pentecostal flame? What new sparks of understanding and compassion fly up if we read Hindu texts on the *guha* alongside Buddhist invocations of the "void" (in the Heart Sutra) or biblical references to Elijah or Muhammad in his cave, Jonah in the whale, Jesus in the tomb? What novel possibilities of semantic resonance are generated by juxtaposing the sacred bird (*hamsa*) of Vedanta alongside the dove of Noah's ark, of Christ's baptism in the Jordan? (A, 51).

Cross-reading follows the anatheist movement of faith passing through experiences of disenchantment to retrieve a more mature and complex faith of which doubt and wonder are integral parts. Those who are able to sustain experiences of friction and alienation brought about by cross-reading can also learn to enjoy the pleasure of discovering new insights. As I have explained elsewhere, reading texts together can nourish the familiar with the unknown and can keep the familiar alive.[11] It means giving the necessary oxygen to meanings. It is always possible that cross-reading brings forth meanings that were concealed in the classical reading of the text. That these texts come alive in unexpected ways is a sign that truth and revelation may be found outside of one's own scripture and tradition. Kearney concludes: "[This semantic exchange] lies at the very heart of anatheism as a return to God after God, that is as an invitation to rediscover forgotten truths of one's own faith by traversing alien faiths" (A, 51).

III

Even though I am sympathetic to Kearney's approach to interreligious dialogue, I have some questions that I want to make explicit in the concluding part of this chapter. I formulate these questions in friendship and with the greatest possible admiration. At the heart of my reflections is the question of how Kearney's anatheism relates to religious particularities, and I will make this more concrete by speaking as a Catholic theologian engaged in interreligious dialogue. What I will try to show is that this particular dogmatic (!) tradition contains theological resources for dialogue even though it also claims that in Christ, God's revelation reaches its climax.

Throughout his book (and the same goes for his earlier works), Kearney urges believers to move beyond what he calls dogmatic approaches to religion, which he associates with certainty, reification, triumphalism, exclusion, and the all-too-real possibility of violence. Clearly, dogmas are not Kearney's favorites—neither are religious claims to finality and uniqueness. Anatheism unsettles dogmas, challenges religious certainties, and embraces agnosticism to open up a dialogical space of interreligious hospitality. To overcome the rigidity of dogmatic theism and to meet the challenges of religious pluralism, anatheism is the way forward: religious reorientation presupposes disorientation and the loss of faith. The outcome—or, better, the goal—is a mature and adult faith, and it is this faith that enables interreligious hospitality. Kearney argues that if we stand back from definite claims, we may also embrace the possibility of welcoming strange gods and the insights and truths they bring with them.

As a Catholic theologian, I hesitate to fully embrace Kearney's rejection of dogmatic approaches to religion. I understand how the firm declaration of dogmas may sometimes function as a conversation stopper, certainly when a dogmatic affirmation goes together with condemnation, accursing, or even excommunication of those who believe differently, as has happened throughout Catholic history. Clearly this is not conducive to any dialogue. However, I do not agree that dogmas necessarily lead to exclusivism nor am I convinced that they necessarily preclude dialogue. I think matters are more nuanced and that a dogmatic tradition, like Catholicism, may also obtain strong theological resources from interreligious hospitality. I do not think we should associate them exclusively with rigid triumphalism.

Dogmas are at the heart of the self-understanding of the Catholic tradition. Historically speaking, the dogmas of the Catholic Church developed over time, and they often (though not always) grew out of lived religious practices of ordinary believers and from progressive insight. As Jon Sobrino puts it, the final formulation of a dogma often marks the climax of a long process of "Christian living and Christian reflective thinking."[12] Liturgy especially has given insight to divine revelation and has been a source and location for emerging theological understanding to be made explicit in dogmas. Connected to the above, the Catholic dogmatic tradition is not static; doctrinal development is a matter of fact and attests to the vitality of tradition. This doctrinal development entails a process of gradually unfolding ideas and insights, of growing understanding over time, and of seeing and grasping new dimensions of revelation. Fidelity to tradition is not seen as blind obedience but as a constructive and creative task, precisely because "tradition is . . . something living and vital, an ongoing process in which the unity of faith finds expression in the variety of languages and the diversity of cultures. It ceases to be [t]radition if it fossilizes."[13] The Church has received a gift the meaning of which she does not fully comprehend; her knowledge of the mystery of the revelation of God is "always fragmentary and impaired by the limits of our understanding."[14] In this context, I am reminded of a passage from Cardinal John Henry Newman, who, not unlike Kearney, refers to Mary as an example of what it means to ponder about God. Unlike Kearney, Newman sees Mary as exemplifying doctrinal development in the Church. According to Newman, Mary, who "kept these things pondering in her heart," not only exemplifies the ideal Christian believer but also symbolizes the faith of the "doctors of the church who have to investigate and weigh and define as well as to profess the gospel; to draw the line between truth and heresy; to anticipate or remedy the various aberrations of wrong reason; to combat pride or recklessness with their own arms; and thus to triumph over the sophist and the innovator."[15] It is, of course, possible that the Church, like Mary, embodies the anatheist mindset. But I doubt that Kearney would come to such a conclusion.

IV

Fundamental theological deliberation and argumentation is often triggered by contemporary challenges and happens in conversation with real concerns and developments in the world. A "need" exists "to find fresh raw materials out of which to develop meaningful responses to ever-changing contexts and the novel questions and experiences which such contexts make possible."[16] As Kearney would probably affirm, one of the most important challenges today is that of religious plurality. Though the Church was always aware of the existence of other religions (she came into being in a world marked by religious diversity) it was only during the second Vatican Council (1962–1965) that the council fathers realized the theological urgency to discuss the relation between the Church and other religions. During Vatican II, the council fathers revisited the Catholic tradition to discover paths that, for various reasons, the Church did not take but could have, which may have opened up a new life-giving future. Exploring what one might call "the untapped depths of the theological tradition," they took the tradition in a new and unexpected direction of dialogue and openness.[17]

The Catholic dogmatic tradition, surely, contains obstacles to dialogue and the Church wrestles to this day with triumphalist inclinations. However, this tradition also holds deep theological motivations to encounter the religious other and to search for God in other religious traditions. To uphold dogmas does not necessarily exclude dialogical openness; in fact, the Catholic tradition is rather generous toward other traditions. This generosity is, at least in my reading, rooted in the superabundance of God's love, which is at the heart of God's self-communication through history. Let me make this more concrete.

According to the Dogmatic Constitution on Divine Revelation *Dei Verbum*, God, in his grace, manifests himself in words and deeds, unceasingly extending himself to all people. God communicates himself (*sese revelavit*). He speaks and thereby invites (and does not impose, decree, or require) people to enter into a relationship with him and thus to come to share in the divine nature. God's motivation to do so becomes evident in the fact that God reveals himself out of love for human beings, addressing them as friends: "Through this revelation, therefore, the invisible God . . . out of the abundance of His love speaks to men as friends . . . and lives among them . . . so that He may invite and take them into fellowship with Himself" (*Dei Verbum: Dogmatic Constitution on Divine Revelation*, §2).

This dynamic of superabundant love is the impulse of God's mission in the world at large; his plan of salvation includes everyone. Thus God not only reveals his Godself, but also graciously *offers* the gift of salvation to all human beings as the Dogmatic Constitution on the Church *Lumen Gentium* argues. God seeks all people and tries to accommodate them where they are according to the needs of their concrete context. The speaking, relational God makes Godself vulnerable by starting a dialogue with God's whole creation. In this way, God runs the risk of misapprehension, misunderstanding, rejection. Indeed, this is not a sovereign God, who stays far removed from the human scene, or a master God who imposes his will. Rather:

> God speaks and through speaking—and this is important—he subjects himself to all the misunderstandings that are part of the use of language. Whoever speaks can be misunderstood; whoever speaks can be gainsaid. That is, the God of Israel is not God who reigns, sits enthroned and is silent. And actually by speaking he makes himself particularly vulnerable. For whoever speaks posits through speaking himself someone over against him who is a dialogue partner, and as a consequence he allows the dialogue partner the freedom to say "Yes" and to listen or to say "No" and to reject. It is an enormous risk that the God of Christianity and Judaism takes. It is not found anywhere else.[18]

This divine vulnerability, is seen preeminently in the scandalous particularity of the incarnation, when God takes on the human embodiment. This too is the greatest expression of the superabundance of divine love: so great is the love of God for his people that he became one of us—this is, par excellence, the expression of divine solidarity with humanity.[19] It is a radical act of kenotic self-disclosure and of kenosis in which God reaffirms his involvement with and love for humanity.

In a first-century Jewish man, Jesus of Nazareth, living in Palestine under Roman oppression, God has disclosed Godself and his plans for humanity in an unsurpassable fashion. He has become human among humans, a carpenter's son. That is why we say that whoever sees Christ sees the father (John 14:9); in him, God is present in a very historical, real, and palpable manner. It is in this sense that God's revelation in Christ is final and of unsurpassable quality.[20] This notion may be offensive to modern thinkers (it has always been offensive), and it certainly seems to preclude the humility so necessary for interreligious dialogue. However, that need not be the case. Emphasizing the scope of human finitude, the Catholic tradition holds that the deeper meaning of God's self-revelation has yet to be fully grasped. The Church, as a pilgrimage community, is called to penetrate the depths of divine truth, knowing that she may not fully succeed. Moreover, *Dei Verbum* holds that an overemphasis on the culmination of God's revelation in Christ might lead to an underemphasis on "the glorious appearance of our Lord Jesus Christ" in the eschaton (DV§4). Until the moment of Christ's coming in glory, the Church must be aware that it sees things in a mirror, dimly (1 Corinthians 13:12). This realization calls for a certain humility.

This humility was expressed again when the council fathers affirmed that God is understood to be active through grace, the spirit, and the seeds of the word in other religions.[21] Profoundly important in this regard is the Declaration on the Relation of the Church with non-Christian Religions (*Nostra Aetate*), according to which: "The Catholic Church rejects nothing that is true and holy in these religions. She regards with sincere reverence those ways of conduct and of life, those precepts and teachings which, though differing in many aspects from the ones she holds and sets forth, nonetheless often reflect a ray of that Truth which enlightens all men. Indeed, she proclaims, and ever must proclaim Christ "the way, the truth, and the life" (John 14:6), in whom men may find the fullness of religious life, in whom God has reconciled all things to Himself (*Nostra Aetate*, §4).

Among Catholic theologians dedicated to the cause of interreligious dialogue, this is one of the most important passages from the Second Vatican Council because it expresses appreciation for other religious traditions, rather than focusing on what they lack. The language used is hospitable rather than hostile, affirmative rather than judgmental.[22] Instead of admonishing from a position of certainty with regard to the final divine revelation, the fathers encouraged trust and openness, calling on the Church to lend a listening ear, to take the challenges of the times seriously, and to initiate a dialogue with the wider world without dogmatic triumphalism. The passage even summons the Church to "recognize, preserve and promote the good things … found among these men." It is a passage that signals openness towards other religions. That was, moreover, also the intention of the council fathers: by pointing to the positive values found in the other religions, they sought to put an end to the prejudices of the past and to establish relations with those of other faiths—to open a space for dialogue.[23]

The declaration *Nostra Aetate* and the dogmatic constitution *Lumen Gentium* affirm that the elements of truth and goodness that may be found in other religions spring from God's desire to reach out to all human beings; they are the result of God's gracious generosity, they are the result of God visiting all human beings and accommodating them where they are (*Nostra Aetate*, §2; *Lumen Gentium*, 17; *Ad Gentes*, 9). To put it in Kearney's terms, God reveals Godself and leaves traces of his truth in all traditions, in ritual practices, and scriptures. If we truly recognize (as *Nostra Aetate* urges) that there is truth to be found in other traditions, then the challenge is to discover what those elements of truth are and how they can enrich and deepen our (mutual) understanding of God's self-revelation. So the dogmatic tradition itself gives strong incentives to Catholics the world over to engage in practices of interreligious hospitality.

V

As a Catholic theologian dedicated to the cause of interreligious dialogue, I attempt to make this call for discernment concrete by doing what has been called "comparative theology." The primary question asked by comparative theologians is, where does God reveal Godself? By refusing to put limitations on God's activity in the world and by being willing to engage in an in-depth study of other religious traditions, comparative theologians seek traces of the divine wherever God makes Godself known and by engaging in a praxis of cross-reading they hope to deepen and even alter their understanding of the divine.

Comparative theology takes a nonclassical approach to the classical theological goal of *faith seeking understanding* by allowing itself to engage in a detailed study of religious texts other than its own. In brief, it is "the rereading of one's home theological tradition ... after serious engagement in the reading of another tradition."[24] When religious texts from different traditions are studied and read together, they begin to interact, influence, and affect one another, and this also has an effect on the reader. These texts begin to move and shift, losing their familiar (and perhaps sometimes even predictable or stale) meaning. Remarkable in this project of comparative theology is that *a scholarly approach* to the religious texts in question is combined with a more *spiritual approach* to the text, in which the reader affirms the authority of the text and surrenders to the world it projects. The close and comparative reading is like a religious act, analogous to the *lectio divina*. By surrendering to the power of two texts and being open to their ability to transform, the religious imagination of the comparative theologian is stretched "beyond established religious boundaries."[25]

Comparative theology is original in the way it recognizes other religions and their textual traditions as theological *loci alieni*. Reading and studying texts from various traditions, the comparative theologian becomes vulnerable to texts from more than one tradition (listening and learning to discern where traces of God may be found).[26] From this perspective, comparative theology is one way of not only welcoming the religious other, but also of receiving the divine other anew. Comparative theology does not intend to alter or rewrite the dogmatic tradition; neither does it seek to produce radically new truths. On the contrary, it progresses cautiously with a concern for the truths already known and revered in the tradition.[27] It does not hastily try to accommodate the tradition to our contemporary context of plurality. Rather, it proceeds at a deliberate and careful pace, refraining from formulating final answers to complex problems. As a cautious undertaking, comparative theology is not intent on developing some grand theology of religions in which the questions about Christology, soteriology, and revelation would be dealt with definitively. On the other hand, comparative theology does not merely repeat what tradition has always said. Rather, it asks, searches, and probes after the truth, trying to see God anew. Comparative theology seeks fresh insights into those familiar truths handed down by the tradition that may lead to new ways of understanding, interpreting, and receiving those truths.[28] This may help theologians to further develop their doctrinal traditions.[29]

VI

Anatheism is an invitation to revisit what might be termed a primary scene of religion: "the encounter with a radical stranger, who we choose or do not choose to call God" (A, 7). It is not a new religion; it is rather a way of believing after triumphalism. For Kearney, faith means "knowing you don't know anything absolutely about absolutes" (A, 170). This tallies with the central anatheistic idea of the divine stranger, who reveals himself where and when we would least expect it. As Kearney puts it, anatheism "begins and ends with the epiphany of the divine in the face of the stranger." Two responses are possible: hostility or hospitality (A, 149).

What I have tried to argue in this contribution is that Catholic theology also acknowledges that *Deus semper maior est.* Not only do we not grasp the fullness of his revelation; his gracious self-communication extends beyond the boundaries of our own Christian tradition. Other religious traditions also contain traces of the divine. When we encounter the religious other and study her tradition, we should be aware that God has already been there and we are challenged to welcome God, who has visited other traditions under the guise of the stranger.

Not unlike Kearney, I make this concrete by engaging in comparative theological practices of cross-reading, and I do this because of a strong belief that God also speaks of Godself in the scriptures of other religious traditions. I do this because I realize that our understanding of God's mystery may be deepened and our triumphalist inclinations may be countered by engaging in such practices of cross-reading. Does this make me an anatheist? I am not sure. I would think that my embrace of the dogmas that are central to my own tradition, and that entail the claim that we do know at least something about God and God's plan of salvation for humankind, is hard to reconcile with the agnosticism that is so central to Kearney's wager. I do hope, on the other hand, that this contribution, which may be an instance of (Catholic-)dogmatic theism, does not necessarily exclude dialogical openness and that it may even contain important theological incentives to open up a space for interreligious hospitality.

MARIANNE MOYAERT is a visiting Lecturer in Theology and Religious Studies at KU Leuven (Belgium), where she belongs to the Research Unit Pastoral and Empirical Theology. She is also Professor at the Free University of Amsterdam (the Netherlands), where she teaches hermeneutics, philosophy of religion, and philosophical and theological anthropology. She is the author of *Fragile Identities: Towards a Theology of Interreligious Hospitality.*

Notes

1. Kearney often commences his articles with this question: *d'où parlez-vous*? Where do you speak from? It is a question that Paul Ricoeur asked all of his students who participated in his classes. Kearney has taken over this habit, and so have I (as many others, I presume). This question bears testimony to the hermeneutical tradition in which Kearney stands; it is a question that acknowledges from the outset that there is no view from nowhere

and that we always speak from somewhere. For better or for worse, we are marked and affected by a variety of traditions. This is not problematic as such. Often, it is our particular hermeneutical perspective from which spring particular questions and from which emerge novel insights. Prejudices become problematic when they are not taken up in the process of reflection, and cannot be contested or critiqued. The question *d'où parlez-vous* is not only a question to name our particular viewpoint, but also to make this viewpoint part of the discussion.

2. For a more fundamental discussion of the relation between philosophy (of religion) and theology see Moyaert, "Why Are Theologians Annoyed by John Hick," in *Studies in Interreligious Dialogue* 22, 191–208.

3. See also Manoussakis, *After God: Richard Kearney and the Religious Turn in Continental Philosophy*, vx.

4. Ricoeur, "Religion, Atheism and Faith," in *The Conflict of Interpretations: Essays in Hermeneutics*, 448.

5. See also Moyaert, *In Response to the Religious Other: Ricoeur and the Fragility of Interreligious Encounters*, chapter 2, 45–68.

6. Corbin, "An End and a Beginning . . . Richard Kearney on Welcoming Divine Strangers and Writing Divine Words," 540.

7. Kearney, "Imagining the Sacred Stranger; Hostility of Hospitality," in *Politics and the Religious Imagination*, 17.

8. Kearney, "Guest or Enemy? Welcoming the Stranger," Religion & Ethics website, June 21, 2012, http://www.abc.net.au/religion/articles/2012/06/21/3529859.htm.

9. See Moyaert, *Fragile Identities: Towards a Theology of Interreligious Hospitality*, 271.

10. See Moyaert, *In Response to the Religious Other: Ricoeur and the Fragility of Interreligious Encounter*, chapter 6, 157–188.

11. See Moyaert, *In Response to the Religious Other: Ricoeur and the Fragility of Interreligious Encounter*, chapter 6, 157-188.

12. Sobrino, *Christology at the Crossroads: A Latin American Approach*, 324.

13. International Theological Commission, *Theology Today: Perspectives, Principles and Criteria*, accessed March 12, 2017, www.vatican.va.

14. John Paul II, *Fides et Ratio: Encyclical Letter on the Relationship between Faith and Reason*, no 13.

15. Newman, "A Theory of Development in Religious Doctrine," in *Fifteen Sermons Preached Before the University of Oxford Between A.D. 1826 and 1843*.

16. Merrigan, "Accounting for the Particular: The Promise and Pitfalls of an Incarnational Hermeneutics of Interreligious Dialogue," paper presented at the International Expert Symposium "Between Doctrine and Discernment," November 14–15, 2014, KU Leuven.

17. Ibid.

18. Danneels, "Geloof en moderniteit," in *Hoe dichtbij is de toekomst? Lessen voor de eenentwintigste eeuw*, 18.

19. Haers, *De theologen op het matje geroepen*, 141.

20. Cf. "For, in giving us, as he did, his Son, who is his one and only Word, he spoke to us once and for all, in this single Word, and he has no occasion to speak further." John of the Cross, *The Ascent of Mount Carmel*, Bk. II, Ch. XXII, 183.

21. Lane, *Stepping Stones to Other Religions: A Christian Theology of Inter-Religious Dialogue*, 70.

22. This tallies with the general tone of the Council. Not a single anathema was pronounced in contrast to, for example, Trent.

23. Dupuis, *Christianity and the Religions: From Confrontation to Dialogue*, 61.

24. Clooney, *Theology after Vedanta: An Experiment in Comparative Theology*, 3.

25. Cornille, "Empathy and Interreligious Imagination," 114.

26. See Moyaert, "*On Vulnerability: Probing after the Ethical Dimensions of Comparative Theology*," in *Religions* 3 (2012) special issue on European Perspectives on Comparative Theology, 1144–1161.

27. Clooney, *Comparative Theology*, 157.

28. Ibid., 112.

29. For the notion of *loci alieni* see Gruber, "Revelatory Alienations: Catholic Tradition and Its Loci Alieni: A Response to Paul Griffiths," 46–56.

9 Buddhist Anatheism

Joseph S. O'Leary

Scion of a distinguished medical family, Richard Kearney offers an auscultation of our deep modern unease about "God" and some pointers for a healthier regime of religious thinking and living. He brings to the task not the cumbersome armor of a theologian, but comprehensive literary and philosophical sensitivity, attuned to the anxieties and aspirations of his times, which he sounds in depth in three cultures—Ireland, France, and the United States of America. Theologians fret about getting doctrinal claims right under contemporary conditions, and may even draw on Buddhism to recalibrate the language of faith and make it a more skillful and salutary communication. Kearney casts his net more widely, bringing in a shoal of "epiphanies" from the poets and thinkers he admires, and also from the experience of life in all its fleshly complexity. Issues of faith and doctrine emerge within this human and spiritual consciousness in a subtle way, as imaginative orientations, inextricably embedded in their experiential matrix.

A hermeneuticist formed by Paul Ricœur, Kearney espouses the entire gamut of modern religious and antireligious attitudes from within, taking all of them as part of our story and part of who we are. The positive outlook of faith that survives this ecumenical embrace, or rather that is born of it, takes the form of a "wager"—not a refutation of atheism or a vindication of theism, but the decision to dwell in our current spiritual situation, in that space of "anatheism" in which atheism and theism are in dialogue. Here, the believer may be the radical doubter while the atheist may testify to gracious ultimacy in a work of art or an ethical achievement. The anatheistic wager is a reading of this entire process as an evolutionary threshold in human consciousness, which spells not a collapse of religious traditions but their salutary mutation.

Kearney organizes his thought as a *perichoresis*—a dance around the empty center or *chora*—which is the space of divine absence but also of a new mode of divine presence. Atheists and agnostics join in this dance on equal terms with everyone else. What distinguishes the believer's steps in this dance is the wager that guides him, the confidence that biblical and Christian language and ritual has a joyful contribution to make. Buddhists, too, can join in the dance, their steps particularly light and dexterous because of their awareness of emptiness and interrelationality. This is very far from Pascal's notorious wager, a grim moral blackmail: Your best bet is to believe because you have so much to lose, so much to gain, if the faith is true; and you can believe if you will to, and if you enact the observances of faith, suspending the skeptical mind. Pray, and become stupid, *abêtissez-vous*, and faith will come in addition.

Kearney's wager opens the mind instead of closing it. Faith is not opposed to the revolutionary openings of modern thought and literature. Rather, it lets itself be nourished by the epiphanies of meaning and purpose they enable. In doing so, it raises modernity into what Teilhard de Chardin called "the divine milieu." Faith no longer needs to prove its epistemological validity, for in its dialogal collaboration with literature and philosophy and art and progressive political engagement, in building up this incarnate milieu, it shows itself to be an enriching and enlightening force.

Buddhism would recognize in this hospitable, mind-expanding faith a "skillful means," a vital and flexible expression of enlightened awareness. The element of choice in this wager is close to that which bodhisattvas exhibit when they choose the timely and appropriate words or gestures that compassionately lead sentient beings to wisdom. The question "but is it all ultimately true?" falls away as the skillful activity is deployed, showing its healing effect at every turn. One might speak of this shift of focus as a "step back" (Heidegger) from the obsession with the metaphysical definition of God to a vital engagement with God and neighbor through the practice of love, in a total life-world pervaded by attention to the signs of grace that emerge on every side. But it is better to call it a "step forward," a step into the space where we already are without knowing it. This space—and not any dogmatic teaching or creedal label such as "theism" or "monotheism"—now appears as the primary datum with which faith and religion concern themselves. Arguments about the existence of God or the problem of evil recede to a secondary place as one surrenders to the attraction of this vital process.

Similarly, in Buddhism, the processes of enlightenment and compassion prevail over the cultivation of correct views; indeed, the latter tends to be viewed with suspicion as setting up fixed certitudes in place of skillful responsiveness to the experiences that draw forth one's energies of wisdom and compassion. Both Buddhism and Christianity are coterminous with the total space of human awareness. Anatheism is a formula for keeping them open to that space, refusing the retreat into compartmentalized religious claims.

A multidimensional incarnational faith, rescued from the fundamentalist distortions to which believers and nonbelievers alike have fallen prey, will shed the accoutrements that are burnt up in the fire of atheistic critique, but, more positively, will integrate the distinctive traits of modern poetic and ethical vision. It will retrieve the twentieth century not as disenchanted, secularized, or godless, but as a deeply religious period, bequeathing resources for a renewal of Christian thought, language, and practice. The unprecedented catastrophes of World Wars I and II generated a soul-searching and a quest for meaning that place modern humanity at a level of religious depth comparable to that of the biblical Job. Thirst for justice, peace, and care for human rights and the environment have created a platform of human understanding that is morally superior to that of any empire of the past and that even overthrows entrenched religious narrowness, as in the push for marriage equality. The arts have shattered traditional conceptions and broken through to a radically new vision of humanity and its potential for transformation, while phenomenological and existential thinkers have sounded in a new way the riddles of humanity and of being. Modernist iconoclasticism rejoins a dynamic at the heart of scripture and the gospels, which constantly urge us to take leave of our narrow conceptions of God to meet God anew as a liberating presence. Buddhism, too, in its quieter way, is a profoundly iconoclastic or subversive religion, constantly weaning us away from objects of clinging and refusing to let us rest in any "view" so that our minds and hearts are freed to join in the dance of emptiness.

This is not to say that faith and religion emerge unscathed from the ordeal of modernity. Rather, their meaning is radically altered. Faith is less a matter of subscription to tenets than of an orientation in regard to reality itself; religion becomes a repertory of skillful means for engaging with reality itself. This change permits a powerful affinity between Christian and Buddhist praxis and vision to emerge. In each, one performs religious acts and uses religious language in order to grow in a rooted and creative engagement with reality, and in that process, the Christian may well draw on Buddhist resources and vice versa. Just as an Irish citizen might be happy to be called a European, so Christian believers can embrace a wider Buddho-Christian identity and can see themselves as contributors to the emergence of a new religious culture that sublates past identities into a dialogal fabric.

Within this new religious *oikoumene*, a Buddhist-Christian interplay might play a key role since both religions have always explicitly aimed at universality and have always developed a keen critical consciousness over against inherited limited forms. Both are explicitly concerned with the same matter—that is, with processes of liberation and salvation that are afoot in the living present. Both see materialism as an amputation of consciousness and a source of suffering and point out that at every step, we run into invisible realities—conscience and morality, truth, love, reason itself—that dislodge the materialistic or naturalistic outlook and keep it from having the last word. Beyond defensive apologetics, both religions enact a richer vision of the world, which is not imposed by doctrine but emerges from the texture of human life itself. The scriptures of both religions can be read as an exegesis of everyday life, and even their most dazzling epiphanies or theophanies lodge at the heart of the human life-world. Some rare theologians, such as Schleiermacher and Tillich, strove to bring this into view, but it emerges more luminously when discovered by artists, thinkers, and even scientists who lack theological tutoring.

Does the love of God or total trust in God imply a clinging to a macro-substance—an impregnable identity, a secure foundation—that becomes a bulwark against the freedom of the spirit? The Buddhist deconstruction of such a God could, in that case, be a service to biblical faith, overcoming a God who is substance for a God who is spirit. Viewed in this light, Buddhist "atheism" becomes a voice in Christian theological reflection, as does the radical monotheism of Islam. All these *-isms* send us back to the concrete incarnational texture of the divine milieu. It is impossible to reject Islamic monotheism or Buddhist atheism as radically mistaken; they must be studied as pointers to great truths. All of these religions are wrestling with the ultimate, unfathomable mystery, before which they fall silent, so it is inappropriate to set them neatly off against one another as holding rival tenets. Historical controversies between them come into view as different hermeneutical slants on the one shared situation of religious questioning and finding, and they change today into a relaxed dialogue where none seeks to refute the others.

The study of Buddhism always throws us back on our own existence, telling us that we must change our lives, and leaving little space for detached philosophizing. Christian theology has often buried itself in well-defended speculations against any contact with the unpleasantness of real life. The phenomenological turn that anatheism gives to talk of God suspends this possibility of disengagement. To speak of God becomes indissociable from talking of justice, responsibility, hospitality, the other, the stranger, peace-making, beauty, creativity, or carnal existence. An apologetic for faith in this God is not helped by metaphysical arguments; the effective apologetics is one that points to this concrete "God-event" and invites one to test its credibility. Classical metaphysical theology remains "true," but its truth is a repertory of tokens, as are the *philosophoumena* of Buddhism, and it is fully and concretely true only when the doctrines become skillful means, used in contexts of salvific liberation.

The incarnational vision of Christianity embraces all of human experience and the whole cosmos, and Buddhism for its part claims to communicate a vision of things as they really are. As each stretches itself out anew in order to match the contemporary horizons of awareness, each realizes more effectively its own universal scope. Buddhism is often embraced by those who want a religion without God or without a personal God—creator and judge—on whom we depend totally. Does this force the anatheist to wager for theism against Buddhism? One can argue that the sense of divine possibility and presence emerging in the anatheistic milieu is something quite other than any god that Buddhism rejects. Indeed, the openings on ultimacy in the Buddhist tradition are incompatible with an airtight atheism. The divine in Buddhism does not give itself the strong profile of the monotheistic God; it is broken down into such elements as absolute reality and universal compassion, justice, mercy, grace, personality (of bodhisattvas and helpful *devas* or gods), and eternity (the ultimate reality of Buddhahood and *nirvāṇa* transcends all temporal categories), which are dispersed in partial form across the field of Buddhist representations. But more than that, the lived practice of Buddhism—and of Christianity—opens up to the real, a growth in compassionate responsiveness and penetrating insight, bringing the two religions into communion with one another.

Some might wager that the real anatheism is simply Buddhism, into which a Christianity without God could be sublated without remainder. Since the Oriental Renaissance of the early nineteenth century, Buddhism has been a refuge for those who seek a rational metaphysics, ethics, and spiritual practice free of the perplexing enigmas of theological speculation. All the old riddles of theology, beginning with the problem of evil, are recycled in Buddhist critiques that dismantle theistic traditions, resolving the riddles by making the divine object that gives rise to them collapse on its inherent contradictions. A Christian might respond to this by apologetics or in labored efforts to show that Buddhist insight is not incompatible with faith. Or, heeding Robert Magliola's plea to "face up to real doctrinal difference,"[1] the Christian might engage in ecumenical dialogue between the opposing views of faith in God and the Buddhist rational self-reliance. But neither of these is an adequate response, because both imply too narrow a conception of Buddhist or Christian truth.

To be sure, despite powerful affinities between the new faith and the philosophical milieu of Platonism in the early church, the fathers did try to spell out the points of agreement and of disagreement, of which the most substantial was the Platonists' ignorance or rejection of the incarnation. One might renew a similar disputation with Buddhism, but this would not be the essential point at issue in the dialogue. In the Christian vision of reality, the figure of Christ emerges prominently as a cipher of divine and human reality. Different figures emerge in the Buddhist horizon, but all of them point beyond themselves to reality itself, to be encountered in wisdom and compassion. Despite the high doctrinal claims for his divine status, the figure of Christ also points beyond himself to the wider reality, though in much Christian thinking he has absorbed all attention at the expense of an opening up to reality in its broadest scope. This revelatory function of Christ must first be lived out in exploration of the horizons opened up, an exploration that can be shared with Buddhists, before one stresses doctrinal claims. These claims are often far less easy to define than was traditionally thought—to the degree that it becomes very difficult to set them up solidly as points of difference over and against Buddhism or Judaism.

In any case, "right view" or "orthodoxy" is not a pressing concern in the anatheistic milieu, where the accent has shifted to exploring living realities. Faith, revelation, and authority continue to be respected, but they no longer control the total horizon any more than does a reductive rationalism that would do away with them. In 1847, Schopenhauer referred to "a boiling-point on the scale of culture where all faith, revelation, and authorities evaporate."[2] All three have certainly undergone a change in status, echoed in the common complaint that *the faith is no longer what it was*. From a Buddhist point of view, one could argue that all three have acquired the status of skillful means, serving as leads to open a vision of reality as a whole rather than as shibboleths of a singular religious identity. We should not stress heavily that the singularity of Christ as historical savior distinguishes Christianity from Buddhism, since the Christ-event, like the Buddha's wisdom, is coextensive with reality itself. It illuminates the very nature of reality and nothing eludes its light. Christ is "the savior of the world" (John 4:42) because he is the light that enlightens all minds (John 1:9); both revelation and salvation are universal. Christianity, like Buddhism, is an empowering vision of reality as such. Both religions constantly think beyond their inherited forms in order to become themselves. When Meister Eckhart said that being is God (*esse est Deus*), he may have been pointing to this universality of religious vision, which demands that each of its key terms be coterminous with reality itself.

"Reality itself" is, of course, a rather indeterminate notion, and it would be difficult to set it up firmly as a criterion of what is dead and what is living in religious traditions. If we accept that reality is the judge of religion, not religion of reality, just as "the Sabbath was made for humanity, not humanity for the Sabbath" (Mark 2:27), then each religion is faced with the task of determining what reality itself is and of aspiring to be adequate to it. Buddhism does this in its general ontology with its notes of emptiness, liberation, and thusness (*tathatā*). If both religions are an embrace of reality, a vision of reality, and an affirmation of reality, and if their particular tenets and claims are to be taken as skillful means stretching out to that universal embrace, then it is counterproductive to start opposing them as contrary belief systems. Both share reality itself and the different inflections or styles of their address to reality are complementary. Even such terms as "theism" and "atheism" indicate nuances of vision rather than stark theses. An infinite, incomprehensible, ineffable divinity on the one side cannot be simply opposed to the empty thusness of reality on the other. The real is not opposed to the real; on both sides there is the same sense of ultimacy, the same movement of freedom. Buddhists and Christians share the same boat—that of human beings adrift on the ocean of reality. They descry together the contours of that mighty ocean, using languages that are mutually challenging and mutually enlightening. Their traditions have a functional role as guides to navigation, and they lose meaning unless they are serving the present living adventure of navigating the sea of the real. The way to save religions from themselves is to take seriously their claim to universality. If Christ and Buddha are speaking to and for the entire world, then it must be possible to "cash" their words as indicating universal reality. The more we seek to draw out the implications of this, the more the narrowness, stuffiness, and stubborn sectarianism of so much in-house religious talk becomes apparent. Theologians in their talk of "God" and "grace" and "salvation" are often merely moving pawns on a chessboard of theory. If their terminology were stretched at every point to be adequate to what it must intend to denote, the entire fabric of theological discourse would change. Buddhist-Christian dialogue has somewhat slumped recently, because people got tired of the speculative language used by so many of its proponents. Drawing on the decadent speculation of the alleged "Trinitarian renaissance," interreligious theologians sought to map the places of other religions in light of the doctrine of the Trinity (or rather of a modern speculative image of the Trinity), sometimes invoking metaphysical tenets of German idealism or process thought for good measure. A Buddhist-Christian encounter rooted in a shared apprehension of reality itself would have to proceed in a very different style, beginning with a renunciation of unreal speculative constructions in favor of a return to the phenomena, a return to where we always already are.

Anatheism registers a change in the nature and function of theism, which is such that atheism ceases to have a clear target. To deny "the existence of God" becomes as difficult as to deny the ocean of being or of emptiness. A sense of divine presence at the heart of things, at the ground of being, is something that "insists,"[3] yet that may not translate as smoothly as was thought into the anthropomorphic language of a knowing, willing, acting personal agent or into the scholastic attempt to give refined metaphysical expression to these representations. An incarnate style of theological hermeneutic will keep the notion of God-in-himself as a vanishing point while assessing the paths wherein believers have felt themselves to be in communication with the divine. The Buddhist notion of conventional or screening truth (*saṃvrti-satya*) makes a play of mobile traces of all religious language, through which the ultimate truth (*paramārtha-satya*) is communicated only as an elusive presence best attested by silence, when all conceptual and linguistic fabrications are brought to rest.

If under Buddhist influence we talk of an "empty God," the implications are comparable to the talk of "God as being" that the contact with Greek philosophy enabled. The biblical God did not disappear into being but asserted his irreducible identity in regard to the language and categories of being. Similarly, today we may expect that the biblical God will not disappear into emptiness, but will assert his identity in a fresh way. In any case, Buddhism urges that our conventional talk of God should have the vibrant effectiveness of a skillful means, conducing at every point to spiritual liberation, and that the ultimate paramarthic reality of God is accessible to us only in and across the play of conventions. This might allow Pascal's "*abêtissez-vous*" to be read in a more positive key: If you want to know the living God, join in the practices that transmit divine presence, without anxious searching after metaphysical definitions and certitudes.

We must let our too-narrow conceptions of God be solicited and shaken by the new horizons that have emerged—solicited not by speculative gyrations, but by a "reality check" that tests them against reality itself. Buddhism, with its astringent vision of reality, based on an intensive analytical empiricism, provides an effective check on the inflatedness of so much Christian discourse. The interreligious space in which such mutual critique and correction is possible is becoming more and more the obligatory horizon of all religious thought, the milieu that mediates and inflects all our efforts to talk of God or of grace and salvation. As we cultivate that milieu, with greater attention to the earth and to the texture of human community, our inherited biblical conceptions of God and even the texture of our prayer will broaden to match the contours of the world in which we actually live. Kearney's wager is that a wider conception of the divine can bear the full brunt of philosophical critiques, including those inspired by Buddhism, and can establish itself in a "poetic" vision of existence as a field of enabling possibility. Thus the clamor of religious and antireligious propaganda today can be seen as reflecting the death-throes of the old narrow conceptions and the birth-throes of something new. "The anatheist retrieval of the sacred in the profane is preceded by an acute acceptance of disillusionment and death" (A, 110). In Buddhism, full acceptance of the three marks of existence—impermanence, suffering, and non-self—to which a fourth mark, emptiness, may be added, precedes the turnabout whereby one retrieves *nirvāṇa* in *saṃsāra*. To build a common platform between Buddhism and Christianity on the basis of contemplating the texture of reality and discovering it to be at bottom sacred or nirvanic, is to set up a space of awareness that will temper and condition our language of a personal, active God. Mahāyāna Buddhism boldly asserts the ultimately nirvanic quality of reality, despite the many miseries of samsaric existence. In Kearney's Christian vision, attention to human suffering, to the stranger, the "the least of these" becomes the very hinge on which the conjunction of the everyday and the divine turns.

On the theme of God, it would be very instructive to contrast the Indian arguments for and against his existence, as well as the Indian determinations of the divine essence, with their Western counterparts. It is hardly a satisfactory result of three millennia of philosophical theology to say that God's existence is unprovable and his essence indefinable. Indeed, this entire discussion now seems a massive distraction from the true quality of life that gives the world a religious dimension. While even the most untutored discourse on God cannot be long sustained without subscribing to some view on divine essence and existence, these views no longer carry much weight. Theologians may insist that even if we posit divine existence merely as a hermeneutical wager, forgoing any effort to establish it by reasoning, and even if we sketch the divine essence in phenomenological terms by exploring the "God-event" of mystics, artists, and activists, making of God a vibrant space of possibility, we need a criteriology to decide when what we call "God" in these contexts can safely be received as "God." But that is a wooden approach, and the unfathomable depths of the divine are not a practicable or useful topic for analysis. Rather, the total texture of a religious culture is what theology should be assessing, a texture within which words such as "God" may figure skillfully or unskillfully.

This shift of focus has been anticipated by countless theologians and religious thinkers who have registered or promoted a softening of tight definitions of God's being in favor of a poetic and phenomenological horizon in which God cannot be clinically disengaged from the totality of existence and life. Schleiermacher's location of God in terms of the sentiment of utter dependence and Tillich's location of God in terms of "ultimate concern" are characteristic examples of this movement. Steep doctrines on the divine nature remain authoritative and even necessary, but their status has become that of a secondary defense of the rich primary language of faith. In Buddhism, likewise, what counts above all is the milieu of liberation. The doctrinal foundations—theories of Buddhahood and of ontology—are constantly bent back to their pragmatic, functional, liberative context.

What anatheism may add to this existential turn is a reconversion of all religious terms into indications of concrete life-orientations. The wager of "I believe in a gracious God, creator of all" is "cashed" as an embrace of life itself as gift, as creatively purposed, as opening out infinitely. Another creedal utterance, such as "I believe the Holy Spirit" can carry the same weight of comprehensive life-affirmation. Thus, a list of doctrinal tenets changes its meaning and become a series of poetic or transforming phenomenological responses to the lived world. Bearing in mind the impossibility of isolating the idea of God from the full context of the divine milieu in which God is known in a wide web of experiences of grace and love, the metaphysical debate can be relocated as answering a concrete, contextual question: "This God that you always refer to, is it real or just a convenient imaginative symbol?"

Starting from phenomenological categories such as "call" and "gift," one could argue that they must be grounded in some ultimate reality. Making fully explicit the nature of the ultimate reality postulated in Christian experience and doing the same for the Buddhist conception of ultimate reality, one could set up a friendly dharma-battle between the two ways of thinking. The debate would soon shift to the plane of ontological presuppositions. For Christian metaphysics, all beings exist in total dependence on the divine source of all being. For Buddhist metaphysics, all beings are radically impermanent, dependently co-arising formations. Christians see divinization as the goal of beings; Buddhists speak of nirvanic release from the painful realm of impermanence. But these oppositions soften as we recognize that the Buddhist analysis of samsaric existence applies quite well to the Christian experience of created being in its finitude and contingency. Meanwhile, Mahāyāna Buddhism, in its paradoxical claim that the samsaric is already nirvanic, comes close to the Christian vision of the transformation of the creature through union with the divine.

This metaphysical discussion may never come to a definitive conclusion, but it should not be discouraged as a distraction. The intellect and its questions are also an integral element in the Christian and Buddhist life and cannot be expelled from the divine milieu. The pursuit of debate with Buddhists about the existence and nature of God could become a precious spiritual exercise as Christian ardor blends with Buddhist serenity, overcoming the centuries in which that ardor turned sour in fanaticism and in which that serenity may have favored an entrenched indifference to the question of God.

Kearney's anatheism thus maps the new dialogal space in which the Christian gospel engages with Western modernity but equally with Eastern religious wisdom. That space has its own coherence and lasting power, irrespective of doctrinal claims and counterclaims. It forms a plateau for future dialogal developments, among which the dialogue with Buddhism is likely to play the most central role. One may hope that rather than muddying the contours of both traditions and diminishing their power of conviction, the anatheistic opening will allow the traditions to be voiced in new styles comprehensible to modern hearts and minds, with a new modesty and vulnerability as they enter into a dance-like interplay with long-despised "strangers." Such a happy future for religion exceeds the anticipation of nervous believers and militant unbelievers alike, and releases both from a centuries-long crisis of doubt and anxiety, replacing the rituals of a tired and bitter conflict with the creativity of a responsive culture of vision, compassion, and joyful trust.

JOSEPH S. O'LEARY is an Irish theologian who has lived in Japan since 1983, where he taught at Sophia University (Tokyo) and did research at Nanzan University (Nagoya). He is the author of a trilogy in fundamental theology: *Questioning Back*, *Religious Pluralism and Christian Truth*, and *Conventional and Absolute Truth: A Key for Fundamental Theology.*

Notes

1. Magliola, *Facing up to Real Doctrinal Difference: How Some Thought-Motifs from Derrida Can Nourish the Catholic-Buddhist Encounter.*
2. Schopenhauer, *On the Fourfold Root of the Principle of Sufficient Reason (1847 edition)*, 180.
3. Cf. Caputo, *The Insistence of God: A Theology of Perhaps.*

10 The Wager That Wasn't: An Education in Shady Chances

L. Callid Keefe-Perry

I

There are perhaps three potential risks posed by the anatheistic wager. Philosophically, the risk is that, when speaking about the presence of the divine, we are actually speaking about nothing. Ethically, the risk is waiting for God, but engaging in violence. Theologically, the risk is that we engage in "aestheticization." In all three of these framings, a constant is that Kearney's anatheism is put forth as a wager whose outcome is definitively unknown. It is a fair gamble—nothing to hedge bets against and no insider information about a fighter who might throw the match.

Kearney wants anatheism to persist in a moment of true tension—or perhaps in a micro-oscillation between theism and atheism—not "a hypothetical synthesis in a dialectic moving from theism through atheism to a final telos," (A, 6) or "an empty secularism that merely aestheticizes religion by removing its faith content" (A, 130). He wants to circumscribe an area in which a true wager can be made, a bet whose outcome we cannot know in advance. And the stakes for the wager are high: as a result of having a truly open space, we may decide "to return to a God beyond both the *qua* God and the *quasi* God" (A, 130). Free from cultural and familial habituation and pressure to affirm either theism or atheism, the anatheistic moment allows one to exercise his or her own agency and make a wager that Kearney assures us cannot be rigged.

Anatheism is framed as that which "neither includes nor excludes a leap of second faith," clears "a landing site for the divine stranger without either prohibiting or mandating a landing" (A, 15), and allows us "to freely recommit to faith if we choose" (A, 130). He refers to it alternatively as "creative not-knowing," the "suspension of received assumptions," the "abandonment of accredited certainties," and as an "attitude of holy insecurity" (A, 7). Following Kant and then Heidegger, Kearney says that "philosophically speaking . . . the anatheist wager is marked by a moment of radicalized 'innocence' (*in-nocens*) that opens the door to ulterior dimensions of truth" (A, 8). This wager must be beyond reproach, must be pristine and—in Kearney's own words—innocent. That is, not *nocens*, not harmful or noxious.

I think Kearney is trying to protect against a kind of fetishization of form without anything really changed under the hood. He wants anatheism to be something other than just faith with a bit of doubt thrown in for good measure. He wants to distance his argument from a tumble into some kind of pro-imaginative determinism in which that poetic act of imagining *necessarily* yields faith. Kearney's anatheism is supposed to stand on its own outside of both theism and atheism, with both equally invited in. If there is not a free choice, then it is not anatheism. Anything else, and Kearney would protest. And yet, I cannot help but wonder if, in fact, the philosopher doth protest too much. I think it is possible that Kearney does indeed hope we will all make the wager, all the while—perhaps unwittingly—holding a pair of aces up his sleeve....

Kearney deserves his due, though, and since he sets the stage in such a way to suggest that those preparing to grapple with the anatheistic moment are in store for "a sense of unknowability calling for risk and adventure" (A, 22), it is worth first considering the possibility that the risk actually is a true one. Since so much of this volume is premised on the wager-li-ness of anatheism, it seems only fair to give that premise room to breathe. What I will show, though, is that even if anatheism is *structurally* a fair wager, it is not without some contextual complexities that pass without much address.

II

When gambling, it is important to consider the discontinuity between what the house wants us to *feel* the odds are and what the rules of the game actually say about the matter. To this end, I will be reading Kearney's anatheism through a lens of Ricoeurian imagination, with some decidedly uneven results. Before continuing, though, I should note that I am not one to quibble with Kearney on his reading of Ricoeur. That would be an act of hubris *par excellence*. I do, however, think it is worth noting that in focusing on Ricoeur's emphasis on metaphor, anatheism bears a particular mark that it might not carry had Kearney decided to turn his gaze more clearly toward Ricoeur's work on imagination. I do not think Kearney has misrepresented Ricoeur in the text, but by privileging certain sections of Ricoeur's canon instead of others, the odds for atheism feel greater than they actually are. After a brief exploration of some Ricoeurian themes that are not very present in *Anatheism*, I will turn back to see how the wager looks in their light.

Always a champion of that space of overlap between hermeneutics and phenomenology, Ricoeur was clear that there is no such thing as "a brute impression, an impression that is direct and unadorned by human structuring. Instead, perception is always structured by physiological and imaginative processes."[1] What

Ricoeur is concerned with is the recovery of a sense of imagination that is not rife with connotations of falsity, distrust, and insufficiency. Other than Aristotle and Kant, Ricoeur said that the entire body of Western thought had generally failed to recognize the interrelation of imagination and perception because imagination had been construed with "what it is to have an image, an image, supposedly in the mind's eye, of reality."[2] In this Platonic conception, the imagination is an inferior, mental reproduction of reality, a cognitive photocopy of some moment or idea, including the degradation of crispness and accuracy that comes from such copying. Ricoeur terms this the "*re*productive imagination" and says that while it does indeed exist he is far more interested in reflecting on the "*pro*ductive imagination."

On this issue, Kearney himself has written that "the fault ... of most philosophies of imagination to date has been their failure to develop a properly hermeneutic account of imagining" (PI, 147). When imagination is merely functioning reproductively, all that is produced by the imagination has already been produced or is some mashing together of things themselves already produced. For example, the result of "imagining a giant, silly, purple monkey," which, while perhaps never previously extant, nevertheless is composed of elements that are merely being reproduced in a new constellation. Conversely, a "properly hermeneutic account of imagining" turns focus to imagination not as something rooted merely in sensorial innovation, but in the renewal of meaning and the emergence of novelty. In its productive form, understood as a hermeneutic act, Ricoeur regards imagining to be an ontological event able to introduce new being into the present order. "The metaphors, symbols, or narratives produced by imagination all provide us with 'imaginative variations' of the world, thereby offering us the freedom to conceive of the world in other ways and to undertake forms of action which might lead to its transformation.... The possible worlds of imagination can be made real by action" (PI, 149).

Why, though, call the act of imagining a hermeneutic move? Because if "there is no such thing as a brute impression, an impression that is direct and unadorned by human structuring,"[3] then the task of perception itself is an interpretive and meaning-making one. Thus, for Ricoeur, "imagination comes into play in that moment when a new meaning emerges from out of the ruins of ... interpretation" (PI, 148). A productive Ricoeurian imagination is that which allows us to hope for water even as we stand by ruins on the sands of the desert of criticism. This seems very resonant with Kearney's anatheism, where there is a "suspension of primary belief, as we enter the world of fiction ... the opening of a space of imagination" (A, 130). Anatheism, then, is a type of second naïveté,[4] what Ricoeur calls an "authentic faith after the dogmatic prejudices of one's first naïveté have been purged."[5] What is being sought after is clearer vision and finer perception—a cleaning of the lens from the specks and smudges of dogmatic prejudices. As a result, since perception itself requires interpretation, Ricoeurian imagining is a hermeneutic act, and as such, claims about hermeneutics are applicable to imagination as well.

Because "hermeneutics is not confined to the *objective* structural analysis of texts, nor to the *subjective* existential analysis of the authors of texts,"[6] neither is imagination merely objective or subjective. And since the "primary concern [of hermeneutics] is with the *worlds* which these authors and texts open up,"[7] so too is this the case for the imagination.

Apropos of anatheism, it seems to follow that just by clearing the space to make a wager, someone caught up in an "anatheistic moment" has had to imagine that there is more than one option on which to place a bet. Emphasizing the wager metaphor for anatheism means that one has to weigh the chances of both atheism and theism, feeling the tension between them while standing in neither. Following Ricoeur, though, even if one—or both!—of these options is fictive, the careful work of perfect neutrality and fifty-fifty odds have already been potentially undone. When we engage with a fiction, "we start with an image without an original," and "may discover a kind of second ontology which is not the ontology of the original but . . . the ontology displayed by the image itself, because it has no original."[8] Even hosting the *idea* of the divine may yield something strange being seen.

If Ricoeur is correct—and I believe he is—and investing attention to a fiction can yield to the opening of a novel horizon, then the mind fully open to either side of anatheism's wager cannot evenly weigh the options. Imagination is potent stuff, and there are so many more stories of theism than atheism that the odds cannot possibly be even. Is anatheism a sneaky guarantor of theism? No—at least, not if the theism in mind is the strong, onto-theological type with its "moralizing deity of accusation and condemnation" (A, 73). However, the lure of a hope for a God of justice and a sense of an ulterior dimension of truth pulls many fiercely. Loaded dice do not always roll the best faces: they just increase the odds of something particular coming up.

If indeed anatheism is a wager, something seems awry. What's more, I think Kearney himself—consciously or not—knows it.

III

The riskiness of a wager is directly related to the odds. If anatheism is supposed to be equally invitational to both sides of the theist versus atheist and sacred versus secular debates, then one would expect each side to have equal time for argumentation. This is not the case. Kearney is attentive to setting the tension between theism and atheism in precise parallel to the coupling of hospitality and hostility, but for all his moves to want the anatheistic moment to be an unfettered one, he spends an unequal amount of time discussing the *hostes* of welcome arms and the *hostes* of armed welcome.

For example, as Kearney is rounding the corner in his conclusion, he asserts that "anatheism tries to introduce reasonable hermeneutic considerations to the theist-atheist debate" (A, 171), and yet when he turns to the kind of "redefinitions of religion" that anatheism yields, his examples are theists of one stripe or another: Levinas, Soroush, Bonhoeffer, Gandhi, Girard, and Vivekananda. If the wager were truly a fair one, then I would imagine we would be seeing just as many atheists on this list. But we don't, and I think that is worth noticing: if the blackjack dealer keeps winking to the player on her right immediately before he hits twenty-one, I think it is within reason to have suspicions about the table.

Similarly, when Kearney follows Merleau-Ponty and offers that suspending confessional truth claims "allows for a specific negative capability regarding questions of doubt, proof, dogma, or doctrine" (A, 95), he then concludes his sentence, "so as to better appreciate the 'thing itself,' the holy thisness of our flesh-and-blood existence" (A, 95). What is the nature of holiness if confessional truth claims have been suspended? How does "holy" persist as a category of reference to either quiddity or haeccity? What could it even mean? Likewise, when Kearney claims that the "reaffirmation of life [is] . . . a recognition that most things in our secular universe are in fact, already and always, sacred at heart" (A, 74) it is hard to imagine how there is any space for an atheist position if "at heart" the universe is itself sacred. What about those for whom "holy" and "sacred" are terms to be dismissed? Are they welcome at the table? What does it mean that atheism is only given a full chance to speak in *Anatheism* when it is challenging a type of theism with strong onto-theological claims?

Finally, consider the following passage from *Anatheism*'s closing epilogue, reflecting on the presumptions and presuppositions that undergird it: "For even though the anatheist wager takes the form of a retrieval of second faith, it does so from out of the future, by giving a future to the past, by surprising us in each messianic instant. It is in this sense that I speak of anatheist time as a time of micro-eschatology. A time of epiphanies when the stranger breaks through the continuum of history" (A, 184).

Ultimately, Kearney pretty clearly wants "the cup of cold water given to the stranger" (A, 134), thinking this hospitable choice is preferable to the hostile one. I agree entirely, and this is perhaps expected given that the subtitle of the book is "Returning to God after God." But why then go through all the motions of a fair choice wager, the "suspension of received assumptions," and an "abandonment of accredited certainties?" This leads us back to Kearney himself and his own clarity regarding the rules of this "wager."

IV

The problem, I think, is not that Kearney has described the rules wrong, but that the odds are off. At first, it seems that on one side of the table is a box marked "atheism" on the other "theism," and we're supposed to stand apart from both, decide to put all our chips in one or the other, and flip a coin. The setup suggests that anatheism is an even game: God either is or is not a thing with a sustained metaphysical referent. Equal chances. The wager, though, is more complicated than this. Contrary to first appearances and the numerous moves to make the wager seem "fair," anatheism is not actually about the choice between God's actual existence or not. The rules do involve flipping a coin, but the outcome is not so much about whether it lands heads or tails, but whether it lands at all. And it does. Consistently.

Tucked into the fourth footnote to his conclusion, Kearney offers what I read as a kind of *raison d'être* for the anatheistic project as a whole.

> My purpose in this book has not been to prove (or disprove) God's metaphysical existence as some sort of superterrestrial Being, but to show—with the help of phenomenological and hermeneutical methods—the "meaning" of the "God event" at a practical, poetic, and mystical level. In short, our question is how does the encounter with the stranger—as radically other, alien, transcendent, "more"—affect our lives for better (or for worse). This is the essence of the anatheist wager. A matter of interpreting and choosing whether what many call by "divine names" (the radically Other) brings life or death, love or hate. It is not at all concerned with metaphysical or physical proofs for God's existence that rely upon laws of probability. (And here we differ also from the calculations of Pascal's wager.) Anatheism is not at odds with science and the natural world; it simply asks how we respond to the radical surprise of the Stranger as an invitation to faith, to make the impossible possible, to bring justice where there is war, love where there is hate, wisdom where there is ignorance (A, 231).

I read here a kind of echo from his early training under the brothers of Glenstal who included coursework on atheism even while confessing that Jesus is risen. Kearney, too, has a profound and passionate hope against hope that we humans are capable of coexisting without blowing each other up, but he refuses to promise us that we will survive. In spite of this significant hesitation, he nonetheless seems to hope to pass through—even if fleetingly—a place beyond the desert of criticism. That is to say, far from being a wager, anatheism as Kearney frames it is actually not even much of a meaningful choice at all.

By Kearney's own words, the book was written "to show … the 'meaning' of the 'God event' at a practical, poetic, and mystical level." It is a book focused "on the meaning of the sacred—after one has abandoned illusions of the Alpha-God—for one's ethical and poetical existence" (A, 183). It is hard to maintain equal space for a robust and thorough atheism when the telos of the project points to "the meaning of the sacred," even if it is a sacrality that differs from classical Christian patristics. All of which raises the question, where does the idea of "risk" and "wager" come from if the substrate of the question itself is embedded with ideas whose very existence suggest a certain schema?

I believe that the focus on the wager-like quality of anatheism is not false so much as it is overly emphasized: the risk of it functions, like Kierkegaard's indirect communication, to affectively express that which could not be received directly. To focus on the riskiness of the wager itself—instead of what the risk expresses—is to read anatheism too flatly. The wager is not an objective wager at all, but a subjective one. We stand and *experience* the anatheistic moment as one that has profound consequences. It is the depth of that feeling of profundity that should draw our attention more than the "wager" it is caused by. Like Kierkegaard, I think Kearney's idea of hope is a "throwing" of oneself, in freedom and beyond reason, toward a choice: a deepening of inwardness and subjectivity. Anything that threatens to objectify that choice, any fixed claim to a positivist certainty of theism *or* atheism, runs counter to anatheism.

It seems as if there are two possibilities moving ahead: Kearney can either: (1) claim that any theism that is not of the strong onto-theological type is not, in fact, actually theism at all, but anatheism;[9] or (2) cede that though his project strives to be one equally charitable to theism and atheism it is in fact a rigged game in favor of God and that his anatheism tends toward a kind of shadowy weak theism. I strongly advocate for the latter position. What's more, I do not think that the failure of anatheism to be truly risky is a problem in the slightest. Anatheism is *not* a wager; it is an education.

My argument is a small one: the project of anatheism is certainly worthy of our attention, so much so, in fact, that it deserves to be named for what it is. What I have tried to show here is that however you come at it, "fair wager" does not quite seem to fit—and it shouldn't. Anatheism isn't objectively a risk, but rather a rich and nourishing hermeneutic and phenomenological course of study aimed at one of the only types of dynamic theism that can persist if one acknowledges all the fractious and complicating factors that Kearney names so well throughout the text. We subjectively experience it as a risk because we are yet grappling with the implications of theism being broader than a necessary commitment to a strong agentive God.

The fact is, though he is charming and perhaps a bit of a disciplinary rogue, Kearney is better suited to the role of educator than that of gambler. He wants to educate us into a hope that does not rest on promises but on possibilities that are yet unfolding. Kearney's anatheism is a kind of teaching akin to what Sylvia McMillan calls a "pedagogy of liminality."[10]

As one of Ricoeur's students, Kearney knows—perhaps better than anyone—that Ricoeur did not name "the masters of suspicion" as skeptics, but as liberators, as workers trying to "clear the horizon for a more authentic word, for a new reign of Truth, not only by means of a 'destructive' critique, but by the invention of an art of interpreting."[11] Anatheism is not the vacating of certainty to leave a vacuum of chaotic anything-might-be-possible-ness. Rather, via what Ricoeur called "double guile"[12] anatheism makes room for surprise, nuance, and an understanding that truth itself both reveals and conceals. Anatheism is an education in theological imagination, a leading out to hope for the growth of discourse around a God that may be and might call out for compassion. A God, in John Caputo's terms, that does not *exist*, but *insists*, calling out to us in the never-quite-arriving event harbored in the name of God.[13]

V

In closing, I should add that I think Kearney himself already—at some level—knows all this. Published a year prior to *Anatheism*, his article "Returning to God after God: Levinas, Derrida, Ricoeur," notes that what he is concerned about is "the development of genuine faith that involves a renunciation of fear and dependency."[14] Much of that text finds its way into *Anatheism*'s third chapter, and so I find it fitting then, to say that the book, too, is about "the development of genuine faith." With that in place, then, references to "the wager" come across in slightly different terms.

It is not the betting that matters, or the odds, but the playing. Anatheism is the deepest kind of play, the kind of "space of free possibility—beyond impossibility" (A, 81) that children discover on school grounds and backyards. The kinds of games that are all made of imagination but are also very much real. The kind of games from which we learn what it means to be who we are and how to be with one another.

L. CALLID KEEFE-PERRY is a member of The Religious Society of Friends (Quakers) and travels in the ministry within and beyond that denomination. He is the author of *Way to Water: A Theopoetics Primer* and serves as the executive director of ARC: A Creative Collaborative for Theopoetics.

Notes

1. Taylor, "Ricoeur's Philosophy of Imagination," 94.
2. Ibid., 95.
3. Ibid., 94.
4. Ricoeur, *La Symbolique du Mal*, 326.
5. Ibid., 202.
6. Ibid., 149.
7. Ibid.
8. Taylor, "Ricoeur's Philosophy of Imagination," 98.
9. I would include at least the weak theism of the sort advocated by John Caputo—much of the work done using Whitehead's process-relational thought, panentheism,

Grace Jantzen's feminist theology, poststructuralist Continental philosophy, or any of the nonrealist arguments along the lines of Don Cupitt.

10. "For this is what hopelessness is: the death of the adventure of subjective liminality in the prison-camp of bondage to objectivity. A Kierkegaardian pedagogy of liminality is one of hope–hope in oneself as spirit constantly sojourning into the risk of liminality." See McMillan, "Kierkegaard and a Pedagogy of Liminality," 57.

11. Ricoeur, *Freud and Philosophy: An Essay on Interpretation*, 33.

12. Ibid., 34.

13. Caputo, *The Insistence of God: A Theology of Perhaps.*

14. Kearney, "Returning to God," 167.

Part III: Poetics of the Sacred

11 Recognition and Hospitality: Coming Back to Odysseus's Coming Home

Pierre Drouot
Translated by Sarah Horton

From the beginning of the Prelude of *Anatheism* (A, 13), Richard Kearney endeavors to identify in the texts of the Jewish, Christian, and Muslim traditions decisive experiences that allow us to infer a consistency in the Abrahamic religions: the existence of fundamental moments of hospitality, of "wagers" that consist in welcoming a stranger even before recognizing his "wholly other" nature—his divinity. The annunciation (like the reception of the word) and before it the identification of the divine are said to take place against the background of an availability to the stranger, of a hospitality that, moreover, threatens to reverse into hostility and thereby to prevent all recognition.

This connection between a primitive welcome and recognition (even if this latter does not have the same object) seems to me also to inhabit the Homeric texts, especially the *Odyssey*.[1] What I propose in this study is to examine how these concepts are there arranged and how the final ordeals of Odysseus help us think this sometimes-thwarted interdependence between the concepts of hospitality and recognition.

I

The notions of recognition and hospitality could initially seem quite foreign [*étrangère*] to each other. One is more theoretical and refers us to the establishment of knowledge or of identity; the other is of a practical order, defining a duty, a demand, and an action of a moral nature. The first evokes a movement of assimilation, of integration by identification (or distinction) of the unknown to the known, and the second, an attitude of openness to the stranger [*étranger*]. From this point of view, they can even appear contradictory, the one consisting in absorbing the stranger whereas the other commands one to make oneself available to him. What motivates this short "course" is, however, the hypothesis that these two notions are intimately linked: less removed from each other than they may appear, they seem to me interdependent, and thinking of them together can permit me to establish, if not to clarify, problems that they raise conjointly.[2] Their first commonality is of a formal nature: the very concepts of recognition and hospitality do indeed have a profound relation, which makes them what I will call "mirror concepts." Both indeed bear within themselves an ambivalence that is of the order of symmetry.

Beginning in the preface to the collection of studies he devotes to it, Paul Ricœur brings out the polysemy of the term *reconnaissance*.[3] Identification by oneself of something other than oneself, it can also apply to oneself, be "mutual," and moreover designate—in French at least—gratitude toward some other. Following him, I retain from these different meanings contained in a same word the "reversal, on the very level of the grammar, of the verb *to recognize* from its use in the active voice to its use in the passive voice: 'I actively recognize things, persons, myself; I ask to be recognized by others.'"[4] Mirror and symmetry: recognition as identification is an act of which I am the subject; social recognition is recognition by the other—received—of which I am the object. In the same notion, two inverse positions are expressed.

In the same way, there is in recognition a symmetry in the relation of oneself to the other. Recognition as identification, as I insisted above, implies a centripetal movement of appropriation, of incorporation, of integration to oneself of a foreign [*étranger*] object that one identifies with the known: I recognize an individual, a thing, a form, a style by relating them to knowledge that permits me to *identify* them, to *assimilate* them (to grasp them as the same or to distinguish them as other). By contrast, recognition as gratitude is, conversely, a centrifugal movement from oneself toward the other by which one assumes a debt with regard to another [*autrui*]: showing recognition is no longer bringing the other back to oneself but offering oneself to another [*autre*]. On the one hand, I incorporate an object by assimilating it; on the other, I offer myself to another subject. Philosophers such as Hegel or Sartre, not to mention Levinas, have, moreover, observed that in recognition by the other and even more in social recognition or mutual recognition, there takes place still more intimately a mirror relationship from oneself to the other, by which each one, recognizing the other, recognizes himself via the other—these two positions, a priori opposed, of identification of oneself and of impetus toward the other are here profoundly intermingled.

An analogous principle of symmetry, if not of confusion of inverses, inhabits the concept of hospitality. This is first due to the oft-noted fact that the term *hôte*[5] that is linked to it designates the welcomed subject as well as the welcoming subject. I could make the same remarks here that I made regarding recognition: the word has the same value in the active voice as in the passive voice—the one who accomplishes the welcome is an *hôte* at the same time as the one who benefits from it. In mirror image, it designates the movement of welcome of the other (from the other to oneself) and the movement toward the other (from oneself to the other). This homonymy cannot be considered as only accidental, as Ricœur still seems able to imagine concerning recognition. This latter indeed does not designate exactly the same action and does not nominalize the same verb when it changes voice: recognizing an object can be similar to but is not the same as recognizing the worth of a man, and still less is it the same as feeling gratitude [*reconnaissance*] for the same or another. As for the symmetry of the word *hôte*, it concerns the same relation (hospitality). It designates the active subject and the passive subject of the same action, of the same verb (to welcome) by which, at the same time and symmetrically, each is the *hôte* of the other.

The other mirror effect that is lodged in hospitality is due to its etymology, masterfully commented on by Benveniste and taken up again by Richard Kearney: its etymology bears within itself the risk of its reversal into hostility. Via their common Latin source (from *hostire*, to compensate, to equalize), hospitality is indeed intimately linked to it. In their common genealogy that the *Dictionnaire historique de la langue française [Historical Dictionary of the French Language]* proposes,[6] we thus find as many terms referring to welcome and to treatment as equals (*hostis*, host/guest [*hôte*];[7] hotel; hospital; hospitality) as we do words suggesting enmity, opposition or violence (*hostia*, victim; *hostes*, enemy; *hostis*, army (enemy); hostage; hostile). In the everyday practice of the language, this relation (or this threat) remains alive: the French *hôte* (or even more the English *host*) is very close to the words *hostile* (*hostile*) or *hostilité* (*hostility*). Hospitality, which rests on a form of recognition of the other as an equal, is thus an uneasy term that leads to the possibility of its perversion, if not its inversion, into its symmetric (or negative) counterpart that is hostility—which is anchored on the contrary in a denial of recognition that it maintains.

II

These successive remarks on the concepts of recognition and hospitality persuade me of their formal commonality: both are inhabited by an analogous principle of symmetry. But it appears that they are also mirrors of each other, insofar as it is the same relation that they allow one to conceive: that between oneself and the stranger, the same and the other. More profoundly, it seems that they are more intimately linked insofar as hospitality rests on a form of minimal recognition: that of a community, if not of an equality, between the host [*hôte*] and his guest [*hôte*],[8] and leads to other forms of recognition (mutual recognition, gratitude, and so on). Conversely, hostility and the denial of hospitality that founds it hinge symmetrically on a crisis of recognition. This is what reading the *Odyssey*, notably the central and ambivalent passage of the visit to "Alkinoös the generous," confirms for us.

The question of the welcome of the other runs through the *Odyssey*, which presents Odysseus disarmed and abandoned by the gods to chance and to the good will of his fellows. Marcel Conche, in one of his *Essais sur Homère [Essays on Homer]*,[9] takes up several passages in which he benefits from this hospitality without condition of chance hosts. Nausikaa: "Stranger, since you seem not like a thoughtless man, nor a mean one ... now, since it is our land and our city that you have come to, you shall not lack for clothing nor anything else, of those gifts which should befall the unhappy suppliant upon his arrival" (VI, 186, 191–193).[10] Her father, Alkinoös, exhorted by the "aged hero Echeneos": "Alkinoös, this is not the better way, nor is it fitting that the guest [*hôte*] should sit on the ground beside the hearth, in the ashes.... But come, raise the stranger up and seat him on a silver-studded chair, and tell your heralds to mix in more wine for us, so we can pour a libation to Zeus who delights in the thunder, and he goes together with suppliants, whose rights are sacred. And let the housekeeper from her stores give the guest [*hôte*] a supper" (VII, 159–166, quotation modified in accordance with the French). Eumaios (Book XIV, 48), or Penelope. Telemachos himself is welcomed as a stranger by Menelaos, and Odysseus, at the very moment in which he does not benefit from it, remembers having frequently submitted himself to this duty of hospitality: "For I, I too have lived happily among men in a rich house, and I often gave thus to vagabonds, without asking either their name or their needs" (XVII, 419–421 and XIX, 75–78).[11] This obligation to welcome from which the man of a thousand ruses profits is perhaps not entirely unconditioned: it is most often justified in religious terms. By Eumaios, for example: "Stranger, I have no right to deny the guest [*hôte*], not even if one came to me who was meaner than you," (XIV, 56–57, quotation modified in accordance with the French). And when he is justifying himself, like Nausikaa before him: "since all strangers and wanderers are sacred in the sight of Zeus, and the gift is a light and a dear one" (VI, 207–208). It nevertheless implies what Conche calls a "sense of humanity": this duty toward the stranger or the beggar, as wretched as he may be, manifests a spontaneous recognition of a common humanity.

If hospitality thus induces a form of recognition, it is that, very general, of the humanity of the other. All other recognition is secondary: one can even say that in this welcome of the suffering, the other is found a form of abstraction from the habitual mechanisms of judgment linked to "recognition as identification." To welcome thus is to refuse to identify the other with his appearance, mistrusting it in order to actively recognize a man in him, whatever his outfit may be. Nausikaa scolds her servants for having fled before the terrifying appearance of Odysseus: "Do you think this is some enemy coming against us?" (VI, 200). His "nobility" and beauty appear to her only once she has welcomed him as a man—and he has washed ("A while ago he seemed an unpromising man to me. Now he even resembles one of the gods, who hold high heaven" VI, 242–243). Alkinoös in his turn wonders about Odysseus's appearance (as soon as he commits himself to welcoming him), imagining that he could be "one of the immortals come down from heaven" (VII, 199). And when he arrives in Ithaka, this latter is unrecognizable: Eumaios before Penelope offers him lodging without recognizing him.

In these experiences of the gift of hospitality a dimension of *occultation of identity* thus shows through: Odysseus, formerly master of dissimulation, is himself dirty, in rags, or disguised—unrecognizable, *inassimilable*. Welcome is given without knowing—or without knowing anything other than the humanity of the received stranger—and in the active refusal of a judgment of appearances. The revelation of the identity of the "stranger," carefully staged, is second in relation to the welcome. First one bathes, one lodges, one feeds Odysseus, and only then does one ask him to introduce himself: "When they had made libation and drunk," the invited ones having returned to their homes, Arete, by the side of "Alkinoös the generous," could finally (and only) address to him "winged words: 'Stranger and friend, I myself first have a question to ask you. What man are you, and whence?" (VII, 227, 236–238) Recognition, against the probably common intuition (and temptation), is thus second with relation to hospitality. Perhaps one can even say that the condition of hospitality *stricto sensu* finds itself in the nonrecognition of the guest [*hôte*], whose foreignness [*étrangèreté*] (he is first called "the stranger [*l'étranger*]" before being "the beggar," "the suppliant") is carefully preserved until the welcome is consummated.

This observation of a primacy of hospitality over recognition is verified in the account of the inverse experience that Odysseus gives to Alkinoös. It is all the more striking (and justly famous) because it immediately follows the moment of hospitality commented on above and is even contemporary with it: it is in Book IX, in recognition of the welcome he has received, that Odysseus, reveals his name. "Now first I will tell you my name, so that all of you may know me, and I hereafter, escaping the day without pity, be your friend and guest [*hôte*], though the home where I live is far away from you. I am Odysseus son of Laertes" (IX, 16–19). Then he narrates his inhospitable adventure. In this very instant of virtuous hospitality that leads to recognition as identification, as mutual, and as gratitude, Odysseus recounts, after the brief account of an unfortunate hostility (pillage, feast, and vengeance), a negative experience of a refusal of hospitality that only draws greater force therefrom: the visit to the Cyclops Polyphemos.

The stake, which concerns the tension between hospitality and hostility, is set from the start of the adventure: Odysseus and his companions, wondering about the Cyclopes, want to verify "whether they are savage and violent, and without justice, or hospitable to strangers and with minds that are godly" (IX, 175–176). The confirmation of the intuition of Odysseus's "proud heart" (IX, 213–215) comes quickly: Polyphemos, whose profusion of riches is meticulously described[12] (his scorn of duties owes nothing to a possible poverty that could explain it, if not excuse it), mocks the request for welcome made "at [his] knees" and "in accordance with the custom of guests [*hôtes*]" that is made by the suppliant: "Stranger, you are a simple fool, or come from far off, when you tell me to avoid the wrath of the gods or fear them" (IX, 267, 268, 273–274).[13] The Cyclops is first a single-eyed monster in the manner by which he excludes himself from the life of humans—the "civilized" life, consisting in respect for the law, for justice, and for the gods: in his *inhospitality.* The presentation of the Cyclopes begins with a long list of their breaches of human rules (IX, 105–115). The eye trained on his force, his interest, and his riches, the monocular monster has no other eye for the gods[14] and duties, and he does exactly the opposite of what everyone owes (and what Odysseus's listener Alkinoös does) to others—instead of sheltering them, he imprisons them; instead of caring for them, he dismembers them; instead of feeding them, he devours them. "[H]e . . . sprang up and reached for my companions, caught up two together and slapped them, like killing puppies, against the ground, and the brains ran all over the floor, soaking the ground. Then he cut them up limb by limb and got supper ready, and like a lion reared in the hills, without leaving anything, ate them, entrails, flesh and the marrowy bones alike" (IX, 287–293).

This transgressive account, by its uncommon violence, thus seems to me to stage cathartically the monstrosity of a denial of hospitality at the very moment in which it is generously accorded. It also hinges perversely on the question of recognition. Polyphemos's first reflex is to seek information about the voyagers, concerned perhaps to know who they are (or, more certainly, to know their number and the promises of meat that they represent). That of Odysseus, as a result, is to resort to ruse—and dissimulation—that aims to prevent recognition by cultivating illusion: first by lying about their docking conditions with "crafty words" (IX, 282, quotation modified), then by elaborating a strategy for flight based on the blinding of Polyphemos. He will proceed by that, consisting in putting out his single eye, but he will rely above all on the fact of keeping silent, and even denying his true identity. If the neighbors of the Cyclops consequently renounce assisting him, it is because they do not understand him when he answers that his aggressor is "nobody": the ruse works because Odysseus gives himself over to nonrecognition and even to annihilation in saying that this is his name when the Cyclops, reserving for him the perverse "gift" of eating him last, asks him his name before making him his guest [*hôte*]. It is to this ruse concerning recognition as much as to the use of the olive-wood pike—the violence of which answers that of the monster—that Odysseus and his companions owe their liberation. And it is to Odysseus's "proud" will to finally reveal his true identity that he owes the curse that will condemn him to return home, many years later, "in bad case, with the loss of all his companions, in someone else's ship, and find troubles in his household" (IX, 534–535).

III

This Cyclopean episode, presented as the inauguration of his curse and his quest, is thus situated by Odysseus himself (before he has even lived it) in relation to another passage of the *Odyssey* that constitutes its temporary outcome and that immediately follows this account told to Alkinoös (it is in one of his vessels, soon cursed in its turn, that he reaches his shore): the return to Ithaka. And now the final books that develop it present precisely these "other pains," promised by Polyphemos, as linked to another denial of hospitality: the wandering of Odysseus, marked by experiences of hospitality, is thus framed by two spectacular ordeals linked to an extreme inhospitality.

The theme of hospitality is not most evident in the passage concerning the return to Ithaka. As Odysseus is indeed arriving *at his home*, it is apparently not so much a question of hospitality as of *property* or *legitimacy*—but that is to forget that he disembarks there disguised as a "beggar," and that it is his experience as a stranger (and a guest [*hôte*]) that is here related. More profoundly, the reader of this passage is first gripped by an account of vengeance in which the dramatic stake concerns more directly the problem of fidelity (and treason), be it that of servants, friends, wife, or son. The question of recognition and of its tests [*épreuves*], which has so greatly interested the commentators, thus can itself seem second: Paul Ricœur, who analyzes it from this point of view, observes that this "history of recognition finds itself inextricably intertwined with one of vengeance. The rhythm of this second story governs that of recognition itself, to the point that the degrees of recognition are stages along the path of vengeance that ends with a massacre of pitiless cruelty."[15] However, if the questions of the recognition of one's own, of its denial, of its successive tests and proofs [*(é)preuves*],[16] and of its final violent establishment are truly those around which the narrative is organized, it seems to me all the same that this quest is triggered by a failure of hospitality, and that this latter is therefore an equally fundamental stake.

Even though it has very often attracted the attention of the commentators, the question of recognition can indeed here seem secondary. Skillfully and constantly delayed, it appears more to constitute a strategy than to represent a difficulty. Thus Odysseus lies first to Eumaios, despite the proofs [*gages*] he could have given: he questions him after welcoming him, but also after confirming to him his fears concerning the suitors. Then he lies to Telemachos, and finally to Penelope, before whom Odysseus at first refuses to appear. When she finally meets him, in Book XVII, she welcomes him in the guise of a stranger before even having glimpsed (and much less, therefore, recognized) him. Their first discussion, placed anew under the ambiguous sign of a thwarted hospitality, could be the moment of the greatly desired recognition: Odysseus, who does not doubt Penelope's fidelity, answers her identifying questions only with a new dissimulation. "Stranger, I myself first have a question to ask you. What man are you and whence? Where is your city? Your parents?" (XIX, 104–105). This is because in this inhospitable experience that is his own, recognition would for the moment be a threat and must be deferred. This dimension of risk—and hostility—is perceived in the following passage itself, when for the first time a human being recognizes Odysseus in spite of him: his nurse, Eurykleia, who, while washing his feet, remembers his scar. Far from joining in the emotion of his faithful servant, Odysseus threatens her with great violence, promising her death if she reveals his identity. "Nurse of mine though you are, I will not spare you, when I kill the rest of the serving maids in my palace" (XIX, 489–490). If there is thus a problem linked to recognition, which will manifest itself at the end of the course with Penelope and Laertes, to whom it will be necessary to give signs of it, it is deliberately created and maintained by Odysseus himself to serve his hostile intentions and confound his enemies, or more exactly to put their sense of hospitality to the test.

Thus, even though it is indeed a question in the end for Odysseus of separating the faithful and the traitors, what first characterizes them is rather the respect or disrespect that they manifest for the duty of hospitality toward the one who wishes to present himself in the guise of a beggar. The friends of Odysseus, to whom he finally reveals himself, indeed first shine by the welcome they grant to the stranger, independently of the recognition of his identity, their fidelity to the vanished king only appearing in a second moment. He is thus first welcomed by Eumaios, the "noble swineherd," who, an attentive livestock farmer like the Cyclops, is a sort of anti-Polyphemos, who saves him from the aggression of the dogs and feeds him. Hospitality is given before all recognition and before all request for identification: "Come, old sir, along to my shelter, so that you also first may be filled to contentment with food and wine, then tell me where you come from" (XIV, 45–47). In the following passage, the swineherd delivers an assured speech in praise of hospitality (referred to his vanished master, who, he confirms, was a great practitioner of it), on the occasion of which he manifests his friendship for the regretted master. After him, the servant Eurykleia, his "nurse," will manifest a hospitable attention before recognizing him. Penelope, for her part, calls to Telemachos (who will himself have the occasion to make himself the spokesperson for the principle of welcome) before the suitors in these terms: "[S]uch a thing has been done now, here in our palace, and you permitted our stranger guest [*hôte*] to be so outrageously handled. How must it be now, if the guest [*hôte*] who sits in our household is made to suffer so from bitter brutality? That must be your outrage and shame as people see it" (XVIII, 221–225, translation modified).[17] Without even having yet seen (and much less, therefore, recognized) him, she grants the "stranger" lodging, care, and food—before manifesting her fidelity, and then, much later, identifying him.

In this virtuous course, hospitality will thus be first, fidelity second, identification third. It definitely seems, therefore, that the absence of recognition does not in itself pose a problem as long as hospitality, before fidelity, is gained: it does not prevent Odysseus from manifesting his satisfaction with regard to Eumaios as with regard to Penelope, and that he "was happy that his livelihood was so well cared for while he was absent" (XIV, 526–527). The effect of a calculated dissimulation, it is, like in the Cyclops's cave, more a strategy than an obstacle,[18] which has as its goal to confound enemies first characterized precisely by their failures of hospitality. What it is a question of recognizing here, as the considered choice of the wretched suppliant's costume testifies, is thus, before the wanderer's identity or legitimacy, the inhabitants' capacity for welcome.

This dissimulation under the guise of an unrecognizable stranger thus permits Odysseus to convince himself of the nobility and fidelity of his household. It also permits him to identify a blatant failure of hospitality on the part of those who thus become his adversaries. This latter first manifests itself by an "impudence" consisting in imposing on the hospitality of Odysseus's family (and especially of Penelope). The last books of the *Odyssey* thus describe a perversion of hospitality by which "suppliants," presented as parasites, resort to "fables" to move the masters of the house. Profiting from their weaknesses, they neither receive nor are received but impose themselves by lies and ruse, rendering impossible all reciprocity and all recognition. Besides these profiteers, the text also denounces the excess of the "suitors, who have no regard for anyone in their minds, nor pity" (XIV, 81–95). Presented as impious ones worse than pirates, they call Polyphemos to mind by their *hubris* as by their scorn of the gods. Deviant guests [*hôtes*], they reveal by menacing it the confidence that is the foundation of hospitality—which is expressed, in a gripping turn of events, by the fact that they are precisely the first to suspect the motives of the true-false suppliant Odysseus, accusing him of putative abuses (which are only their own) and suspecting him of preferring alms to work.[19]

This *impudence* of the welcomed one that threatens hospitality is found equally in the manner that suitors and servants treat the anonymous suppliant under the guise of which Odysseus chooses to continue dissimulating himself. Among them, the goatherd, Melanthios, is the first to reveal his "impertinence" in Book XVII: attacking the "bothersome beggar who spoils the fun of feasting" (XVII, 220), he strikes him with his staff. He repeats these insults and threats in Book XX: "Stranger, are you still to be here in the house, to pester the gentlemen with your begging? Will you not take yourself outside and elsewhere? I think that now you and I can no longer part, until we have tried our fists. There is nothing orderly about your begging" (XX, 178–182). His sister, the servant, Melantho, also lashes out at him twice: in Book XVIII, she calls him a "[w]retched stranger ... whose wits are distracted" (XVIII, 327) and wants to frighten him in Book XIX: "you may be forced to get out, with a torch thrown at you" (XIX, 69). It is faced with another suppliant, the "public beggar," Iros, "known to fame for his ravenous belly," that Odysseus finds himself condemned to impose himself as a guest [*hôte*].[20] Among the suitors, Antinoös, like Eurymachos after him, manifests a sometimes violent aversion to the suppliant (he threatens him with a "stool") in several places and, above all, a marked denial of hospitality. Seeing in him a "bum [*gueux*]" (or simply "that"), he questions Eumaios: "Do we not already have enough other vagabonds, and bothersome beggars to ruin our feasting?" (XVII, 376–377).

Such reactions can serve as foils giving to Odysseus. "Give, dear friend. You seem to me, of all the Achaians, not the worst, but the best. You look like a king. Therefore, you ought to give me a better present of your food than the others have done" (XVII, 415–418). To Eumaios, Telemachos, and Penelope they are the occasion to remember anew the terms of this duty. Equally, they permit the denouncing of a profound human fault, which rests on a vicious hospitality. It is from this, as before, in the *Iliad*, where Menelaos justifies war by the abuse of hospitality that Paris supposedly committed, that ensues hostility and the desire for vengeance, if not for recognition. Odysseus, faced with the impudence of the suitors, from then on feels warranted in the violence he exercises precisely against the least hospitable of them, aiming first at Antinoös (his first arrow being for his "tender neck"), Eurymachos, the servants guilty of having taken pleasure with them (including, therefore, Melantho), and finally Melanthios, whose cruel punishment is commensurate with his moral failure. "They cut off, with the pitiless bronze, his nose and his ears, tore off his private parts and gave them to the dogs to feed on raw, and lopped off his hands and feet, in fury of anger" (XXII, 474–476). This end of wandering, which one is accustomed to presenting as happy, reveals, however, a paradoxical Odysseus who, in the name of the duty of hospitality (and of the failures thereof which he was able to judge), authorizes himself to furiously massacre the suitors, sparing only those close to him. Ultimately concentrated on the desire to find again his goods and his household, he is deaf to the pleas of the suppliants and finishes them off with the greatest violence, which only the intervention *ex machina* of Zeus and Athena will prevent from degenerating into a full-scale war.

This ambivalent ending warns us anew of the necessity of hospitality, the beauty and fragility of which the *Odyssey* has for several millennia ceaselessly painted for us. A fundamental demand taking precedence over the search for recognition, it is nevertheless the condition of all recognition and ultimately concerns nothing less than social peace.

PIERRE DROUOT is a French philosopher and cineaste, specialized in antique and deconstructionist thought. He teaches philosophy and cinema at the Lycée Kirschleger in Munster (France).

SARAH HORTON is a doctoral student in philosophy at Boston College. Her main area of study is twentieth-century French philosophy, and her research interests include ethics, philosophy of literature, and the phenomenology of friendship.

Notes

1. Unless otherwise specified, all citations from the *Odyssey* refer to Richmond Lattimore's translation. Further, all spellings of names from the *Odyssey* follow Lattimore. Page references are indicated between brackets in the text.

2. According to the introductory expression of Paul Ricœur in his *Parcours de la reconnaissance*, the title of which he justifies by opposing it to the pretention of a "theory." Ricoeur, *Parcours de la reconnaissance*, 14. [*The Course of Recognition*, xi.]

3. The French *reconnaissance*, as Drouot will explain, means both "recognition" and "gratitude." Except for one instance in which I rendered it as "gratitude" (followed by *reconnaissance* in brackets), I have translated it as "recognition" throughout, but the reader should bear the other meaning in mind. [Translator's note.]

4. Ricoeur, *Parcours de la reconnaissance*, 13. [*The Course of Recognition*, x. Translation modified.]

5. The French *hôte* means both "host" and "guest." When I have translated it as "guest," I have included the French word in brackets to remind the reader of its linguistic connection to the term "hospitality." [Translator's note.]

6. I am referring especially to the illuminating and stimulating table that he proposes in complement of the article "Hôte". *Dictionnaire historique de la langue française*, dir. Alain Rey, Le Robert, Paris, 1992.

7. As Kearney explains in the passage Drouot references above, the Latin *hostis*, like the French *hôte*, means both "host" and "guest." [Translator's note.]

8. Note that this phrase could also have been translated as "the guest and his host." [Translator's note.]

9. Conche, "L'humanité d'Homère," ["Homer's Humanity"] in *Essais sur Homère*, 113–138.

10. Translation slightly modified, following Drouot's quotation of Philippe Jaccottet's French translation. [Translator's note.]

11. Here Lattimore's translation differs significantly enough from Jaccottet's that I have simply translated Jaccottet's French. [Translator's note.]

12. The recurring expression "fat flocks" that designates Polyphemos' beasts is all the less gratuitous because it is thanks to their fleshy paunches that Odysseus and his companions will be able to escape from him (and steal them from him).

13. Translation from Jaccottet's French. [Translator's note.]

14. He is capable of this because he is not properly human and benefits from the divine protection of his father Poseidon.

15. Ricoeur, *Parcours de la reconnaissance*, 125–126. [*The Course of Recognition*, 72–73. Translation modified.]

16. Here *épreuves* means "tests," and *preuves* means "proofs"; the play on words cannot be translated into English. [Translator's note.]

17. Compare the reproach to Melantho at the beginning of Book XIX.

18. He will reveal his true identity to Telemachos in a beautiful scene of recognition close to, though reversed from, that of *Temps retrouvé* [*Time Regained*] (commented on in Ricœur, *Parcours de la reconnaissance*, 105–116 [61–68]) only when this is necessary to organize the combat (Book XVI, 188: "I am your father ...").

19. Notably in the mouths of Iros and Eurymachos in Book XVIII.

20. Book XVIII, 1–2. One should note that Odysseus, for his part, says that he is ready to share the hospitality of the masters of the house ("This doorsill is big enough for both of us," 17) and that the conflict which follows, to the great entertainment of the suitors who rejoice in the wretchedness in which they maintain the suppliants, is the doing of this begger who desires exclusivity, finally condemned by Odysseus: "But you must no longer try to be the king of guests [*hôtes*] and beggars," 106. [Quotation modified in accordance with the French.]

12 The Twofold Face of God: An Anatheistic Reading of the Sacrifice of Abraham

Jacob Rogozinski

I

Anatheism: "faith beyond faith in a God beyond God" (A, 3). How are we to think of this twofold "beyond"? *Who* is this God beyond God? How does he reveal himself, and in what sense can he still be called "God"? *Anatheism: Returning to God after God* by Richard Kearney raises these questions, among others. According to Kearney, the conversion, the *metanoia*—or, to say it in Hebrew, the *teshuva*—which leads to anatheism, implies the crossing of an "atheistic moment," the experience of distress at the "death of God," the opening of a new, unique, heretofore unheard-of experience of the divine. But this ordeal through which the human subject passes coincides with a strange *metanoia* of God himself—"*ana-theos*, the return of God after the disappearance of God" (A, 5)—as if God needed to fade away, to be lost before returning, transfigured. Kearney does not hesitate to describe this double movement as a *kenosis*, a self-emptying and a death of the sovereign God, the almighty Lord, a "kenotic emptying out of transcendence into the heart of the world's body, becoming a God beneath us rather than a God beyond us" (A, 91).

Does this new face of God only arise out of a religious crisis? Does it only approach us *after* a moment of doubt and despair? Or has it been present from the beginning, hidden behind the glorious mask of the "omni-God?" Is anatheism only posttheism, the possibility of a sobered faith, more humble and more ecumenical, in times of triumphant secularism? Does it allow us, too, to come back to the secret truth of faith, a truth "hidden since the foundation of the world" (Matthew 13:35)?

It is the latter of these options that Kearney chooses. The anatheistic *metanoia* is rooted indeed in a singular experience, a "moment of epiphany," that he detects in the inaugural scenes, the founding moments of the three monotheistic religions. From Abraham's welcome of the three unknown men, to the visitation of Mary, to Muhammad's ecstasy in the Mount Hira cave, each case deals with the meeting of an "unexpected guest." Each case presents us with the figure of a stranger who reveals himself afterward to be the very face of the divine. But this epiphany of the stranger is characterized by a radical ambiguity: is he friend or foe? Truth or deception?

There is a "constitutive ambiguity" of the experience of the stranger—also marked in the word *hostis*, signifying both guest and foe—and this ambivalence "makes every dramatic encounter between the human and the divine into a radical hermeneutic wager: compassion or murder. You either welcome, or refuse the stranger. Monotheism is the history of this wager" (A, 22). This is a wager that concerns the divine as much as the human, that concerns the stranger as much as the host, that comes from the outsider as well as from the one who welcomes him. As Kearney emphasizes, "the Stranger before me both *is* God (as transcendent Guest), and *is not* God (as screen of my projections and presumptions)" (A, 15). He is both a projection on the other of my own phantasm that hides from me the otherness of the other and, at the same time, a truth that traverses that screen.

How can we distinguish the truth of the divine and its nontruth, disentangle these two aspects of the same phenomenon that intermingle in its self-givenness? This demarcation must be possible: it is the very possibility of an ethics and a faith delivered from phantasm. In the five moments of the anatheistic wager, Kearney therefore reserves a major role for what he calls *discernment* (A, 44–47). This term, which belongs to an old tradition of the church, means for him a "carnal response to the arrival of the Other," a "pre-reflexive response" that underlies and directs critical thinking (A, 44–47). The call to discernment means here—against Derrida, and perhaps against Levinas too—that we do not have to offer anyone unconditional welcome because not everyone is divine. There is one who kills and another who gives life, one who loves and one who lies. And it should always be possible to differentiate them. If not, "each encounter with the divine would be like a blind date (A, 44–47)," similar to the ordeal of the absurd that Kierkegaard discovers in the story of Abraham, that of a believer who receives from his God the terrifying order to sacrifice his own son.

Against the Derridean undecidable, against Kierkegaard's paradox, which "paralyzes" the one who faces it, Kearney here opposes a wise wager supported by discernment: "Abraham already knew this trial of two opposing calls, one that told him to kill his son and one that ordered him to save him. He discerned and made a wise choice, that of love against death." Strangely, interpreting the story of Abraham in this way, Kearney abdicates the whole decision to the human subject, as if Isaac's father had simultaneously heard two voices and decided to obey only one of them. But we know that the biblical narrative depicts two successive calls, one that orders the sacrifice and the other that interrupts it; and Abraham obeys *each* of these two contradictory calls. What is at stake is not the choice of the human subject, his ability to "discern" good and evil, the true call of the other and the false one. It is the ambiguity of the call itself, of this twofold call, which seems to order two contrary actions. Thus, the paradox cannot be so easily discarded. We need to further analyze the episode related in Genesis 22. Perhaps doing so will throw a new light on the meaning and scope of the anatheistic wager.

II

Known as the "sacrifice of Abraham" or, in the Jewish tradition, as the *Aqedah*, the "binding" of Isaac, the story confronts us with the ambiguity of a call that comes from the stranger. What is at stake here is the limit of faith: can faith justify murder, including the murder of one's own child? It seems that such a faith could justify the fiercest fanaticism—the Crusades, the Inquisition, or, nowadays, jihadist terrorism. But who is the God who commands murder? Can we believe in such a God? It is not only Abraham, but also the reader who is put to the test, for the text remains deeply enigmatic. At first, we cannot understand Abraham's submission to the terrifying order; especially if we remember that, before the destruction of Sodom, he did not hesitate to oppose God in the name of justice. His obedience raises the question of the relation between faith and ethics, for the ethics of the three monotheisms is grounded in the prohibition against murder. We can find it not only in the Ten Commandments, but also in Genesis 9:6, just after the flood, when God blesses Noah and his progeny and gives a primordial law to the future mankind: "Whoever sheds the blood of man, by man shall his blood be shed, for God made man in his own image." In any case, the story of Isaac's binding would lose all meaning, if it were not considered in the context of this prohibition. We thus find a contradiction between two divine orders: by obeying God, Abraham breaks God's law. He sets God up against God himself.

Who is the God of Abraham? What kind of God is one who "tests" his believer in such a cruel way? And why did he have to test him? If he is the all-knowing, he must have known the result beforehand. Is he such a perverse God? Could this trial be a kind of devilish temptation? Moreover, we know that Isaac is not an ordinary child: he is the "child of promise," of the promise that God has inscribed in Abraham's name, which makes him *Av-raham*, literally: the "father of multitudes." By ordering the killing of Isaac, God seems to contradict himself, to become unfaithful to his own promise. And he will soon contradict himself again by canceling the first order. In this sense, the text not only confronts us with the ambiguity of God but, more radically, with his possible lunacy.

The story of Isaac's binding has been interpreted in different ways by modern thinkers. It often rouses indignation, for instance in Kant and Hegel. In *Fear and Trembling*, Kierkegaard deals with it in a different manner: for him, the case of Abraham shows us that faith is an "incredible paradox," "capable of making a murder into a holy act, well pleasing to God."[1] According to him, ethics and faith are two separate spheres, and we can pass from ethics to faith only by a "leap." Indeed, he defines ethics as the reign of the general, of "what is applicable to everyone," whereas faith is "exactly this paradox, that the single individual is higher than the universal."[2] In the sphere of faith, every ethical norm or law is suspended: because faith is a singular relation to God, an "absolute relation to the Absolute," to "an absolutely Different, without any distinctive clue." God is the absolute exception, which justifies all exceptions. "If faith is not this, then Abraham is lost": he is only a murderer or a madman.[3] Does this mean that any believer should imitate Abraham, by committing murder for the sake of God? Certainly not: it would be, says Kierkegaard, the "most horrifying misunderstanding." The absolute singularity of Abraham's experience is incommunicable, impossible to imitate, and "it is only by faith that one acquires a resemblance to Abraham, not by murder."[4] However, it is obvious that Abraham's faith is inseparable from his trial. If God had not required his son's life, the paradox of faith would have been annihilated, and Abraham would not have been Abraham.

Unlike Kierkegaard, unlike most Christian and Islamic commentators, the Jewish tradition has sharply rejected any interpretation of Abraham's story that could justify murder by invoking an arbitrary order of God. For that reason, some rabbis tried to look for a "sin" that could rationally explain Abraham's trial as a "punishment." They alleged that God wanted to punish either his attitude in regard to Ismael and Agar, who he banished to the desert, or his territorial compromise with the Cananean king, Abimelekh.[5] Here, part of the Jewish tradition gets embroiled in the fatal slope of theodicy: it tries to justify the unjustifiable. In the same way, some current Jewish thinkers have "justified" the Shoah as a divine "punishment" of the sins and unbelief of their people. We find here again the perverse, the sadistic God who is presupposed by most common interpretations of Abraham's sacrifice.

Nevertheless, from a Jewish point of view, it is possible to defend an ethical interpretation of the episode without accepting the postulate of a divine infliction. This reading has been assumed by Levinas. He opposes his conception of a faith ruled by ethics to the "violence" of Kierkegaard's thought. His "hardness" rises at the precise moment when he attempts to "overcome" ethics, by entering a religious stage that no ethical law could justify: "so begins the contempt for the ethical foundation of Being."[6] According to Levinas, this claim to overcome ethics is based on a misinterpretation: the Danish thinker identifies ethics with the abstraction of the general, where the singularity of the ego has been lost. He does not perceive the primordial ethical relation between the ego and the other, an always singular relation where the face of the other calls the ego to its infinite responsibility. From this ethical perspective, the episode of Isaac's binding can receive another signification. Above all, we must avoid focusing only on the first call without taking into account the second, which cancels the first: Kierkegaard has not understood that "the attention lent by Abraham to the voice which brought him back to the ethical order by forbidding him the human sacrifice is the highest moment of the drama. That he had obeyed the first voice is surprising. That he had, in spite of this obedience, enough distance to hear the second voice, here is the most important."[7]

However, Levinas's analysis raises several questions. He tries to shift the emphasis from the first call to the second, as if the second alone carried all the meaning of the story. Is this true? Does the second call succeed in erasing the scandal of the first? It is apparently the same God who commands successively the murder and the prohibition of murder, the break of the covenant and its confirmation. By refusing to hear the first call, Levinas does not take into account the ambiguity of God. Moreover, he seems surprised by Abraham's obedience to the first call, and he presupposes that Abraham could hold a certain "distance" from the divine injunction. However, what would it be like to be obedient to a God who is not unconditioned? In Levinas's ethics, our exposition to the other is also unconditioned, as a "devotion without promise," a "gift without return," without any kind of distance or reserve. In a certain sense, the Levinasian other, who commands of me an absolute sacrifice of myself, is not so different from the God who imposes on Abraham his terrifying trial. But Levinas's ethic is situated from the point of view of the sacrificed and not that of the one who sacrifices: as if Levinas were speaking in the place of Isaac himself, bound on the altar and agreeing to his own sacrifice.

We can remark too that Levinas refuses to name "God" the author of the first call. He faithfully adheres to an old Jewish tradition, which does not accept that God could break his own law by commanding a murder. The author of such an evil injunction can only be an evil angel, the devil himself: this was already the teaching of the *Book of Jubilees* (about the second century BC) and then that of the Talmud. In Treatise *Sanhedrin*, we can indeed read this:

> After what words did God put Abraham to the test? After Satan's words. Because it is written 'Abraham made a big feast the day of the weaning of Isaac.' Then Satan addressed the Holy One, blessed is He, and said to Him: 'Master of the Universe, you offered a son to this hundred-years-old man and during this feast he did not even think of offering you a turtledove.' God answered him: 'But if I said to him: bring me your son in offering, he would sacrifice him immediately.' At once follows the verse: 'and God did test Abraham and said to him: 'take now your son, your unique son' (89b).

This attempt to overcome God's initial ambiguity by dissociating it in two opposite figures is characteristic of rabbinical Judaism. Here, the Talmud projects on Abraham's story a schema forged earlier in the Book of Job. But this theodicy succeeds in saving God's goodness only by limiting his omnipotence and by breaking his unity. Like all Gnostic "explanations" of evil, it only elides the difficulty. The problem then consists in knowing why his opponent could tempt

God and why God allows the devil to test Job, Abraham, and the multitudes of humbled and tortured victims of human history in such a cruel way. A God who agrees so easily to evil, a God who seems to be a passive accomplice of Satan—does such a God not have something satanic about him?

In any case, the story of Abraham's sacrifice is so paradoxical that it could arouse the hypothesis of a devilish temptation. We must notice that, in the Muslim tradition, the devil, called Satan or Iblis, comes to tempt Abraham too. As Islam emphasizes Abraham's submission to the divine will, the tempter is not the one who gives him the order to immolate his son. On the contrary, the devil strives to dissuade Abraham from performing the sacrifice, claiming that the order is coming . . . from the devil himself. Standing in his way, the evil one says to Abraham: "By God, I think that Satan has come to you in a dream and commanded you to sacrifice this little son of yours"—"But then," continues the narrative, "Abraham recognized Iblis and said to him: 'Go away, O Enemy of God! By God, I am obeying the command of my Lord in this matter.'"[8]

Abraham's paradox thus locks us into apparently insuperable aporias. If we try to exonerate God by considering the trial of Abraham as the punishment of a sin, we make God a merciless torturer and we justify a priori the worst injustices of human history. If we assert that God requires the sacrifice of his son to test his faith, such a perverse God is no better than the devil. But if we refuse to accept that, if we attribute to the call a diabolical origin, we drift then towards a quasi-Gnostic dualism and we still do not understand how God could authorize the devil to tempt Abraham. Is there any possibility of escaping the aporia? Of asserting the divine origin of the call without demonizing the God of Abraham? Of maintaining the initial ambiguity of God without cleaving his attributes?

III

To answer these questions, it is necessary to return to the letter of the text. What exactly does God ask of Abraham? To lead his son to Mount Moriah in order to "offer him in *'olah*." Never in this passage do we find the term *qorban*, which means a ritual sacrifice. The Hebrew word *'olah* does not hint at the killing of a victim: it means literally "rise." We thus deform the text when we translate this term by "burnt offering," as do all of the English translations, or by "*holocaust*," as do most of the French ones. The only French translation that follows the Hebrew—that of Chouraqui—translates as "*fais-le monter en montée*" ("make him rise in a rise"). To translate the expression into German, Buber and Rosenzweig forged the term *Darhöhung*, which means at the same time "exposure" and "elevation" (in the sense of a spiritual experiment). These translators remained faithful to another Jewish tradition, which has insisted on the nonsacrificial meaning of the narrative. The interpretation of *'olah* as "rise" appears for the first time in the *midrash*, or rabbinical comment, *Genesis Rabbah* (probably written in the fourth century CE). According to it, Abraham blamed God for contradicting himself by ordering to sacrifice the child of promise, but God replied, "I have not contradicted myself when I said, 'take your son,' because I have not told you 'slaughter him,' but 'raise him.'" Rashi, the great medieval commentator, specifies: "He did not say to Abraham: 'immolate him,' because the Holy One, blessed is He, did not want that he slaughters him, but only that he made him rise on the mountain as an offering. And after he would have made him rise, He would say to him: 'Make him come down!'"

Nevertheless, we can notice that the word *'olah* appears very often in the other books of the Torah, for instance in *Leviticus*, where it obviously means a "holocaust" in which an animal victim is completely burned in offering to God. Moreover, it has the same meaning at the very end of the Moriah episode, when Abraham will immolate a ram "by an *'olah*." But nothing proves that this word has the same meaning in *the beginning* of the story. The order given to Abraham can thus have a sacrificial sense or a very different one, and nothing in the context allows us to decide. The divine order seems essentially equivocal, as were the Greek oracles. If the sacrificial meaning of *'olah* seems here the most obvious, the ambiguity of the word leaves open another possible interpretation, which preserves a horizon of hope and allows us to keep faith in the promise. Abraham however decides on the opposite interpretation: without any kind of ethical "discernment," he chooses the sacrificial meaning. Perhaps because the call reveals here the secret desire of its addressee. It reveals Abraham's desire for murder, a desire that he refuses to assume, which he projects onto the other. It is necessary to resist any temptation to "psychoanalyze" Abraham, by trying to decipher his unconscious desire.[9]

Let us listen, instead, to what the story says: it is speaking of a murderous desire, which looks for a justification in an alleged divine call. It reveals thus which conception Abraham has of God. By interpreting the call in such a way, he shows that he remains captive to a mortiferous relation to the divine. He imagines God as a bloodthirsty tyrant who denies his own promise and requires a holocaust. We have heard of this fierce God who demands the life of the firstborn sons: the heathen tribes of Canaan celebrated his worship. His name was Baal or Molokh, and the Torah never ceased denouncing his cult as an abomination. When Abraham gets ready to sacrifice Isaac, he proves that he has not really broken away from idolatry, that he still confuses God and Molokh.

What is an idol? A god "made by man's hand," a human, all too human representation of God. The rejection of idolatry, as notes Kearney, preserves the strangeness of the divine stranger by refusing to lock it into a visible figure that men could manipulate and control. Whatever it might be addressed to, idolatry is grounded in an alienating *projection*: the idol is always an image or a part of myself, which I have projected onto the plane of the other and which appears to me *as if* it were coming from the other. Jean-Luc Marion is right to define the idol as an *invisible mirror.* When the human glance stretches out towards the divine, the idol is this visible figure that stops the glance by reflecting it, by returning to itself its own sight: "the idol masks the mirror because it fills the gaze. . . . Because it offers to the gaze its first visible, the idol itself remains an invisible mirror."[10]

It is for this reason, let us add, that every idol is sacrificial (including the modern idols of politics and spectacle). The projection that, each time, constitutes my idol is an alienating identification, a primordial sacrifice of myself: it is my own flesh, my own life that I illusively transfer to my image in the mirror. Idolatry is not a "false religion" that it would be possible to oppose to the "true" one. A worshiper of Amon-Ra, Zeus, or Shiva may very well, even as he bows down before their statue, have overcome idolatry in his heart. On the contrary, a devout monotheist, who has no words strong enough to condemn the worship of idols, may have kept an idolatrous relationship to his god; for example, when he believes he gratifies him by sacrificing his son to him, or by slaughtering "heretics" and "infidels." Idolatry, or rather, *idolization*, is one of the most originary modes of our relation to the other. It happens on this surface of projection, this invisible screen on which we project our own phantasms or, more precisely, what I have designated as the *remainder* of our flesh.[11] This projection disfigures the face of the other and forbids us any access to him or her, including the divine other. Nobody knew this better than Augustine. He said that the adorers of images "see a mirror, but they stop there: they do not see through the mirror the One who must be seen through the mirror; so, they do not see that this mirror which they see is a mirror, in other words an image."[12]

IV

What is at stake in Isaac's binding becomes clear: in its ambiguity, the biblical text summons us to decide between an idolatrous sacrificial representation of the divine and another conception. Who is the God of Abraham? Once again, the letter of the text gives us a decisive indication. At the beginning of the episode, when it is said that "God did test Abraham," the Hebrew name for God is *Elohim*. Then, at the climax of the story, when he is on the verge of killing Isaac, the call that stops his hand is no longer coming from *Elohim* but from the holy name, the unpronounceable name of God: YHWH (translated in English by the periphrasis *the Lord*).

How should we interpret this change of name? Some scholars use to classify the texts of the Torah according to the various names given to God: these would belong to different sources, which would have been later collected in a unique text. In this passage, the change of the divine name intervenes however at the very core of the narrative, when the sacrificial order is evicted by the prohibition of murder, and this change gives all its impact to the narrative. It is possible to consider it as a first revelation of this unspeakable name, which will be explicitly revealed to Moses on Mount Sinai. This is still an indirect revelation because it is not revealed to Abraham—only to the reader. It is, however, a true revelation, in which another dimension of the divine is unveiled. For the Jewish tradition, each of God's names reveals one of God's faces—that is to say one of his attributes—and we must remember that, in Hebrew, the word meaning "face," *panim*, is a plural, just like the word *Elohim*. Among the different names of God (*El, Shaddaï, Tzebaoth*, and so on), two of them have a major significance: *Elohim* and YHWH. According to the rabbinic teachings, whereas the first one designates God's "attribute of Rigour," his "attribute of Mercy" is called YHWH. For instance, in the *Midrash Exodus Rabbah* (3, 6): "the Holy One, blessed is He, says to Moses: 'is it my name which you want to know? I am called according to my works.... When I judge created beings, my name is *Elohim*.... When I am merciful to the world, my name is YHWH.... Hence, *I shall be what I shall be*, according to my works.'"

But what is the "rigour," what is the "justice" of a God who requires infanticide? This classical conception of "divine attributes" does not enable us to face the paradoxical ambiguity of God, his wildness, his primordial violence. And it is also too static to allow us to understand the sudden changing of the divine name, which happens in the climax of Abraham's drama. We have thus to approach in another way the difference between the divine names.

At first, we must notice that *Elohim*, which has the grammatical form of the plural, is a common name: it is the generic name of divinity, which, in the Bible, also indicates the heathen ones. It probably derives from the root *alah*, which means "to adore." It is thus the name of the undifferentiated divine, of all the entities which men can adore. At this level, no demarcation is possible between the sacred and the holy, between the idol and the invisible other. According to some other authors, *El, Elohim* would come from a Semitic word meaning *power*, creative and procreative strength, which is also found in the name of the ram, *eyl* (and, several centuries after, in the name of the God of Islam). He is sometimes called *El Shaddaï*, the Lord of the Mountain, the High and Almighty God. Opposed to these symbols of a powerful strength, which the God of Israel shares with Baal ("the Lord") and Molokh ("the King"), is the name YHWH. Here, we are not dealing with a common name anymore, but rather with a proper, absolutely idiomatic one, which for that reason has to remain secret, unpronounceable.

Who is YHWH, and in whom does this name distinguish itself from those of the idols? Just before revealing to Moses his unspeakable name, YHWH expresses the enigmatic sentence "*ehyeh asher ehyeh*," literally: "I shall be as I shall be." Instead of reading this sentence as an ontological thesis ("I am the one who is," "I am the being itself") as mainstream Christian theology does, the Jewish tradition understands it as the assertion of a *being-with*. According to Rashi, God so announces to Moses that "*I shall be* with you in this distress *as I shall be* with your people in all distresses to come." Ricœur is close to this tradition when he detects here a "non-Greek sense of Being," enlarged to "a being-with or being-faithful" (quoted in A, 79). In another text, the French philosopher insists on the "dissolving power of the theology of the Name," whose revelation implements a "reduction" of any kind of anthropomorphic figurations of the divine: the revelation of Mount Sinai means "the Name against the Idol."[13]

The unspeakable name does not appear anymore as the universal attribute of a cosmic power, but as the sign of a singular relation between an I and another I, as the certitude of a support, the promise of being-with. God does not appear as the almighty Master who requires absolute obedience, but as the one who frees from servitude ("It is me, YHWH, your *Elohim*, who made you escape out of Egypt, out of the house of slavery" (Exodus 20:2)). He does not fill up the glance by showing the glorious image of a first visible, but forbids the cult of images and any attempt to represent the divine in the visible. Finally, far from demanding of his believers a total sacrifice, he is the One who forbids murder and refuses bloody sacrifice and *'olah*.[14] We understand henceforth why the call to holocaust comes from *Elohim*, whereas the second call is the call of YHWH.

V

It seems nevertheless impossible to oppose these two calls, as if two different Gods had uttered them: otherwise, we would return to a quasi-Gnostic cleavage of the oneness of Israel's God. What is the relation between these two divine names? Are they merely two equivalent ways of naming the same God? Or would one of these two names be *truer*, closer to the truth of God than the other one? It seems that an anatheistic approach would undoubtedly benefit from a rereading of Schelling, the only modern philosopher who explored the fundamental ambiguity of the divine. In his *Philosophy of Revelation*, he analyses the story of Abraham and the substitution of divine names. According to him, *Elohim*, the "still indistinct" God, is opposed to YHWH, the "differentiated God" who reveals himself by being named. If *Elohim* is the "first God," the archaic divinity of ancient times, then YHWH is *Ehyeh*—that is to say, "I shall be": the coming God, the God that *will be*. But his revelation is not immediate: the truth of God can appear only through that primordial obscure principle from which he is inseparable. "The true God," writes Schelling, "is only the one who appears and he thus presupposes continuously *Elohim* as the substratum, the medium of his apparition."[15] There would thus be an inner differentiation, belonging to the very process of God's self-revelation. The duality of *Elohim* and YHWH would imply that his revelation passes from the sacrificial idol to a God beyond any image; and it reveals the twofold face of a unique God. If there were two Gods, or a dualistic opposition between an evil and a good principle, their antagonism would be quite static, whereas the Bible presents here the movement of self-revelation, or *teshuva*, of the one God. In other words: anatheism requires monotheism.

Kearney calls us to an "anatheistic kenosis" that would free us from the idolatry of the almighty. No doubt we must also free ourselves from the idolatry of the all-knowing. If God knew in advance how Abraham was going to act, the trial would have made no sense—unless it were a sadistic joke hatched by a divine pervert. If we want to deliver ourselves from this terrifying representation of God, we must admit that, before it happened, God did not already know how Abraham would pass through the test. Maybe he did not know himself which of his two faces would reveal itself at the moment of the sacrifice. We must recognize in God a part of unknowing, of untruth, unconsciousness, blindness, forgetfulness.

The revelation of the name is thus a *self*-revelation, where God's truth is revealed to God himself; and it is not only Abraham that God puts through this test, but above all himself. It enables God to understand what his true name is, *who* he is, what kind of God he *may be*. The coming God is an *ana-theos*, a God who comes back to himself, passing beyond "God" by confronting himself with the dark Ground, with the part of blindness and primordial violence, which he also carries within him. Dare we to say that the "anatheistic wager" does not concern only man's relationship to the divine, but also the relationship of the divine to itself? God, too, wagers that he will overcome the first phase, still wild and undifferentiated, of his self-revelation.

Another question can be raised here: the God who reveals himself to himself and to Abraham on Mount Moriah—shall we say that he is a God of mercy and love, a God who comforts and protects? Nothing allows us to say this. The words he addresses to Abraham (which the text refers to as the "messenger of YHWH") only forbid murder, without offering him love or comfort. Ricœur was not wrong to say that "it is the same god, that threatens and consoles"; that the archaic figure of the divine that commands absolute obedience, until murder, is just another face of the father that protects; and that we need to further engage in the mourning of the father and the reduction of the Idol in order to enter into "a tragic faith beyond all assurance and protection."[16]

In what sense can we say, however, that the second phase of self-revelation is *truer* than the first one? That the passage from idol to name brings us closer to the truth of God and brings God himself closer to his own truth? We have seen that idolatry is not limited to the worship of images and statues. Idolatry means a fundamental relationship of man to the other and especially to the divine other, a constantly recurring illusion that consists of projecting onto the other our phantasms and affects, our envy, our hatred, our desire, our love. When the call of YHWH stops Abraham's hand, it interrupts this projection whereby a man illusively attributes to a divine order his own desire for murder. By prohibiting murder, the call of YHWH not only provides an ethical commandment: it frees

Abraham from the imaginary warrant authorizing him to kill, and brings him back to the enigma of his desire. The call is thus a revelation of truth.

How can it be that the crossing of a "godless moment" is necessary to overcome idolatry? Why do we have to cross it again and again? As Schelling observed, the "dark Ground in God" can be overcome by the self-revelation of God, but it will still persist as an opaque and unyielding core within him. We must undoubtedly admit that the ground can always spring up again in the very movement of revelation; or, in other words, that the passage from the "first God" to the "truth of God" is always reversible and must each time be replayed in our own experience. The irruption of the stranger through the screen of phantasm is always precarious and could at any time be covered again by new phantasms. Kearney is therefore right to emphasize that "the decision of hospitality over hostility is never made once and for all; it is a wager that needs to be renewed again and again, anatheistically" (A, 19). These are the stakes of the "atheist moment" that allows us to break away from the ever recurring fascination of the idol.

How could Abraham not cross this moment of doubt and despair when attempting to sacrifice the child of promise? How could Isaac not experience it too? The text of the Bible tells us nothing about that, but Kierkegaard has staged it in the first pages of *Fear and Trembling*: "When Abraham turned to pull up the knife, Isaac saw that his father's left hand was clutching in despair and that a shudder was shaking his body—though Abraham took the knife. Then they came back home and Sarah hastened to meet them, but Isaac had lost his faith."[17]

If the trial has enabled God to reveal himself in truth, what has it provided to Abraham? He seems only to have moved from one approach to God to another, by submitting himself each time passively to the divine calls. In fact, there is no reason to think that, were he to hear another call commanding him to perform a ritual homicide, he would refuse to comply with it again. However, the text gives us a clue, which shows that his relation to the divine has been deeply transformed following the trial: after the "messenger of YHWH" forbids him to sacrifice Isaac, he decides to immolate a ram instead of his son. Perhaps this means that Abraham has not yet broken away from the archaic religion grounded on bloody sacrifice; that he has not yet understood that a nonsacrificial approach to the divine is possible, which would respect every life, whether human or animal. Maybe, as is suggested by the proximity between the name of the ram (*eyl*) and that of *El-Elohim*, it is the "ancient God" himself, the wild idol of strength and power, whom Abraham sacrifices here to another name, another face of the divine. It is this hypothesis, which Lacan defends: that the ram is a metaphor of the fierce *Urvater*, the totem of Abraham's tribe; and that "the one whose Name is unpronounceable designates to be sacrificed" instead of Isaac. It would be his own *Elohim* that Abraham sacrifices after having heard the call of YHWH. "Here," writes Lacan, "we see a sharp divide between God's jouissance and what, in this tradition, is presented as His desire," that is to say between two dimensions of the father, the imaginary and the symbolic ones.[18]

Nevertheless, his subtle analysis misses an essential element of the story: it is not the unpronounceable name that orders Abraham to sacrifice the ram instead of Isaac. It is Abraham himself who freely makes this decision. Could it be that he misunderstands the meaning of the second call, a call that forbids any "murder," that is to say *any kind* of bloody sacrifice? Does he therefore remain idolatrous? In a certain sense, it does not matter: what is decisive here is that he has progressed from his passive submission to the divine call to another attitude, where he is free to decide on his own approach to the divine; as if the revelation of God's truth has freed him from his bondage, his subjection to a transcendent other. The event of Moriah thus gives us the same teaching that a descendant of Abraham gives much later: *the truth will set us free.*

VI

To conclude, I shall content myself to return to Mount Moriah where the unspeakable name is given and heard. It is thus that the Jewish tradition understands the word: *mori-yah*, literally, "vision of Yah," that is of YHWH, whose name is given even before his "messenger" addresses Abraham. The *vision of YHWH*: an expression that is ambiguous in light of the double meaning of the genitive. It could indicate the place of the interrupted sacrifice as a place where *YHWH sees* (sees what? the truth of Abraham's desire? of his own desire? of both intertwined?). And the enigmatic place where the invisible YHWH gives himself *to be seen*, not directly ("nobody can see me without dying"), but by showing the result of his call: the interruption of the sacrifice, the prohibition of murder. Either way, "Moriah" is the secret signature of the *ana-theos*, which inscribes in the narrative the revelation of his name and enjoins us, through an infinite reading, to decipher it.

JACOB ROGOZINSKI is Professor of Philosophy at Strasbourg University, where he succeeded J. L. Nancy in 2002. His research focuses on phenomenological thinking of the ego and the body. His recent works include *The Ego and the Flesh; Guérir la vie: La Passion d'Antonin Artaud; Cryptes de Derrida*; and *Ils m'ont haï sans raison.*

Notes

1. Kierkegaard, *Fear and Trembling*, 46.
2. Ibid., 47.
3. Ibid., 47.

4. Ibid., 25.

5. The last interpretation (which seems quite convincing from a "historical" standpoint) is that of a medieval commentator, the Rashbam—cf. de Launay, "L'exigence de la promesse," in *Le sacrifice d'Abraham*, 67–68.

6. Levinas, *Noms propres*, 84.

7. Ibid., 90.

8. Al-Tabari, *The History of Al-Tabari* (IX° century), vol. II, 92.

9. As, for instance, Marie Balmary tries to do in her interesting essay, "Le sacrifice interdit," 1986.

10. Marion, *God without Being*, 12.

11. I refer here to my book *The Ego and the Flesh*, chap. 10.

12. Augustine, *De Trinitate*, II–24.

13. Ricœur, *The Conflict of Interpretations*, 388.

14. Cf. Isaiah 1:11–16: "'The multitude of your sacrifices, what are they to me?' says YHWH. 'I have more than enough of burnt offerings … They have become a burden to me … Your hands are full of blood; wash and make yourselves clean. Take your evil deeds out of my sight!'"

15. Schelling, *Philosophy of Revelation*, Twenty-Ninth Lessons, 123.

16. Ricœur, *The Conflict of Interpretations*, 441, 455.

17. Kierkegaard, *Fear and Trembling.*

18. Lacan, *On the Names of the Father*, 88.

13 The Apparent God: Biblical Poetics and the End of Time

Theo L. Hettema

I

Richard Kearney's *Anatheism* brings God to the forefront once more. The hermeneutic approach expressed in the notion of anatheism recalls a God who has seemed to have disappeared from the philosophical scene. Once, metaphysics offered a solid triad of God, human beings, and the world, though this tripartition made God into a questionable substitute for being. Nineteenth- and twentieth-century attacks on metaphysics disputed the contents of such a being, and even deconstructed any possibility of thinking of such concepts as being and grounds. Consequently, the solid edifice of a metaphysical God was demolished, neglected by philosophical attention, or transformed into a void in postmodern deconstruction. Yet once the identification of God with being has been deconstructed, there appears the possibility of denoting God and the divine in terms of otherness, which defies any attempt to ontologically identify God and (the ground of) being, or God and the existent.

Kearney's philosophy addresses the challenges of thinking of the divine in terms of otherness. For, what Kearney presents with his *Anatheism* is a philosophical endeavour, in which mental acts and attitudes such as imagination, humor, commitment, discernment, and hospitality create a space in which philosophical meaningfulness may be given to encounters with the other and with God as an other.[1]

For Kearney, the other is that which appears as strange, not connectable with one's own mind-set, that which appears as fundamentally foreign, and even appallingly dangerous. The other has a twofold face. He or she may appear as a guest, asking to be invited, making of us hosts, but he or she may also appear as a dangerous stranger, a potential offender who intends to break through the safety of our home or our body. The encounter with the other can never be understood in predefined criteria. The other remains a stranger in the sense that the other cannot be possessed and incorporated into the whole of my presumptions.

The space of dispossession is particularly the space of expressing the divine other, God as the stranger who refuses to be included in our presumptions. With such a view of God or the divine, Kearney places himself between theism—having a metaphysical and absolutist background in the belief in God—and atheism—posing its dogmatic, absolutist position against the divine.

Thus we meet a fundamental tendency in Kearney to take a middle position: in between metaphysics and postmodernism, or in between theism and atheism. Such a position does not suggest a compromise between two opposites or a dialectical sublation of thesis and antithesis; it is rather an expression that the middle position refuses the absolutes that are presumed by extreme positions. Anatheism seeks a stance that precedes any absolute fixation of the meaning of the other. As such, it is a regressive movement, a return to a stage before literalism and the fixation of meaning. At the same time, it is a progressive movement, always urging someone to make a choice for now and the future, over and over again. Anatheism is the everlasting wager of perceiving the divine as intriguing other and stranger, again. In Kierkegaardian terms, it is a repetition forward (A, 7).

Such a philosophical program had already been presented in Kearney's *The God Who May Be* and had been elaborated in his *Strangers, Gods and Monsters*. Whereas *The God Who May Be* stressed the need to be philosophically sensitive to the potential in order to interpret the notion of God, and *Strangers, Gods and Monsters* showed the richness of interpreting figures of the divine other, *Anatheism* focuses on the element of choice in responding to the divine other, a response fed by imagination, humor, commitment, discernment, and hospitality.

These five components of the wager have in common that they all contain a poetic element. They are all fed by literature, music, and art. They feature metaphoricity—that is, the art of seeing the other as like me but also unlike me—and express translatability, the conviction that the call of the other can be understood, though a fundamental otherness remains in translation (A, 15). The anatheistic wager contains a poetics in which "the figural saves God from the literal" (A, 14). Poetics saves the divine other from being dogmatized. In short, Kearney's anatheism offers a fusion of religion, philosophy, and poetics, meant to offer a hermeneutics of living with and responding to the other.

II

It is this blend of religion, philosophy, and poetics that explains Kearney's use of literature, the narratives of inspiring lives, and religious texts such as the Bible and the Quran. The poetics of an anatheistic wager can be fed by all kinds of cultural expressions, presented in art, film, literature, and music, as well as in religious expressions. The anatheistic wager can be nourished by sacred books such as the Bible and the Quran, which, as a matter of fact, have functioned as sources of cultural inspiration throughout their existence.

As for the Bible, this sacred book is, for Kearney, the "other formative source of Western 'wisdom' along with Greek philosophy" (A, 8). With this point of view, we may understand how biblical stories have a place in the anatheistic wager; they offer a poetics that, by imagination, shapes our sensitivity to responding to the other. The encounter with the other is always a wager: we cannot know beforehand what the character of the other is that presents itself to us. This ambiguity of the other explains why Kearney has a great interest in biblical stories that speak of meeting a stranger who might be a divine stranger: Abraham's encounter with three visitors at Mamre (Genesis 18) and the Annunciation (Luke 1:26–38). Stories like these poetically explore the possible responses of hostility and hospitality towards the divine stranger (A, 17–30).

It is at this point that I want to connect to Kearney's philosophical endeavor: biblical poetics as a means of encountering the divine other as stranger. I am convinced of the fruitfulness of introducing biblical poetics into systematic reflection.[2] I derive this conviction from the work of Paul Ricoeur, who recognized the value of biblical stories for philosophical reflection, interpreting these stories not as mythological or protological counterpoints to thinking, but as figurative forms of reflection.[3]

My intention to put forth biblical poetics as a means of reflecting on the merits of anatheism comes from a systematic theological point of view. I have good reasons to put forward such a view, because Kearney himself favors a theological locus, namely the locus of eschatology. For Kearney, the other is principally not someone or something present—that is, at hand. The other is always appearing; the other arises in front of me, unexpected, uncontrollable. Exactly this element of uncontrollable appearance makes the other a stranger with a twofold face, at once terrifying and friendly. The problematic of such an uncontrollable appearance rises to greater heights when the other is interpreted as divine. God is not present in the sense that he is at hand in a controllable experience. His appearance is in a mode of arrival, in a perpetual act of coming.

In traditional dogmatics, eschatology refers to God's coming at the end of time. Kearney transforms such eschatology into an unremitting appearance of God as coming. One cannot speak of God apart from being the other who is coming to us. God's coming is not restricted to a certain moment in the future, but is the fundamental aspect of his appearance in time and place, here and now. Kearney's eschatology is an "*amor mundi*, love of the world as the embodiment of infinity in the finite, of transcendence, of eschatology in the now" (A, 166). The divine appearance can only be a real appearance here and now, but we must keep in mind that it is an appearance that is not subject to the rules of the here and now. It is in this tension that eschatology develops its view of the divine.

It is not only in *Anatheism* that Kearney uses the tenets of eschatology as a means of exploring the character of the (divine) other. Already in his earlier hermeneutics of religion he uses the notion of eschatology to express "the other's future possibilities which are impossible for me (to realise, possess, grasp)"

(GWMB, 12). In other words, "I understand eschaton here precisely in the sense of an end without end—an end that escapes and surprises us, like a thief in the night—rather than some immanent teleological closure" (GWMB, 12). Kearney observes how the otherness of the divine leads to two different attitudes. On the one hand, it gives rise to an exalted mystical communion, as a "saturated phenomenon" beyond any name and identification (GWMB, 32–33). On the other hand, there is a tendency to favor a "dark god"—an ambivalent deity which transcends our conventional moral notions of good and evil and summons us to discover our innermost unconscious selves, to "follow our bliss." In this order of spellbinding sublimity, "God is horrific" (GWMB, 33).

Between such extremes of nonverbal communion in the divine presence and "apocalyptic traumatism," Kearney searches for a third way, which "might help us to eschew the excesses of both *ecclesiastical mysticism* on the one hand (Marion and certain negative theologians) and *apocalyptic postmodernism* on the other (Zizek and the prophets of the sublime)" (GWMB, 34). Kearney has continued this search for *interpreting otherness* by exploring the poetic expressions of both extremes in literature, art, and film. Again, his conclusion is that an eschatological reflection offers a hermeneutic alternative to the philosophical dilemmas of the extremes as described.

> Such an eschatological Kingdom ... has not abandoned the hope that the God who makes the impossible possible may return to Being in hitherto unimagined ways. There is an ethical urgency to eschatological expectation. There is an awareness that if the 'possible advent' indeed comes as an unpredictable surprise, like a thief in the night, it always comes through the face of the most vulnerable—the cry of the 'smallest of these,' the widow, the orphaned, the anguished, the hungry; those who ask: 'Where are you?' To reply to this ethical call, it is crucial to be able to say *I am* here. And this *being present* here and now before the summons of the fragile other requires that the *eschaton* still-to-come already intersects, however enigmatically and epiphanically, with the ontological order of being as loving possible (SGM, 228).

III

So far, we have seen that Kearney's anatheistic project is fundamentally poetic, in all its five elements of being a philosophical wager, and is fundamentally eschatological, directed to the other as coming. At this point, the question arises: how do these two facets connect? Does the poetic support the eschatological and vice versa? And how is this relation established in biblical poetics? My contribution is directed at answering these questions.

My interest in these questions arose when I observed how Kearney treats various examples of biblical passages in the books mentioned above: Abraham's meeting with the three visitors, Moses's encounter with God at the burning bush, Jesus's transfiguration on the mount, and the Annunciation of Gabriel to Mary. It strikes me that these examples each support Kearney's search for figurations of the advent of the other in encounters of hospitality, which cannot be anchored in fixed patterns of conventional expectations. The examples show how the eschatological aspect of the appearance of the other is expressed in the imagination of biblical poetics, in its narrative and lyricism. The question for me is whether such support also holds in other biblical cases. In my contribution I search for a more extreme form of biblical poetics as a means to put to the test the relation between poetics and eschatology as concerns the appearance of the other. To this end, I turn to the book of Revelation.

The book of Revelation is a piece of apocalyptic literature, which means that it reveals a hidden message of an imminent catastrophe on a cosmic scale, in which God makes a final judgment of the world. When it was written (around AD 96), it had at its disposal a rather young tradition of Jewish and Christian apocalyptic literature. Elements of this literary tradition are refigured in an exuberant way that makes the book an extreme work in many senses. First, it is a book that stands at the limit of the Christian biblical canon. It is the last book of the New Testament, but it is also the most disputed and even sometimes removed book from the New Testament canon. Its canonical authority has been far from undisputed. Second, the book explores the boundaries of time and space. The book describes the final days of the present earth, in which time turns to eternal bliss and woe. The limits of place are explored: the entire world is implicated in the description of cosmic catastrophes that scourge the earth, the world's fate is summed up in the description of a single place, the city of Jerusalem, and this single place is pushed beyond its limits when a new, heavenly Jerusalem descends to take its place.

Third, in describing these events, the book of Revelation comes to the limits of communication. Communication is important for the author of Revelation. The unveiling of his message is meant as a vital encouragement for persecuted Christians. The idea that the present course of a history of persecution and martyrdom may lead to an ultimate goal of heavenly glorification encourages the persecuted to persevere in their faith. Therefore, the author explicitly addresses his readers in seven introductory letters, stresses the inevitability of the course of events and their ultimate goal, and provides the reader with many explanatory passages, given by guiding angels and even by the most trustworthy messenger of all: Jesus Christ, appearing as the eschatological "Son of Man."[4] At the same time, the author meets the limits of communication. He needs all the imagery of Old Testament prophecy and the tradition of apocalypticism to convey his message. However, this imagery also leads him to encounter an impossibility of communication: some messages are not yet ready to be revealed (Revelation 10).

The worldwide catastrophe as foreseen by the author leads him to the limits of narrative and hymnal expression, in an exuberant stylistic attempt to encompass what cannot be encompassed. We meet Jesus Christ as the "Son of Man," explaining the visionary images of the author as apocalyptic events (Revelation 1:9–20); but there is also a heavenly elder, in eternal praise of God's heavenly throne, who provides explanation (Revelation 7:13–17) and we read of a guiding angel who leads the author away in the spirit, as formerly the Old Testament prophets experienced (Revelation 17:3; 21:9). The wish for interpretative clarity leads to a multiplicity of voices.

Another illustration of almost breathless exuberance is the way the author uses the number seven in his narrative. Seven is the biblical number of completion. In a sevenfold series, the author of Revelation expresses the entirety of his addressees and the intentional completion of a series of events for the whole world. However, with this stylistic numerology, we stumble on the sevenfold series. We encounter seven churches as addressees, represented by seven spirits in heaven and expressed in seven lampstands and seven stars (Revelation 1:4–20). Then we follow seven letters to seven churches in the book of Revelation. In a vision, the heavenly king is seen writing on seven scrolls. Their unsealing leads to a sevenfold series of events (Revelation 5:8). The event of the seventh seal consists in the blowing of seven trumpets by seven angels, introducing a new series of seven catastrophic events (Revelation 8:11). Seven thunders cover what may not be spoken (Revelation 10:4). A fearful beast has seven heads (Revelation 13:1). Seven angels pour out seven bowls of God's wrath (Revelation 16). The steady assurance of a sevenfold series, meant to bring the believers to perseverance, rather leads by its exaggeration to total confusion.

The limits of sevenfold stylistics become clear in Revelation 17:11, where the author refers to the beast with seven heads. It must have been common knowledge for the original readers of Revelation that these seven heads refer to the seven emperors of Rome. But there is also an eighth king: "He belongs to the seven and is going to his destruction."[5] Here, the sevenfold series needs both an inclusion and extension that cannot be kept in a series of seven. There is another instance where a series breaks down. It is in Revelation 9, where the fifth angel with a trumpet starts a first "woe," a destruction of a part of the earth. Two more woes are to follow (Revelation 9:12). Indeed, the sixth trumpet blow announces the events of a second woe (Revelation 11:14). Now, one should expect a third woe at the blowing of the seventh trumpet. But this seventh blow announces the appearance of the reign of God, without any devastating woe. As a matter of fact, there are more scenes of demolition to follow after this chapter, but a third woe is never mentioned again.

We should not interpret the exuberance in style that follows as an expression of literary incompetence. The author shows a firm grip on the structure of the book by presenting chiastic units.[6] An introduction to the book as a whole, directed to its readers (Revelation 1:3), is mirrored by a conclusion and appeal to the reader (Revelation 22:7–21). A block of sevenfold series of events (seven seals and seven trumpets) (Revelation 4:11) is mirrored by a similar block with the vision of seven bowls of wrath leading to a final vision on the heavenly Jerusalem descending on earth (Revelation 15:1 and 22:6). These blocks encompass a central block of text (Revelation 12:14) without any sevenfold series, but exhibit a crucial scene, in which Jesus himself is persecuted before any apocalyptic praise of his glory and heavenly elevation can be given. It is not that the author lacks any literary command, but he is willing to go to the extremes of what is literally acceptable in his manifold use of repetitions and exuberant images.

There is a fourth point of extremity, concerning a question of faith. The Old Testament has told of an earlier devastation of the earth, by means of a great flood in the time of Noah, after which God declares to Noah: "Never again will all life be destroyed by the waters of a flood" (Genesis 9:11). It must have been a problem for the first Christians how the firm confirmation of a covenant of life could lead to another disaster.[7] Is it indeed a God of salvation that the reader encounters in the dreadful vision of John of Patmos? The book of Revelation meets these doubts by providing many scenes in which God is honored by a heavenly court, consisting of elders (twenty-four, a doubling of the number of Israelite tribes) and martyrs. It is their praise that grants to God his identity as king over heaven and earth.

We may add to these stylistic and substantive extremes a fifth extremity: the extremity of interpretation. Any encounter with the other, we learn from Kearney, may lead to an attitude of indeterminateness, or to an attitude of horror. Understanding that any encounter with the other takes place between these two interpretative extremes reveals much about the book of Revelation.

One such extreme is given when the reader directly identifies her or his living conditions with the contents of the book of Revelation. The rule of dictators, suffering and martyrdom, wars, and natural disasters can all be identified in the images and numerology of Revelation. Direct identification makes the book of Revelation an externalization of one's fears and wishes for revenge. Such wishful thinking has a bearing on the image of the divine other, which becomes an exaggeration of hidden fears and forces. For the book of Revelation, the "monster God" of direct identification leads to an interpretation in which any advent of the other goes together with imminent destruction. Not only do devilish beasts destroy the earth; God, too, sends out his angels with fearful trumpets and bowls of wrath—images that feed any interpretive move of identification with one's feelings of revenge.

The other extreme of interpretation is laid down in an attitude of indeterminateness. Such an approach to Revelation is beautifully expressed in the deconstructive analysis by Jacques Derrida.[8] Derrida observes that the apocalyptic text of Revelation intends to reveal a truth about the end that is to come. But when this apocalyptic tone is considered, its claim is not about a certain matter of truth, but about truth itself: "Not only truth as the revealed truth of a secret on the end or of the secret of the end. Truth itself is the end, the destination, and that truth unveils itself, is the advent of the end."[9] The aspiration of the apocalyptic tone is high. But its character is always one of an advent that is coming and never present, preceding any event of truth. Finally, then, the apocalyptic tone of Revelation is deconstructed into an imperative "Come!" without any determination. "'Come' does not address itself, does not appeal, to an identity determinable in advance," Derrida writes. "It is a drift underivable from the identity of a determination. 'Come' is *only* derivable, absolutely derivable, but only from the other, from nothing that may be an origin or a verifiable, decidable, presentable, appropriable identity."[10]

The claim of a revelatory truth, taken to its utmost, leads to an indeterminate, never-ending call for coming. That apocalyptic tone not only expresses the tone of revelation, but of philosophy as a whole, for Derrida, in which any truth claim is deconstructed.

We should not expect Kearney's hermeneutics to provide a middle ground between these two extremes of interpretation, though I can imagine that Kearney has a certain sympathy for Derrida's interpretation, which expresses that the other cannot be identified in advance. However, there is one aspect that makes the two extremes of interpretation counter the assets of Kearney's hermeneutics: neither interpretation allows for a genuine encounter with the other. When Abraham meets three strangers at Mamre, the other is unpredictable: the men may be strangers who are after Abraham's life and savings, or they may be bearers of a divine revelation for Abraham's identity and future. But there is for Abraham a possibility of encounter and a moment of decision: it is up to him to decide if he is willing to receive the strangers. Similarly for the Annunciation scene: there is the possibility of a hostile stranger seeking lust and the possibility of a divine revelation of Mary's future. But it is up to Mary to make this event into an encounter with the divine—it is her decision.

All this seems so far away from the world of Revelation, in which the words "encounter" and "decision" do not seem to fit. This is, for me, the sixth and most confrontational extremity: the book of Revelation unfolds scenes of disaster and judgment in which no encounter with the divine incites one to make a decision. The book does not present an appeal to conversion. Its message is one of perseverance: stay to the faith that you have chosen. Of course, the book shows some direct communication from the Son of Man or an angel to John of Patmos, but the narrated content unfolds without any influence or action by the receiver of the message. Is such a manifestation of the coming of the other without any human decision the end of the revelation of the divine other? In other words, is this the point where the divine other deforms into a monstrous other or loses its contours?

At this point of considering extremities, I turn to the center of the book, the textual block of Revelation 12–14. In this scene, we read about a woman who gives birth to a son. A dragon wants to devour the child, but the child is snatched up to God (Revelation 12:5). It is clear that the child is Christ, who is called a lamb in the continuation of the scene (Revelation 12:10–11, 14:1). This lamb collects the believers who have persevered into an eternal bliss. As the apocalyptic Son of Man, Christ judges the earth as in a harvest (Revelation 14:1).

This crucial scene extends to all other parts of the book. It is a recurrent theme that Christ is both the vulnerable lamb and the judging Son of Man, who gathers the martyrs and believers in heaven. A superficial reader of the book would expect an order like this: a situation of belief and disbelief, a subsequent judgment of God in which believers and infidels are separated, the believers are rewarded, and the infidels are punished. The actual order in Revelation is rather: a recognition of the martyrs who have died by gathering them around God's heavenly throne, an identification of Christ as lamb and as judge, a judgment, and a final collection of all believers into the glorification of God on earth and in heaven.

It is the act of perseverant belief and suffering that bears any eschatological appearance of God and Christ. It reminds the reader of the kernel story of New Testament martyrdom: the death of Stephen in Acts 7:54–60. In this scene, Stephen, facing his death, sees Jesus as the eschatological Son of Man standing at the right hand of God. Dying for one's faith becomes an eschatological, and even apocalyptic encounter with God and his son, who will come to reign over the world. In the book of Revelation, a further identification between Jesus and the suffering believers is established: the triumphant Son of Man is also the vulnerable lamb, persecuted and killed, as the martyrs have been persecuted and killed.

I conclude that God's act of coming in the book of Revelation is an appearance that is borne by the suffering and death of believers. Any poetic figuration of God as the one who comes does not lead to a faceless monstrosity, nor to an indeterminacy of the divine other, but bears the traces of believers who have experienced a revelatory encounter with God in their suffering and dying.[11]

IV

Does the poetic support the eschatological and vice versa? At first sight, it seems that the imaginative figurations of the poetic collide with the indeterminacy of the eschatological, the appearance of the other as one to come. The biblical poetics of the Book of Revelation, at least, express a figuration in which the fundamental character of God as coming into the world is borne by experiences of encountering God in the extreme experience of suffering and dying.

We have a present perception of martyrdom that differs from this poetics. Islamist fundamentalism and terrorism have provided us with a picture of martyrs who are willing to die for a holy cause and to receive heavenly bliss as a reward. Such a perception makes it difficult for us to perceive martyrdom as an identity marker for the revelatory appearance of God, in which every martyr refers to the eschatological coming of God as the other for the world, and to the identity of God's son as one who has suffered and died, as to annihilate violence and death. However, we have to take into account that the biblical world of interpretation presents another view on suffering and dying: not as heroic examples, leading to violence and terror, but as experiences that refer to an eschatological coming of the other.

When Kearney treats biblical stories in his *Anatheism*, he focuses on stories of encounters with strangers. I would like to urge him to turn to other biblical texts that might, at first sight, seem to erase the face of the other or lead to an apparent monstrosity. When taken seriously, however, both the eschatological character of the other and the force of biblical poetics may allow the ever-appearing other to emerge, even in literature that, from a twenty-first century perspective, may seem rather grotesque.

THEO HETTEMA is Lecturer at the Seminary of the Alliance of Free Evangelical Churches in the Netherlands. His research involves pneumatology, spirituality, hermeneutics, the philosophy of Paul Ricoeur, missionary ecclesiology, and the identity of the free evangelical churches.

Notes

1. The five components of the "anatheist wager" are presented in (A, 40–56). On the aspect of discernment, cf. Hettema, "When the Thin Small Voice Whispers: Richard Kearney's Anatheism and the Postsecular Discernment of Spirits," 2015.

2. Cf. Hettema, *Reading for Good*, 1996.

3. See Ricoeur's work—from his programmatic statement "The symbol gives rise to thought" in Ricoeur, *La symbolique du mal* to Ricoeur and LaCocque, *Penser la Bible*.

4. The expression "Son of Man" is derived from the Old Testament Book of Daniel (7:13–14), for an eschatological figure to whom God gives eternal rule of the world.

5. It is supposed that reference is made to Emperor Domitian, the eighth emperor from Augustus (leaving out the four emperors from the turbulent year of 69 AD).

6. I refer to the exegetical commentaries for a discussion on the topic of the structure of the book of Revelation. There is no unanimity on the literary structure of Revelation. In developing my own interpretation, I considered the works Giblin, "Recapitulation and the Literary Coherence of John's Apocalypse," in *Catholic Biblical Quarterly* 56, 81–95; Resseguie, *Revelation Unsealed: A Narrative Critical Approach to John's Apocalypse*, 160–167; Fiorenza, "Composition

and Structure of the Book of Revelation," in *Catholic Biblical Quarterly* 39, 344–366; and Sims, *A Comparative Literary Study of Daniel and Revelation: Shaping the End*, 119.

7. Cf. a similar treatment in 2 Peter 3:7 where a second destruction of the earth is explained as destruction by another means (by fire instead of by water).

8. Derrida, "Of an Apocalyptic Tone Recently Adopted in Philosophy," in *Semeia* 23, 63–98.

9. Ibid., 84.

10. Ibid., 94.

11. Cf. the elders worship before God's throne (Revelation 4:4–24); the 144,000 sealed believers from the tribes of Israel (Revelation 7:4, 14:1); the great multitude in white robes before God's throne (Revelation 7:9); the believers at a sea of glass (Revelation 15:2); the multitude in heaven (Revelation 19:1); millennium reign for martyrs (Revelation 20:4); the dwelling in a new Jerusalem (Revelation 21:3).

14 Kearney's Other and the Anatheist Shadow

Patrick Burke

I

On the cover of Richard Kearney's first novel, *Sam's Fall*, Sam's face is engulfed in shadow while that of Jack, his twin, is only shadowed partially. The theme of the shadow is central to much of the narrative in both *Sam's Fall* and his second novel, *Walking at Sea Level*, not in a light way such as the reference to "shadows from the rhododendron bushes" (SF, 190) (although this recalls other rhododendrons at the close of *Ulysses*—to be discussed later) or "a shadow crossed Jack's heart" (WSL, 62), but in a constitutive way, as in the taking-up of the Gnostic claim regarding God's shadow. These novels are about twins, about doubles—Jack and Sam, Raphaelle and Hannah, Carpocrates and his "secret sister"—and for the Carpocratian Gnostics, even God has his double, "the formless matter … the nether part, the shadow of his being" (WSL, 105). Even Christ has his double: "Christ became a lie the day they buried his double, the day they hid his shadow in the empty tomb" (WSL, 198). And Raphaelle writes, "If God is double, then we are shadow selves. So argue the Gnostics against the God of the Jews, the God of Augustine" (WSL, 211).

Without claiming that he is a Gnostic (a problem I will take up later), I would like to get at what Richard Kearney is trying to get at in all of this by asking: what is the shadow in the empty tomb? Raphaelle provides the answer. In discussing monasticism with Sam, the novice monk, she asks: "Why such a quest for perfection meant treating women as temptresses, or seeing desire as a way of tempting men away from God. From Eve in Eden to the erotic apparitions of the Desert Fathers. She just couldn't comprehend, Raphaelle said, why this world had to be seen as a derivation from God, rather than the route itself. Why women, throughout the history of religious art, were represented as imaginary fantasies rather than real beings" (SF, 127).

As I read it, the shadow in the empty tomb is the other who has been suppressed, marginalized, dominated, objectified, depersonalized, and dehumanized—namely each woman in her female embodiment and her female transcendence.

Like the face of Sam on the cover of the novel, a woman's face is left in shadow revealing that something is hidden, "a shadow veiled Raphaelle's countenance as if she were carrying precious things inside of her" (SF, 168). Each woman is the ultimate stranger, desired to be sure, but to whom hospitality has not been offered historically. On the back of a photo that she later sends to Sam, Raphaelle writes, in a truly panentheistic fashion: "We do not renounce the world to reach God: we rediscover the world in God. Deep calling upon deep" (SF, 134). For Raphaelle, and for Richard Kearney, the search for the absolute is not incompatible with wagering that living one's own desire is never an obstacle to transcendence but rather the path. We reach God through the stranger and "she embodies something *else*, something *more*, something *other* than what the self can contain or grasp" (A, 152), "a surplus of meaning" (A, 178), of value. This surplus is heard in the "yes" of Molly Bloom and the Shulamitte woman, the "yes" of female transcendence, of female embodiment that is, as I will argue, the "yes" of promiscuity properly understood by Richard Kearney as a sacramental "yes."

What Raphaelle has articulated in her responses to Sam is the central message of an important book by Richard Kearney, *Anatheism*, that takes its place along with his other works at the very center of the contemporary philosophical discourse on religion, responding to the problem of the estrangement of the stranger who historically has passed beyond the horizon of reflective understanding into the invisible, unspeakable, unthinkable darkness of radical undecidability, into the darkness of the empty tomb. When phenomenology took the "turn" toward the theological, toward the question of the nature of post-metaphysical divinity, the question of the stranger became one of the pivotal questions in Continental thought. It is a question to which Richard Kearney has devoted his major research since *Poetique du possible: Phénoménologie hermenetutique de la figuration*, which he published in 1984. Kearney has contributed significantly to the contemporary discourse on the stranger by arguing for a diacritical hermeneutics of alterity beyond the romantic hermeneutics of Gadamer and the radical hermeneutics of Caputo. His trilogy, entitled "Philosophy at the Limit" is completed by *Strangers, Gods, and Monsters*, which explores the main debates on the enigma of the other ranging from religious anthropology (Eliade/Girard/Levi-Strauss) and psychoanalysis (Freud/Lacan/Kristeva) to deconstruction (Derrida/Lyotard/Caputo), phenomenology (Husserl/Heidegger/Levinas) and hermeneutics (Gadamer/Greisch/Ricoeur). Kearney seeks through the ensemble of these voices multiple traversals between seeming incompossibles, always a middle path of what he calls gracious affinities and interlacings of alterity, making us more hospitable to strangers, gods, and monsters but without succumbing to mystique or madness.

As in *The God Who May Be*, in *Anatheism*, Kearney makes a wager favoring a middle path between theism and atheism, between belief and nonbelief, between the sacred and the secular. Rather than interpreting divinity as either pure being in the manner of ontotheology or as pure nonbeing in the manner of negative theology, Kearney wagers that it is wiser to take the mediating course of narrative imagination and to practice a hospitality that remains open existentially to the divinity that might show itself as the stranger, the god of little things that comes and goes, like the thin small voice, like the burning bush, like the voice crying on the street, like the "yes" of Molly Bloom or the Shulammite woman, like that of the Mary of the Annunciation in Christian scripture.

Through narrative imagination and its companion diacritical hermeneutics, it would seem that Kearney wants to name the unnamable, say the unsayable, imagine the unimaginable, and tell the untellable, making the foreign more familiar and the familiar more foreign to acknowledge oneself as another, and to retrieve one's selfhood through the odyssey of hospitality and otherness. All of this gets played out in *Anatheism* through a series of chapters entitled "In the moment," "In the wage," "In the name," "In the flesh," "In the text," "In the world," "In the act."

II

There are two women, mentioned above, who are at the center of Richard Kearney's scholarly life and, for that matter, in his own personal odyssey of hospitality and otherness: Molly in Joyce's *Ulysses* and the Shulammite woman in the Song of Songs from the Hebrew Bible. Let us first take up the figure of Molly Bloom, whose "yes" is, according to Kearney, a "eucharistic" event, an epiphany, a mutual transfiguring instance of the holy in the ordinary and vice versa. Permit me to cite the text itself:

> The sun shines for you he said the day we were lying among the rhododendrons on Howth head in the grey tweed suit and his straw hat the day I got him to propose to me yes first I gave him the bit of seedcake out of my mouth and it was leapyear like now yes 16 years ago my God after that long kiss I near lost my breath yes he said I was a flower of the mountain yes so we are flowers all a womans body yes that was one true thing he said in his life and the sun shines for you today yes that was why I liked him because I saw he understood or felt what a woman is and I knew I could always get round him and I gave him all the pleasure I could leading him on till he asked me to say yes and I wouldnt answer first only looked out over the sea and the sky.[1]

Kearney claims that Molly's "yes" "epitomizes the anatheistic move," neither theistic nor atheistic. The "yes" becomes "yes" through the kiss remembered, the kiss within which Molly inserts the seedcake into Leopold's mouth. The kiss as the primordial site of the sacrament, as the giving and receiving of the sacrament, as the transubstantiation of breath into flesh, as the most intimate encounter of the incarnate spirit. The "yes" of her kiss grows like a wave from her inner pushes and desires and memories and feelings, through a stream flowing from her unconscious into a crescendo of affirmation: "And then I asked him with my eyes to ask again yes and then he asked me would I yes to say yes my mountain flower and first I put my arms around him yes and drew him down to me so he could feel my breasts all perfume yes and his heart was going like mad and yes I said yes I will Yes."[2]

It is fascinating to see how Kearney roots his analysis of the Eucharistic sacramental character of the kiss in Merleau-Ponty's discussion of the "chiasmic crossing of ostensible contraries." In *Phenomenology of Perception*, Merleau-Ponty draws a parallel between the real presence of God in the transubstantiation of bread and wine into body and blood and the relation of the sensible to the sentient. He writes that "sensation is literally a form of communion"[3] by which seer and seen are transfigured one into the other. Merleau-Ponty privileges the handshake in his unveiling of the meaning of chiasm: my touching hand is touched by the hand of the other which I am touching, each both touching and touched, both subject and object, in an intertwining within which their roles are perpetually reversed. But, to exemplify chiasm and the primordial sociality that it institutes, it would be more fruitful to take the kiss between Molly and Leopold—the kiss that, by its very nature, is much more intimate than the handshake and clearly more promiscuous as it involves the mix of all the senses. The kiss in both its erotic and ontological sense in which Molly and Bloom not only touch each other with lips and tongue and nose and cheeks, but also hear and smell and taste each other, where her breath is in his breath and his in hers, yes, *in each other* in a moment of such voluptuous abandon that action and passion, subject and object, become almost indiscernible in an intercorporeity more fundamental than either.

What had been regarded traditionally as incompossibilities in systems where the *-ism* was a term of exclusion and not of emphasis (e.g., materialism or spiritualism)—where the visible and the invisible, self and other, freedom and determinism, concept and word, idea and image, mind and body, spirit and matter mutually cancelled each other out—now become through the anatheistic notion of chiasm each the other side of the other, each enfolded into the other, as a fold of the other. As a result of this process of invagination, this doubling up or folding over within being and of the negativity thereby engendered through which being breaks open in the kiss as openness upon its other, as a primordial 'yes' to the other, and through which the visible, for instance this red, the red of a dancer's dress, the red "of the eternal feminine," the red Molly wants to wear or the rose in her hair becomes for Merleau-Ponty "a sort of straits between exterior and interior horizons ever gaping open."[4] These horizons are the two leaves or "lips"[5] of what Merleau-Ponty will name "flesh," and he proposes that by studying these two leaves or lips "we ought to find the structure of being."[6] In fact he describes the prototype of being as carnal being, as flesh, "as a being of depths, of several leaves or several faces, a being in latency, and a presentation of a certain absence, is a prototype of Being of which our body, the sensible sentient, is a very remarkable variant."[7]

Because the constitutive paradox of the body is that of every visible thing, Merleau-Ponty can speak of the "flesh of the world" and describe the relation between the body and the world as a form of copulation, "the insertion of the world between the two leaves of my body, the insertion of my body between the two leaves of each thing and of the world."[8] This place of copulation, of engulfment and insertion, of one in the other [*ineinander*] is the place of promiscuity, the wild region under the ravishing rhododendrons, where all the dimensions of wild flowering being are in the tension of the chiasm, intertwined, each the reverse of the other. Molly is Bloom's mountain flower (the rhododendron was classified originally as "the alpine rose") "yes so we are flowers all a woman's body yes."

The rhododendron, the alpine rose, pronounces itself across space and time, and gathers within itself all the echoes it arouses and echoes them back in a perpetual utterance of "yes." Because it has this flesh, the factual rose that Molly would wear in her hair or the metaphorical rose that she says is the woman is also the dimensional rose rising as a relief within being and executing a distinct style of cohesion and coherence upon the spatio-temporal field, thus enunciating a propinquity and a promiscuity with the roses of the past and the roses of the future and with all that the rose has ever meant in the myriad cultures where it bloomed. The "yes" of Molly, of the rose, is the "yes" of promiscuity, rooted in the primodial unconscious. Merleau-Ponty describes it as "the initial 'yes,' the indivision of feeling,"[9] the "indivision of my body and of other bodies: of its cavities, reliefs, and those of other bodies, and of these between them ... the encroachment of corporeal schema on each other ... body-images intercourse—their distance, their reconciliation, as at the circus where the parts of the body are intermingled, an investment in the promiscuity of powers, of powers and of others, and of others among them."[10]

Like the problem of the relation between the visible and the invisible of which it is a variation, the self/other problem can also be resolved through the anathe-istic and chiasmic notion of copulation where, as with Molly and Bloom, "two intentions have one sole *Erfüllung*."[11] Let us listen again to this lovely passage from Merleau-Ponty that in turn echoes the love making of Molly and Bloom:

> For the first time, the body no longer couples itself up with the world, it clasps another body, applying itself to it carefully with its whole extension, forming tirelessly with it hands the strange statue which in its turn gives everything it receives; the body is lost outside of the world and its goals, fascinated by the unique occupation of floating in Being with another life, of making itself the outside of its inside and inside of its outside. And henceforth movement,

> touch, vision, applying themselves to the other and to themselves, return toward their source and, in the patient and silent labor of desire, begin the paradox of expression.[12]

In his journal, Sam admits at the end that Raphaelle had been the other voice in him, the voice that said the desires of the flesh were not to be banished but, in seeking to be fulfilled, were paths to divinity. It would appear that here we have echoes of Klaus, the ex-novice monk in his Carpocratianism which the early Church Father Ireneus condemned for its libertinage, its excess of sexual expression outside any context of law.

In *Anatheism*, Kearney references the desires of the Shulammite woman from the Song of Songs and develops this theme extensively in an earlier essay, "The Shulammite's Song: Divine Eros Ascending and Descending." Here, he pits the theistic medieval Christian allegorical readings of Ambrose, Jerome, and Gregory of Nyssa against contemporary atheistic psychological readings by Lacan and Bataille, wagering always for the third way in which the desires of the Shulammite are an affirming "yes" to the summons of a superabundant God "who seeks the beloved before she seeks him" (SS, 307). The Shulammite says "Let him kiss me with the kisses of his mouth" and Kearney puts in the Shulammite's mouth Molly's words to Bloom: "Yes, I say, yes I will. Yes" (SS, 307). It is a yes to God's desire for us and ours for him. And because it is in the first person pronoun, Kearney writes "it is a woman's song from first to last and it keeps the heroine at center stage" (SS, 309) not as the passive and reified woman left in the empty tomb of Christ.

In his anatheistic manner, Kearney reads the Song of Songs as a double crossing, of the ontological understanding of desire as lack and the eschatological understanding as a movement to fullness. Put another way, Kearney writes: "The lover's discourse in the Song of Songs testifies ... to the double traversing of sensuality by transcendence and of transcendence by sensuality" (SS, 309). Thus an amorous eschatology persists in the text, in its dips, folds, and invaginations as Kearney writes, revealing "that desire ascending is a response to desire descending—an eros that precedes the upward movement of the soul and comes to meet it halfway down, indeed all the way down, in the kiss of perpetual incarnation" (SS, 322).

In *Sam's Fall*, a French girl named Violaine "became more desirable the more she was desired. It seemed part of her magic, that desire of desire" (SF, 70). The Shulammite's desire for her beloved's desire renders him more desirable as does his for her. Such are the "fluid reversals of erotic roles" (SS, 306) being played out in this text, not simply between the Shulammite and Solomon but between her and God, theoerotics with human erotics.

Through this chiasmic interweaving of desires expressed through the narrative imaginary, we find traces of the God of love actively engaged in the world, and this may save Kearney from any charge of Gnosticism. In *Walking at Sea Level*, Klaus, the ex-novice monk, tells Jack that no one escapes the dark double, that we are all Gnostics, all part of God's shadow. Kearney's response to this is that "the sacred is *in* the secular, but it is not *of* the secular per se" as certain monistic Gnostics might have it. (But can Kearney maintain this principal consistently?) Kearney affirms enthusiastically Raimon Panikkar's reference to a "deep temporality in which the divine dwells as a seed of possibility calling to be made ever more incarnate in the human and natural world" (A, 141). Panikkar describes this faith commitment as *cosmotheandrism* which connotes "the creative cohabiting of the human and divine in the lived ecological world." Kearney sees Panikkar aligned intimately with anatheism in its seeking to rediscover the God of life at the heart of our incarnate temporal existence.

In his discussion of Saint Francis, Kearney refers to Francis's "*mystical panentheism*—the view that God is in all beings" (A, 100). He sees Merleau-Ponty and Kristeva in their visions of sacramental and sensible incarnation as deeply Franciscan. I find Kearney to also be deeply Franciscan, but we have to ask whether it is really a panentheism that is at work in Kearney's thought by looking at his recuperation of Merleau-Ponty who he nonetheless describes as a methodological agnostic. Panikkar's "deep temporality" resonates well with Kearney's reference to the "nascent logos" described by Merleau-Ponty, that force of transcendence within the immanence of nature. In his 'Working Notes' to the *Visible and the Invisible*, Merleau-Ponty describes a "vertical past" that adheres to the present independent of consciousness, a past existentially sedimented in the present, entailing a displacing of latent intentionality from the lived body to the world, yielding a kind of "intentionality within Being."[13] The intentionality, which encompasses the vertical past, can be explicated as a kind of carnal temporality or duration, somewhat in the manner of Henri Bergson and, for that matter, Panikkar, as an ongoing process whereby the present, in its novelty, both incorporates the past and opens to an ever-emergent future, a duration inherent to material events and processes and not simply to consciousness. This latent intentionality or duration is an active process of self-differentiation. It unfolds in a succession of heterogeneous phases and constitutes a qualitative multiplicity of interrelatedness as an ever-emergent creative novelty. The sheer advance of the present over the past involves the ascription of some minimal novel agency internal to the present event and the adherence of the past to the present, its survival in the present, internalized at the moment of being transcended. This intentionality operative within being is the primordial desire or longing, the original creativity, which is another name for *logos endiathetos*, for wild being.

But can this logos be identified with God? Kearney does not claim such identity, although he alludes to it in phrases such as "by relocating transcendence within the immanence of nature, Merleau-Ponty is restoring logos to the flesh of the world. *Deus sive natura*" (A, 94). In response, let us note that in Merleau-Ponty's later writings two terms are almost used interchangeably, namely *logos endiathetos* and *esprit sauvage*. Merleau-Ponty's use of esprit refers to prereflective consciousness, with its attendant passions and drives. It implies both mind and spirit. It is called *sauvage* when it is being taken in its most rudimentary ontological sense as that which is untamed by cultural acquisitions, that which is the being-ground for the cultivated mind, that is, as a spirit whose roots are anchored in the deepest recesses of nature, as the invisible of nature, as its organizing, energizing, and directing principle.

Although Merleau-Ponty's use of esprit does not bear any explicit reference to the divine principle, there are some phrases, although elliptical, which indicate that his usage may not be wholly antithetical to this. In a note dated October 1959, Merleau-Ponty seems to line "the unmotivated upsurge of brute Being" with "the hidden god."[14] In *Eye and Mind*, he speaks of the "depth of the existing world and that of the fathomless God" and he ties this into phrases such as "abyssal being" or "the being of God for us is an abyss."[15]

Despite these references and related nuances in his use of "esprit," there is not sufficient textual warrant to equate the divine being with *Logos Endiathetos*. In fact, if Merleau-Ponty is a panentheist as Kearney claims, we must note that the Logos Endiathetos is not only in the world but is of the world. The analogy operative here is that of the relation of the soul to the body which according to Merleau-Ponty is to be understood as the relation of the concave to the convex: "the soul is the hollow of the body, the body is the distention of the soul."[16] The mind, as one of the structures or powers of the soul, is the reverse side of the body. It is the mind of the body.[17] It is not some secondary level of positivity, cluttered and clamored with concepts, judgments, and so forth. It is "quiet as water in the fissure of Being."[18] It is of the invisible and is to be conceived as a movement of transcendence within the openness that is generative of the visible and tangible body.[19] The soul and mind are thus defined by and are expressions of an originary negativity, a primordial openness, which comes to the world through the doubling up of Being upon itself, whereby each is of the other. Kearney writes "of Eucharistic embodiment as recovery of the divine within the flesh, a kenotic emptying out of transcendence into the heart of the world's body, becoming a God beneath us rather than a God beyond us" (A, 91) and citing Merleau-Ponty's citing of *Claudel*, Kearney affirms that God "dwells in and authenticates our darkness" (A, 91).

This raises a question: which preposition is Kearney privileging, the *in* or the *of*? He tells us that anatheism is not

> a pantheism (ancient or New Age) that collapses the secular and the sacred into one, denying any distinction between the transcendent and the immanent. Anatheisim does not say the sacred is the secular, it says it is *in* the

> secular, *through* the secular, *toward* the secular. I would even go so far as to say the sacred is inseparable from the secular, while remaining distinct. Anatheism speaks of interanimation between the sacred and secular but not of fusion or confusion. They are inextricably interconnected but never the same thing. That is why Anatheism should never be confounded with Hegelian dialectics (A, 166).

On the face of it, then, Kearney clearly rejects the Carpocratian Gnosticism of Klaus who claims "God is all things—good and evil" (WSL, 197). But does his recuperation of Merleau-Ponty bring him dangerously near to this—note Merleau-Ponty's emphasis on sacramental copulation with all the others who are *both* in and of the world?

III

In order to address this question, we must ask: who is the God in the world? Kearney asks: what do we mean when we speak of God, especially after declarations by Nietzsche, Marx, and Freud of the death of the God of the philosophers who was said to be perfect in power, goodness, and knowledge? Can we still speak of the beneficent Lord of history in the wake of the Holocaust, and by extension Hiroshima, the gulags, the killing fields of Cambodia, Rwanda, and other atrocities of the twentieth century? Kearney wonders whether the only God worthy of belief is a vulnerable and powerless God who suffers with us, who comes to us not as a mighty monarch but a solicitous stranger, whose voice is heard, as James Joyce suggests, "in the cries in the street." And this question is constitutive of Kearney's wager.

In taking-up this latter question, Kearney discusses two major thinkers who suffered the Nazi persecution: Dietrich Bonhoeffer who was executed in April 1945 just a few weeks before Hitler committed suicide, and Paul Ricoeur who lived five years in a Nazi camp but survived. Kearney aligns his anatheism with both of them, first with the writings of Bonhoeffer whose secular reading of the divine "affirms the life of the world in its darkest moments" even if we "are related to God only by his silence and absence" (A, 68). In his *Letters and Papers from Prison*, Bonhoeffer writes of a "religionless faith" in which Christ is no longer an object of religion but one who helps us by virtue of his weakness and suffering rather than his omnipotence (A, 68). For Bonhoeffer, God is weak and powerless in the world. That is the way—the only way—he is with us. Only the suffering God can help, the God who accepts the cross in order to reveal clearly who he is. God abandons us in order to establish a real and personal relation with each one of us. For Bonhoeffer—and for Kearney—to live without God, to live without any abstract or a priori religious guarantee, is the necessary condition for living before God and with God. For Christians, the only response to the horror of this world is to "watch with Christ in Gethsemene" by keeping deep human and personal company with the afflicted, the homeless, the disenfranchised, the marginalized, the stranger—to participate in the sufferings of God in the secular world.

After examining the work of Bonhoeffer, Kearney highlights the anatheistic currents at work in the postwar essays of his friend and mentor Paul Ricoeur. Ricoeur argued for a postreligious faith—one which entailed an "atheistic purging of the life-denying components of religion, of taboo and escapism and with these also the God of ontotheology whose power rested therein." Such postreligious faith "allows us to restore our originary affirmation of life, our primordial desire to be" (A, 75). Ricoeur aligns himself with Bonhoeffer when he describes his postreligious faith as "a faith that moves forward through the shadows, in a new 'night of the soul' . . . before a God who would not have the attributes of 'Providence,' a God who would not protect me but would surrender me to the dangers of a life worthy of being called human. Is not this God the crucified one, the God who, as Bonhoeffer says, only through his weakness is capable of helping me?" (A, 76).[20]

In his chapter entitled "In the Act," Kearney discusses the work of Dorothy Day and Jean Vanier and their active service to the rejected of society with whom they found Christ in solidarity. Attending to her publications *The Long Loneliness* and *The Catholic Worker*, Kearney writes that Day's politics was a praxis of the flesh, turned toward a public ministry of the afflicted. It pertains to everyday acts of love and justice in the secular world, transfiguring misery into care, hostility into hospitality. Like St. Francis, she welcomed the poor and afflicted as guests in her house that was always open. She understood through this praxis that Christ was both host (emptying himself out of love for the least of human beings) and guest (the recipient of hospitality by a Good Samaritan).

Another model of sacramental service is that manifest in the work of Jean Vanier who founded the L'Arche project, "an open door ark for the estranged and rejected" (A, 159), establishing over 130 communities in thirty-three countries and on six continents, whose servant-hosts live with disabled people such as persons with Down syndrome, the wounded of the earth who are so often left to perish in the shadows. Vanier discovered that his service to these discarded people enlarged his spiritual vision, that his love for Christ increased in direct relation to this involvement, that these persons constituted a concrete opportunity to learn to know and love Christ, and that they were his teachers. Service had become sacramental hospitality where host and guest were in chiasm with each other, or as Merleau-Ponty says, in one another, each transformed by the other.

Another example of sacramental hospitality is to be found in the Guestbook Project directed by Richard Kearney that seeks to bring divided communities together, that enables their respective community leaders, students, artists, and refugees to encounter each other across political, religious, and cultural divides.

It involves a process of exchanging narratives from both sides of the conflict, and requires a compassionate listening and empathic imagining as a way of hosting the other. Its sacramentality is expressed in a process of transubstantiation that moves in reciprocal directions, from word to flesh, from flesh to word. Children from opposing sides, for instance, agree to speak to one another in the bodily presence of face to face in a moment of enormous vulnerability. Levinas writes that trust precedes truth, and clearly here, the movement from face to face of the flesh requires the trust that each will listen compassionately to the other's truth. In listening to the other's words, a new flesh can be born, the flesh of hospitality, of peace and welcome. Here we see Kearney putting into practice his own philosophy of hospitality, moving from word to flesh.

IV

And so we return to our original question once more: does Kearney's recuperation of Bonhoeffer and Ricoeur's understandings of God allow him to refute the charge of pantheism? Let me clarify. If anatheism wants to steer a course between atheism and theism by claiming the transcendent is *in* the immanent and vice versa, we have to ask what are the qualities or attributes of the transcendent that justify the claim that God is *in* but not *of* the world.. Would these not be the qualities already articulated by philosophers for centuries, namely that God is eternal and infinite in power, goodness, and knowledge? For many theologians it is standard fare that God is in the world in the persons of the Son and the Holy Spirit, but he is not of the world, given that he is omnipresent, omniscient, and so forth. In other words, how can panentheism not embrace, although in a highly qualified manner, the God who transcends finitude and death?

Perhaps Schelling's speculation about the dark ground of God may be for Kearney another way of coming to terms with this question. For Schelling the *Urgrund*, the groundless abyss of indifference, somehow differentiates into the ground of god's existence and his actual existence, into a two-fold will, the obscure will of the ground and the clear will of love. But given that God is in a process of self-revelation, given that there is strife and opposition in his very being, it would seem the *chora* is an intrinsic principle of his development. And so I am wondering if Derrida may be on track in pointing to a certain undecidability that disturbs and haunts our world from within and calls for a religious response, a movement of faith, that the God to whom we pray, the God of love, is still struggling, as Klaus says in *Sam's Fall*, with his shadow, with the obscurity of his own ground.

But perhaps the above question is the wrong question to put to Richard Kearney. Perhaps he is not a panentheist at all. Kearney responds with the anatheistic paradox, namely that we can only return to God after we have abandoned

"God." But isn't the "God" that we abandon the dead God of the philosophers or else the God of the Baptist preachers, the God of death and fear, while the God to whom we return is the God of life? But is this a *strong* paradox? When I commented some years ago at SPEP on Richard's book *The God Who May Be*, I pointed out that the God of ontotheology was the postmodern God described and rejected by Heidegger who was educated in the dreary German scholasticism of the Suarezian type, namely metaphysical essentialism, and not the God of Thomas Aquinas who desires the perfection of all creatures, who freely and contingently loved all created things. For Thomas, God desires that all persons be saved on the condition that, through a responsible exercise of their freedom, they keep his commandments, cooperate with his grace, and so forth. The kingdom of God, the kingdom of love and justice, was indeed at hand but we humans had to achieve it, freely choose it and work fervently toward it; our profound dignity as persons rested on the fact that we were able to do this. Thus Thomas could say that God depended on us, albeit contingently, to realize the kingdom. Yes, we are related to God, as Bonhoeffer claims, only by his silence and absence; but for Thomas, God's silence and absence are his providential love of our freedom. Without the existential reading of Thomas by Etienne Gilson, I find the anatheistic paradox too facile.

V

Rather than trying to outdo Polonius, let me conclude as I did in my SPEP commentary on *The God Who May Be* by noting that perhaps we have not listened closely to Kearney's words. Perhaps we have not understood that Kearney is effecting a nuptial chiasm between ontology and eschatology, with an emphasis on the latter. The eschatological focus is principally on the ethical, not the ontological, on the God who is responsible for having made promises to us and we who are responsible for fulfilling the promise made to God to trust his promise. The promise of God transforms God into the promised God, a very different sort of God of the gaps, in this case meaning that there is a gap in the divine, a free space gaping at the very core of divinity, the space of the possible. This is not to deny *esse* of God in the way in which Thomas understood *esse* but to defer God's full *esse* to the promised future. God takes leave of his full being in order to make us partners in achieving the kingdom; thus he is not all powerful, because he takes from himself and confers on us the power to freely bring forth his being as the reign of love and justice. And the latter is what is at stake in the anatheistic wager: by accepting the wager we stand to gain the historic responsibility of a personal relation with the divine in completing creation. By denying it, all meaning and value remain anchored in the old notion of the radically transcendent God as disembodied cause outside the phenomenal horizons of experience accessible only by a blind leap, and we are left alone, exclusively responsible for social evil in the world.

It is Kearney's revelation of the richness and depth of the other in shadows—his female imaginary in the person of Raphaelle, Molly Bloom, the Shulammite, Dorothy Day, and many others who have been traditionally hidden and buried in the empty tomb—that helps to bring Christ back to the streets after his long sojourn at the right hand of the Father.

PATRICK BURKE is Professor of Philosophy at Gonzaga University in Florence (Italy). He specializes in Renaissance Philosophy of Art and Contemporary Continental Philosophy. His latest book is an edited volume with Jason Wirth, entitled *The Barbarian Principle*.

Notes

1. Joyce, *Ulysses*, 731.
2. Ibid. 732.
3. Merleau-Ponty, *Phenomenology of Perception*, 212.
4. Merleau-Ponty, *The Visible and the Invisible*, 132.
5. Ibid., 152.
6. Ibid., 264.
7. Ibid., 136.
8. Ibid., 264.
9. Merleau-Ponty, *Themes from the Lectures*, 179.
10. Merleau-Ponty, *Nature*, 279.
11. Merleau-Ponty, *The Visible and the Invisible*, 241.
12. Ibid., 144.
13. Ibid., 244.
14. Ibid., 211.
15. Merleau-Ponty, "Eye and Mind," 177.
16. Merleau-Ponty, *The Visible and the Invisible*, 233.
17. Ibid., 271.
18. Ibid., 235.
19. Ibid. 248.
20. I am reminded here of a story told by St. Bonaventure about St. Francis of Assisi. As a young man, Francis was horrified by poverty and by all forms of suffering, but he was disgusted by leprosy. His charity toward lepers was condescending and not without moral disapproval. But when he discovered the crucified Christ was, according to the prophet, despised as a leper, he began to render human service to the lepers with deep personal concern and devoted compassion, even to the point of kissing their hands and their mouths. I have argued earlier that Kearney is himself deeply Franciscan in spirit. This story, perhaps, reveals all the more the influence of Francis on Kearney's anatheism.

15 Trauma, Resurrection, and the Anatheistic Wager

Shelley Rambo

I

Like many postapocalyptic novels, Cormac McCarthy's *The Road* presses readers over the edge of the known world and its destruction into the unknown. We meet a man and a child, wandering along a road, looking for food and shelter. They are heading south, hoping that they will find relief from the cold. The road is the only compass they have, and yet the road is a site of perilous encounter, as they meet others who are fighting to stay alive. Civilization has devolved into cannibalism, as the desperate ashen landscape yields no nourishment and no color. The father's words about "carrying the fire"[1] purpose the journey, keep the son moving forward, and yet even those words give way. This coming-of-age story collapses into itself as readers are reminded that the world has already ended. Previous frameworks of meaning no longer function to orient persons in the aftermath. The chapterless prose conveys a sense that events are porous and unmarked by time. Differing interpretations of the ending revolve around whether a novel that has presented a world of mere survival can offer a vision of new beginnings. Is there a promise of renewal, or is this mere survival ongoing and endless? While readers may desire a promising conclusion, the question of whether McCarthy offers a refusal or an opening rides on a reading of these cryptic lines in his closing paragraph: "Maps and mazes. Of a thing which could not be put back. Not made right again."[2]

Little reference is made to the event that brought about the end of the world, but McCarthy's prose ensures that there is no going back. McCarthy's traumatic terrain testifies to a rupture in experience and not simply a wrinkle in it. Thus, he offers a visual landscape to mark the phenomenon of trauma. The ongoing challenges of traumatic integration refuse both clear-cut endings and pure beginnings. Life "after" cannot be thought of in terms of a simple return to an old life or even a piecing together of the past. With no going back, what might a forward look like?

In Kurt Vonnegut's "The Shape of All Stories," his 'failed' master's thesis, he charts eight major plots for storytelling and notes that all works of fiction fall within one of these eight. The New Testament plot, as he identifies it, moves from originary goodness, to the depths of hell, and then to the forward and upward swing, to "off the charts bliss." The cross marks a significant turning point in the plot, and resurrection is part of an upward swing to everlasting life.[3] But could resurrection be mapped differently? Vonnegut's "Which Way is Up?" plot is perhaps the most unsettling as it removes the highs and lows of the others, and presents the ambiguities of life without the familiar markers of right and wrong. Instead of a miraculous recovery story, this plot offers life's ambiguities without end. The arc-less ongoingness of the McCarthy novel follows in this vein.

What happens if the concept of resurrection moves outside of its familiar plotline within the New Testament story and into the fraught territory of McCarthy's aftermath? This begs the question of whether resurrection can be thought in this way, or whether it stands as merely a remnant of an unrecoverable world, confined within the New Testament plot. The stakes in probing how this story is told are wrapped up in thinking about whether resurrection, within Christian theology, can testify to the ambiguities of living in the aftermath of trauma, and ultimately whether it can testify to divine presence in ways other than a triumphalistic account of life overcoming death. Is it possible to think of an ongoingness rather than an overcoming? Can the gospel be retold outside of a New Testament story, as Vonnegut presents it, and as a "Which Way is Up?" story?

Working with Richard Kearney's notion of anatheism, the answer is yes *and* no. Framing resurrection as a return rather than a beginning, Kearney offers a route to an alternative vision of resurrection within the posttraumatic realities that McCarthy presents. He helps us imagine what resurrection might look like beyond this rupture. By proposing a "return to God *after* God," (A, xvi) Kearney displaces resurrection from its theistic moorings and repositions it within the anatheistic encounter. Emphasizing the strangeness of the return of the "posthumous Christ," (A, 27) he provides a way to think about resurrection outside the exclusive realm of theism. I will examine Kearney's vision of resurrection within his proposed framework—as a stranger story.

This essay pursues a testimony to resurrection in the aftermath of a world "not made right again."[4] Following Kearney's proposed movement will require Christian theology to release resurrection without promise of a return. While presenting it outside of an explicitly theological conversation, Kearney keeps resurrection within the sphere of belief and a particular articulation of Christian thought. There is no reason for him to do this, especially given his disclaimers at the beginning of the book: "I have no scholarly expertise in theology and little concern to legitimate my reflections with respect to one particular orthodoxy or another (with no disrespect to any)" (A, xv). I suggest that traces of a theistic trajectory remain and are carried forward, perhaps unwittingly. I want to imagine, from within Kearney's anatheistic wager, what it would look like to fully release resurrection without the promise of its return.

II

Resurrection, as narrated within Christian theology, may be understood as falling solely within the realm of theism. In fact, resurrection is often presented as the doctrine within Christian theology that is employed to secure claims of belief. It seems the least pliable for an anatheistic project, given that it is often used to argue for the truth or triumph of Christianity. While Kearney does not directly pursue a new reading of resurrection, he includes a resurrection account within his larger reading of stranger stories in the various religious traditions. Each of the gospel accounts of Jesus resurrection feature the return of God within the sphere of life, only to be mistaken by those with whom he is most familiar. It is easy to see why Kearney turns to these postdeath appearances for his project.

Kearney is interested in recasting the God debates as a return of the sacred in unrecognizable form. The various religious texts feature moments in which God appears to people in unexpected ways, prompting them to respond to divinity in their midst. They each feature the figures of strangers, foreigners, and outcasts appearing in the midst of life and confronting those that they meet with a decision about whether they will welcome the "other." Divinity appears in this strange and estranging form, and the dynamics of the encounter provide a reorientation in and to the world as a result. Outlining the contours of this encounter with the divine Stranger, Kearney claims that they provide a new framework for "the possibility of a return to a God beyond God (*hors-dieu*), a God who may come back to us from the future" (A, 39).

When he turns to the Christian tradition, Kearney uses one of the resurrection accounts to illustrate this encounter and return: the story of Jesus's posthumous appearance to two men as they are walking along the road to the town of Emmaus. Assuming Jesus to be a fellow traveler, they include him in a conversation in which they are discussing the crucifixion events. Encountering him as stranger, they must wager whether to take him into their home and offer him a meal. It is not until the moment when he breaks bread with them that they recognize him as Jesus, the Christ. Kearney claims that Rembrandt's portrayal of this Emmaus scene emphasizes the "incognito of the departed one, the posthumous Christ" (A, 27). The elements of risk and surprise are present, as hospitality wins out over hostility. Whereas traditional readings of this encounter emphasize the importance of the disciples coming to recognize Jesus as the Christ, as accepting the truth of who he is, Kearney places emphasis elsewhere. He is interested in how the disciples are positioned in relationship to the stranger—that is, how they act in the face of what is unknown. They risk taking in the stranger and extend hospitality to him. Divinity appears in their midst by way of a wager; terror turns into communion, he says (A, 27).

Kearney offers two important ways of recasting resurrection. First, he takes resurrection outside of the realm of belief and truth, and places it within the realm of ethics. Kearney's resurrection proposal is not about propositional faith (i.e., do you believe in resurrection?); it is less about coming to knowledge—truth—as it is about entering into the unknown—which requires a release from a hold on truth. Although he does not claim to be addressing a theology of resurrection, reframing resurrection in terms of hostility and hospitality shifts attention away from the ways that it is often discussed within Christian theology: as the miraculous event that secures the claims of Christian faith, the event that proves that Jesus is the Christ. The resurrection appearances often depict the disciples coming to this truth. Contra resurrection within the framework of classical theism, resurrection in anatheism is not about shoring up belief but about losing one's way and discovering the divine in response to the everyday by wagering in each moment. Kearney's wager is about a positioning or posture rather than a principle or creedal affirmation. The wager replaces the assertion of belief, as it calls for action and response. The encounter, rendered in this way, is more complex and provides a more tangled process of faith than what is often offered within theism. The wager is not a decision about whether or not to believe in God. Thus, doubt and unknowing are not counterpoints to faith that must be overcome; instead, they are always present, facilitating the anatheistic encounter.

Second, he offers the possibility of repurposing the theological within what can be identified as the "secular." While theism can read resurrection narrowly, Kearney provides ways of linking the resurrection accounts to other instances of resurrecting. He presents the sacred and the secular in "reciprocal interdependency" (A, 141). The example that he provides is Raimon Panikkar's alliance between politics and religion. For Panikkar, "a politics of transformation and a religion of incarnation" not only coexist but, through their interaction, productive, expanding both the religious and the political in the process (A, 141). This opens up a way of linking the therapeutic (the "secular") and the theological, providing a meeting point for thinking differently, yet together, about the forms of life that might arise in the aftermath of death.

Insofar as they share a vocabulary of healing, a traditional theistic reading ties healing to Christian accounts of redemption and salvation, to which many clinicians would be averse. And yet Kearney invites a "cross-reading" or a "transversality" which he features in terms of the crossing of religions but could also be conveyed in terms of a crossing of life-and-death stories, as narrated within therapeutics settings (A, 50). While resurrection may be inscribed within Christian thought, the accounts of persons coming to life again after a "death" are also, as

Kearney presents them, resurrection stories. The sacred stories, when released from the strong grip of theism, might resonate with stories of resurrecting narrated by persons within multiple spheres of loss.

III

In an interview titled "Terror and Religion," Jacques Derrida turns the tables on his interviewer and presses Richard Kearney on the question of resurrection. "At some point, you, Richard, translate your faith into something determinable and then you have to keep the 'name' of the resurrection."[5] Identifying it as the "thinnest difference" between them, Derrida asserts that one must be ready to give up the hope of resurrection for the sake of "the most rigorous relation with the other," and suggests that Kearney is not willing to do so. It is the determinacy of faith that Derrida refuses to accept. A representative of the "turn to religion" within continental philosophy, Kearney describes his work outside of the sphere of the theological. And yet Derrida questions whether traces of theology (or a theological impulse) remain in his thought. He observes: "the indeterminacy of the messianic leaves you unsatisfied."[6] The problem lies, for Derrida, in the grasp of determinacy; once faith is given a determined end, it ceases to be faith. Derrida says that Kearney still holds onto "determined hope."[7] Derrida groups resurrection together with reconciliation and redemption, identifying them equally with the impulse to circumscribe an ending; they represent an onto-theological grasp in which faith ceases to be faith and presumes to be knowledge.[8]

Maintaining his position as interviewer, Kearney does not respond directly, but *Anatheism* might be interpreted as a belated response to Derrida's charge. I pick up on Derrida's concern and yet reframe it within the context of Kearney's proposal of providing "a third way," (A, 3) a route for a return. Derrida witnesses it as Kearney's restless relation to Christian terms, and yet *Anatheism* expresses it in terms of a path between the well-worn debates between theists and atheists. The term *anatheism* is Kearney's way of outlining another possibility, a point of crossing or passage in which the sacred or divine can be glimpsed.

The project of returning to God *after* God positions theology uniquely within the context of McCarthy's ending. To speak of resurrection *otherwise* means releasing it from the grips of theism while not abandoning it altogether. The question is not whether resurrection needs to be given up or wholeheartedly embraced. Instead, Kearney seems to be forging a way in which resurrection can be re-approached. And yet I want to show briefly here that traces of a particular theistic reading of resurrection linger in his presentation of anatheism, implicitly carrying remnants of a theology that render him subject to Derrida's critique. Kearney releases only so much. Given his statements about theology, we could say that he is not forging an alternative theological conception of redemption. But it is what remains in place, precisely a certain transactional view of redemption (more precisely, the crucifixion), that leads me to question whether the wager itself retains traces of uninterrogated theism. Does Kearney sufficiently let go of a former conception of resurrection in order to allow for a return? Another way of asking this is whether Kearney's concept of resurrection is anatheistic *enough*. Is a Christian vision still mooring anatheism? I am less interested in indicting anatheism on this count and more interested in imagining an anatheistic account of resurrection without this mooring.

Kearney's reading of the Emmaus story emphasizes that Jesus returns only after an experience of estrangement. He appears to the men on the road, and they do not recognize him. The experience of the cross is not explicitly mentioned; his reference to estrangement assumes it. A particular interpretation of the cross and the meaning of his death are implied here, though readers outside of the Christian tradition may not recognize it. The return of Jesus is laced with theological import. Kearney writes, "He has to leave in order to come back. He has to die as estranged outcast, as a broken reed, a nobody and nothing, before he can live again" (A, 27). The emphasis on *has*, on requirement, is not innocuous. The necessity of Jesus's death is tied up in a larger salvific story. A traditional reading of the cross argues that God, the father, willed the suffering of the son in order to bring about the redemption of the world. In this reading, the son *has* to die in order to bring about God's plan of salvation.

Critiques of traditional atonement theologies, largely coming from within Christian scholarship, call into question the necessity of the cross and also its centrality in narrating salvation.[9] There are other ways of interpreting cross and resurrection, and Kearney is aware of this, as he cites Rene Girard's challenge to a sacrificial reading of the cross in a footnote elsewhere. In "Writing Trauma," he follows the citation of Girard with this: "but it remains the case that the father-son drama in whatever form became the dominant story in the western Abrahamic tradition."[10] Interestingly, Kearney preserves this dominant reading of the cross and, thus, of resurrection. This imported reading of atonement—stressing the necessity of the death—keeps him tied to a particular way of reading, not only the death of Jesus but of his subsequent return to life. The son's death brings about new life.[11] While Kearney might not intend to carry forward the transactional view of the cross, he is invested in the father-son drama as a formative trope of western literature.

What's at stake in doing this is that resurrection, read as a stranger story, loses the force of the wager that Kearney wants to insist involves real risk, without the assurance of an ending. The Jesus who returns does so in the form of a stranger, but he returns *according to the will of the father*. The consequence of folding this view of atonement into his reading of the stranger story is that it makes death necessary and thus, the return (resurrection) inevitable. Death inevitably yields life. Thus, the real stakes of the wager are removed in the divine stranger story.

This inevitability is reflected in this statement: "In short, the death of God gives birth to the God of life" (A, 69). Thus a certain version of atonement remains, which calls into question whether the resurrection involves a wager at all. Given the familiarity of resurrection, the question arises whether the incognito Jesus carries the assurance of redemption with him, however unrecognizable he may be. While Kearney rejects the God of onto-theology, the wager may still be linked to a transactional logic that encircles Christian theologies of redemption.

Kearney makes clear that he is resisting Christian triumphalism (A, xiii). One way that he does this is by rejecting sovereignty (strong God) in favor of the weak God. Jesus returns as one who has "traversed the dark" (A, 38). His journey on the cross and through hell is extreme. Although resurrection accounts often present Jesus as the victor over death, Kearney's vision is more tempered, as he emphasizes Christ's estrangement. The Christ is revealed in his weakness, as one who survives the darkness and returns, not as victor, but as the paradoxical hero of the Christian story.[12] Kearney emphasizes, via the portraits of Etty Hillesum and Dietrich Bonhoeffer, that the return counters the picture of God as omnipotent; the vision of Jesus reflects the weak power of God: "Only the suffering God can help."[13] Kearney's emphasis is on paradox and weakness, on struggle and not knowing. The God of anatheism, he writes, is "not a stopgap God then but a God of the gaps who, in all its radical powerlessness, solicits the fullness of our existential power" (A, 69).

Thus, the emergence of life is more fraught, less certain, and more tenuous than in traditional depictions of resurrection in Christian thought. Traditional accounts present the vision of life as an overcoming of death, as moving beyond it. While the term "return" can be read literally as the event of Jesus's return, Kearney's notion of return complicates the directionality of resurrection account—as a return that positions life *after* death and what lies *beyond* it. Kearney is clear that he is not presenting resurrection in a Hegelian synthesis. He writes: "This is why anatheism should not be confounded with Hegelian dialectic. It refuses the temptation of subsuming singular persons and events into some Grand Finale" (A, 167).

And yet the return is purposed and patterned—willed, as if the life that arises is inevitable. While Kearney does not fully enter the theological territory, he carries forward something familiar, even as he is defamiliarizing readers from a theistic mooring. Theological reworkings of atonement, evident in the writings of many womanist and feminist theologians, challenge this transactional logic of the cross, and offer different visions of redemption. They contend with the conception that the death is part of an overall plan of salvation willed by God and that the death is necessary to bring about life.[14] What is important to Kearney is that Jesus is an estranged figure and that the dark night is experienced by him. His "theological" vision features a way of suffering *in extremis* and a *reversal/paradox* of strength and weakness. But what remains in place in Kearney's thought is telling. While he emphasizes that hermeneutics is the "struggle with angels of death and life," the struggle, in the end, yields life. There is always a return. If what is known is released, it *will* be returned. This assurance of a return appears most prominently in his presentation of Paul Ricoeur, which he concludes by stating, "Nothing is lost in anatheism" (A, 76). The anatheist will lose, but this loss will be retrieved; something will come back to him.

A clear difference emerges here, as Kearney's anatheist has not been subject to the end of the world but, rather, is a subject in the face of it. McCarthy's ending presents a traumatic ending and its aftermath. And while Kearney presents a landscape of loss, there is still an active agent operating who can display courage in the face of endings. While the encounter is risky, the subject in Kearney's depiction of anatheism is agile. Kearney does not presume that loss has been done to him; it is still his or hers to lose. There is a tension and, at times, conflation within Kearney's work between two postures: the existentialist and the traumatic. His default is existentialist vocabulary in which the subject still remains active in the face of the dark night. But the traumatic, as I am presenting it via McCarthy, is distinctive. Whereas existentialism features paradox and reversals, the traumatic features rupture and departures.[15] Is there a conflation of existential disenchantment and cataclysmic rupture in Kearney's work? The existential hero undergoes great hardship but he still overcomes, emerging from the dark night, marked by that experience but not overcome by it. But traumatic survival resounds with a counter-statement: All is lost. And as such, McCarthy's "Not made right again" is a statement declaring the tenor and scope of trauma.

IV

While not seeking a theological analysis of resurrection, there is potential within Kearney's project to interpret resurrection *outside* of its traditional boundaries. He prompts us to think that in releasing one vision of resurrection (a vision made impossible by McCarthy), the release may open up to something else—a testimony to a world that cannot be made right again. Within the study of trauma, discussions about healing hover around the question of the nature of life that arises in the aftermath of trauma. This discussion is always forged through the impossibilities of life arising, recognizing that the world lost cannot be regained.

And yet a Christian theology of resurrection, in its iteration of life, does not make this refusal but insists, however tenuously, on a restoration. Kearney's anatheism gestures toward something more radical. Instead of securing life, it invites readers to release it. The release is not an act of agency prompted by the will of an agent. The release comes about because life is no longer the (guaranteed) thing it was before. Life, as we have known it, *is* gone. The wager of resurrection is a wager on life when all bets are off. And insofar as Christian theology makes resurrection inevitable, it fails to account for the shock of death and resurrection—that life is lost, indefinitely, without recovery. The concept of the wager is so central to anatheism, and yet I wonder if it can be carried into the territory that McCarthy describes, a territory designated as posttraumatic.[16]

Kearney prompts me to think: might a theology of resurrection be released and returned to Christian theology again? Kearney turns to the sacred stories in the Christian scripture and loosens the grip of theism on them. Reading them in their strangeness, he breaks the hold of truth and, instead, re-imagines this resurrection landscape in terms of ethics. "Is this story *for good*" versus "Is this story *true*"? Maybe the story of resurrection is never one to be grasped or understood but one to be received again and again in its strangeness. Resurrection is an open question, handed over, without resolve. As the figure of life's return, Jesus is not recognized as such by those to whom he appears. They must come into a different relationship to him, released from their prior ways of knowing. Thus the wager involves an unraveling of an old optic. What makes this encounter sacred is not its insistence on life triumphing over death or even emerging from it; it is the return of life unrecognizable—seeking a home, a place, and curiously seeking bodies to inhabit.[17] Will life return? Kearney invites me to revisit resurrection, asking whether, given the irreparable loss, anatheism can speak about wounded strangers meeting on different terms.

The traumatic renders life more precarious and the encounter more fraught. The afterlife of life itself is presented in Judith Butler's work.[18] Situating her reflections within the context of the abuse of prisoners in Abu-Ghraib, Butler raises the question of the status of life's appearance in the public sphere, especially as framed through the lens of the media. Her analysis indicates a shift from thinking that life is something secure, assumed, and recognized by all to the precarity of life, as it is negotiated and determined by the frames through which it is viewed. Life is *not* a given, according to Butler; it must be recognized and reclaimed anew. Life seems so obvious a thing. And yet, Butler joins a host of scholars challenging the optics of modernity by warning that life can be distorted and denied by looking at it through particular frames. Those things that we have assumed to be most basic—such as life and the human—are now no longer guaranteed for all. Some lives count and are counted. This attention to the conditions under which life may or may not be recognized *as such* adds another dimension to Kearney's anatheism, namely the layers of culture, economics, and politics that can obscure vision. The anatheistic encounter involves multiple factors that blur the appearance and disappearance of the stranger.

The postapocalyptic genre functions to interrogate the present. It exposes what happens when all bets are off. It is because life is wagered in the public sphere that theology, as I envision it, needs to operate as a tracking device to locate places in which life is negotiated and wagered by the powerful at the expense of the weak. A vision of resurrection, if thought anatheistically, could enact a theological intervention in bio-politics, even when (especially when) a certain dominant theological vision pulses below the surface (one that can be called necrophilic).[19]

In Kearney's vision, life is hard-won but nonetheless guaranteed to emerge. The difference between Kearney and me may be thin, but I insist that traumatic loss would frame anatheism in more perilous terms: "All is lost in anatheism."[20] The time for wagering is over. And it is here that the resurrection story may be a story of estrangement beyond recognition. I want to entertain the notion that Kearney's anatheism can only be truly what he claims if this theistic drive to resurrection is released *without the promise of return*. The importance of theological release is for the sake of testifying to the impossibility of life's return as witnessed in trauma. This testimony to impossibility, situated in respect to trauma, may be a holy refusal of the forward sweep of repair that is often enacted by theologies of resurrection. But perhaps theology needs to be released to witness life as unrecognizable for the sake of finding lives irreparably lost.[21]

SHELLY RAMBO is Associate Professor of Theology at Boston University. She is author of *Spirit and Trauma: A Theology of Remaining* and editor (with Stephanie N. Arel) of *Post-Traumatic Public Theology*, which reflects ongoing commitments to strengthening the capacities of religious leaders to respond to violence and trauma. Her forthcoming book, *Resurrecting Wounds: Living in the Afterlife of Trauma*, examines the figure of resurrection wounds as it meets contemporary expressions of posttraumatic life.

Notes

1. McCarthy, *The Road*, 83.
2. Ibid., 287.
3. Graphic designer Maya Eilam charted Vonnegut's thesis and based it on excerpts from his published works in "The Shapes of Stories: A Kurt Vonnegut Infographic," Maya Eilam Art & Design (website): http://mayaeilam.com/2012/01/01/the-shapes-of-stories-a-kurt-vonnegut-infographic. To glimpse Vonnegut's graphing of stories, see Vonnegut, *Palm Sunday: An Autobiographical Collage*, 284–288. Vonnegut also presented these ideas in the USC Aiken Lecture Series, September 23, 1997. Special thanks to Blake Huggins for introducing me to Vonnegut's thesis. While I point to it here, Blake's work will further disrupt the eschatological certainties of the "New Testament" taxonomy.
4. While a theology of resurrection is not Kearney's concern, I am interested in what Kearney offers to my constructive theological work on resurrection.
5. Gratton and John Panteleimon Manoussakis. *Traversing the Imaginary: Richard Kearney and the Postmodern Challenge*, 26.

6. Ibid., 20.

7. Ibid., 26.

8. Ibid. This discussion of God as *khora* is well-cited within a particular corner of Continental thought, but it is interesting to note that the question posed here is whether resurrection can be thought *otherwise*, or whether it is part-and-parcel of ontotheology which espouses an "anthropo-theologic God of Revelation."

9. Kearney notes elsewhere that the "sacrificial" notion of the cross has been challenged by persons such as Rene Girard. See Kearney, "Writing Trauma: Narrative Catharsis in Joyce, Shakespeare and Homer" in *Giornale di metafisca* 1, n35. But he says this within a footnote in which he is discussing "inescapable existential traumas" that point to primal scenes in western literature as testifying to original trauma (via Freud, Agamben, and Levinas). The pattern that he points to in each is that of primal wounding and intergenerational trauma passed through generations between fathers and sons. The inescapability—inevitability—of trauma is interestingly linked here to the logic of necessity in the Christian reading of father and son.

10. Kearney, "Writing Trauma," n35, 22.

11. Within his reading of the Emmaus account, he says of Jesus: "He has to die an estranged outcast, as a broken reed, a nobody and nothing, before he can live again. Unless the seed dies it cannot grow," (A, 27). Later, he repeats this phrasing: "Resurrected here and now, again and again. For each new reader or community of readers. Unless the seed dies … the wheat cannot grow and the bread cannot be shared" (A, 129).

12. In "Writing Trauma," he presents Odysseus as the returning hero/stranger.

13. Bonhoeffer, *Letters and Papers from Prison, 360–361*, as cited in (A, 70).

14. See Williams, *Sisters in the Wilderness: The Challenge of Womanist God-Talk*; Brock and Parker, *Proverbs of Ashes: Violence, Redemptive Suffering, and the Search for What Saves Us*; and, Ray, *Deceiving by the Devil: Atonement, Ransom, and Abuse*. For a collection of essays featuring a variety of contemporary responses to atonement, see Trelstad, *Cross Examinations: Readings on the Meaning of the Cross Today*.

15. I am picking up on Cathy Caruth's references to "a new language of departure" in Caruth, *Literature in the Ashes of History*, 14.

16. Rambo, "Beyond Redemption?: Reading Cormac McCarthy's *The Road* after the End of the World," 99–120.

17. In the gospel of John, the Holy Spirit is promised to the disciples, and the promise expresses similar movements to Kearney's *ana*. The spirit, as expressed there, will be in, above, around, and with them; the divine breath and human breath (spirit = breath, wind) are indistinguishable as presented in the final chapters of the gospel.

18. Butler, *Precarious Life: The Powers of Mourning and Violence*.

19. See Jantzen, *Becoming Divine: Toward a Feminist Philosophy of Religion*, 128–155.

20. Gratton and Manoussakis, *Traversing the Imaginary*, 20.

21. See Matthew 10:39, "Whoever finds their life will lose it. Whoever loses their life because of me will find it."

Epilogue: From Wager to Art and Back Again

Chris Doude van Troostwijk and Matthew Clemente

In the introduction to this volume, we attempted to open up the question of what is at stake in Richard Kearney's anatheistic wager by emphasizing the uniqueness of Kearney's thought. Though clearly influenced by other philosophers of the wager—namely Pascal, Kierkegaard, and James—Kearney, we said, offers a wager all his own. Anatheism is not about metaphysical calculation or blind leaps of faith. It is more existential than epistemological, more a doing than a knowing. And yet it is deeper still. Kearney tells us that "the wager is operative at birth." It is, he claims, both hermeneutical and phenomenological—a carnal hermeneutics that "goes all the way down and is therefore already from the start also a phenomenological experience."[1]

In this regard, one might argue that Kearney's wager finds yet another forerunner—and perhaps its deepest influence—in the "hermeneutic wager" of his teacher and mentor Paul Ricoeur. Indeed, Kearney himself cites the "narrative wager" of Ricoeur as a main source of inspiration for his work (A, xvii). Yet if Ricoeur is, in a sense, a proto-anatheist, he is a proto-anatheist theist. He answers the wager in the affirmative, returning to God after his detour through religion, atheism, and faith (to play on the name of his famous postwar essay).[2] But if Ricoeur ultimately concludes with a return to God, still anatheism persists. Indeed, if it is to remain true to itself—if it is to truly be "a third way" beyond the extremes of theism and atheism (A, 3)—then anatheism must remain open to the possibility of the loss of faith. It must not shutout the atheist who "lives without God but who is not against God" (as Emmanuel Falque says above). It must be prepared to stare deeply into that abyss and refuse to look away.

I

When Nietzsche has his madman announce the death of God, does he abandon the possibility of God altogether? Or can we perhaps read in Nietzsche a gesture toward the atheist side of Richard Kearney's anatheistic wager? According to the madman, "God is dead. God remains dead. And we have killed him."[3] We have killed God by abandoning God. We have destroyed him by denying him. The God of omnipotence and power, the God of punishment and reward, the God of justice, logic, reason, morality—that God has been deposed. We have knocked him from his throne and have thus freed ourselves from his grasp. But in doing so, we have uprooted ourselves from he who had once been our ground. We have torn ourselves from the safety of his shelter and have thus sacrificed "whatever is comforting, holy, healing; all hope, all faith in hidden harmony, in future blisses and justices."[4] The God of explanation, of justification, of meaning and purpose; the God who has a plan, who sets things right, who orders and structures our existence; the God of truth and goodness, of righteousness and rightness, of reason and dignity and rights—he is the God we have abandoned. He is the God we have killed.

The madman's pronouncement, then, is not simply an observation. It is an evaluation—an indictment of our present age. Indeed, Nietzsche is perfectly aware of the risk inherent in destroying the almighty. He understands better than most the danger involved in playing "the wicked game."[5] "What were we doing when we unchained the earth from its sun? Whither is it moving now? Whither are we moving? Away from all suns? Are we not plunging continually? Backward, sideward, forward in all directions? Is there still any up or down? Are we not straying through an infinite nothing?"[6] By murdering God, have we, like the patricidal Oedipus arriving at Colonus, come to the place of our demise? Have we taken the last step to the edge of the abyss? Do we stand peering down into the darkness—ready to leap?

This, Nietzsche realizes, is the most perilous of situations. Man without meaning cannot live on this earth. Nihilism is a sickness that leads only to death. And if God is dead, what hope is there? Nihilism seems like our one option. Once God is done away with, will man not inevitably follow? What reason could we have to prevent us from taking that final leap into the void?

Yet even as he identifies the great danger, still Nietzsche refuses to look away. Faced with the death of God, he leaves us not with the last man, not with nihilism's fatal slouch toward oblivion, but with a wager. He asks us to decide: die with the transcendent God of old or invite divinity back into the immanence of the everyday. (Indeed, it is when the situation is most perilous and all seems lost that the self-blinded Oedipus stands, walks, and fulfills his destiny). In this sense, anatheism has to reckon with the re-naissance of "god," a renaissance that goes along with the emergence of sense in the ethical encounter between human beings. Anatheism comes after the death of God, yes. But it also reflects the never ending process of God's being reborn again.[7]

In the face the sheer meaninglessness of our deicidal existence, Nietzsche challenges us to love life, to affirm its goodness, to revel in the abundant joy of every instant.[8] But this, he realizes, cannot be done without making a return to god after the death of God.[9] For though Nietzsche is often remembered as one of philosophy's great atheists, his atheism is not closed off to the anatheistic wager. This thinker, swinging his *atheist's hammer*, even claimed for himself the title of "disciple of a still *unknown God*."[10] He sensed the possibility of a divine return, and maybe even aspired to one himself.

But if this is true, what kind of divinity could play the role of the god of Nietzsche? To what god would he have us return after he had pronounced the death of God?

"The name Dionysus," he tells us in his 1886 preface to the *Birth of Tragedy*, "was added as one more question mark."[11] And indeed, Dionysus is the god of the question mark. A god not of answers, not of theodicy, not of covenant or commandment, not of morality, not right and wrong, beyond the dichotomy of good and evil, "an entirely reckless and amoral artist-god who wants to experience, whether he is building or destroying, in the good and in the bad, his own joy and glory."[12] He is a god who suffers and who celebrates, who weeps and laughs. A god of art, of tragedy, of music, of aesthetics.[13] This god—this strange and unexpected artist-god—this is the god to whom Nietzsche would have us return after the death of the God of metaphysics and doctrine. And he is, in some ways, the god to whom we do return in and through Richard Kearney's anatheistic wager.

II

It is perhaps surprising to locate in Nietzsche a forerunner to Richard Kearney. It is strange to think of him as a sort of proto-anatheist—a herald ushering in the death of God not to do away with the divine but to return to god anew, to retrieve and reintroduce (to repeat forward, as Kearney might say) the strangeness of a god long since forgotten. After the death of God, we find ourselves in a situation comparable to Oedipus who left the *polis*, where, in Nietzsche's interpretation, law and order reign under Apollonian protection. We too lack protection. We lack the comfort and stability of the God of onto-theology. We are no longer able to find shelter in the familiar God of old. And yet, we live on. We live in the face of the death of God and must continue to work and rework our lives in order to avoid succumbing to an obsessive repetition—a nostalgia for what has been lost.

But can what has been lost be found again? Can it return to us anew—not as nostalgia but as something at once different yet similar, strange yet familiar, unknown yet remembered? Can we return to the miracle of the everyday? It is perhaps telling that Nietzsche gives to his alien god a name both foreign and familiar, a name of a god of old. (Further, he bestows on his first prophet the name of the world's oldest philosopher: Zarathustra).[14] Thus what is old becomes new again. The end is found in the beginning. It repeats forward and recurs eternally. "[T]he death of God gives birth to the God of life" (A, 69).

Kearney, like Nietzsche, recognizes the insufficiency of the God of metaphysics. He sees the need to make god anew, here and now, in the world of lived experience. (Though, it is worth noting that Kearney does not share Nietzsche's irrational, Bacchic, mad-making energies). This, perhaps, is what is at stake in Richard Kearney's anatheistic wager. Anatheism declares that the God of power, the God of answers, the God of theodicy is dead. He remains dead. He cannot be made right again. But if we open ourselves to the stranger, to the unexpected, to the god of the question mark, then maybe, just maybe, the impossible will happen. Maybe the divine will return to us in new and unexpected ways. And maybe we will return to God—not through understanding, not through philosophy and theology, not through knowledge, not through proofs or logic or argumentation, but by doing: through poetry and politics, imagination and art.

The wager, then, is a way forward. We find ourselves confronted by the death of God. We cannot not face it. But as Nietzsche taught, even as we stare deeply into that abyss, still we can say "yes." Still, we can make the impossible movement: We can go on. We can create. We can, like Oedipus, remain open—returning to God anew and receiving divinity in new and unexpected ways. The wager of anatheism is not a wager of logic. It is not Pascal's wager of knowing, nor is it purely practical. It is, rather, an existential wager—but one more in line with Nietzsche than with Kierkegaard. It is a wager of doing and receiving, a wager of making and wondering, a wager of creating and of sensibility, a wager of art.

Nietzsche tells us that art is "the truly *metaphysical* activity of man."[15] He proposes aesthetics as his first philosophy.[16] After the death of God, man must create. "Here, when the danger . . . is greatest, *art* approaches as a saving sorceress, expert at healing."[17] Similarly, Kearney's anatheistic wager leads to a philosophy of *theopoetics*.[18] His "belief in the inherent divinity of 'all things'" calls for "a sacramental reimagining of everyday experience."[19] This reimagining takes place in and through artistic creation, which is always re-creation—the remaking of God who is himself the first creator. "This play of mutual recreation between human and divine is what we call theopoiesis. It involves creatures co-creating with their Creator. In this view, God codepends on us so that the promissory word of Genesis may be realised [*sic*] in embodied figures of time and space, image and flesh, art and action."[20]

But it is precisely at this point that Kearney's anatheism moves beyond the aestheticism of Nietzsche. Here it enters the realm of ethics. For Kearney, *theopoetics* and *theo-praxis* go hand in hand. One cannot create art and neglect the art of living well. And living well means living like the one who brings life and brings it more abundantly. Yet the arrival of God as cocreator in the artistic process is never certain. He may appear or he may not. Thus "theopoetics is always a wager—a risk that can go either way."[21] The wager is not done away with. Faith necessarily implies a risk. It implies the possibility of the loss of faith—the risk of faithlessness. Thus the wager must be lived and acted out, created and recreated, risked and repeated whether God arrives or not.

Notes

1. See *A Conversation after God* above.
2. See Ricoeur, "Religion, Atheism, Faith," in *The Conflict of Interpretations.*
3. Nietzsche, *The Gay Science*, "III," 125.
4. Nietzsche, *Beyond Good and Evil*, 55.
5. Ibid., 205.
6. Nietzsche, *The Gay Science*, "III," 125.
7. See, Doude van Troostwijk, "The Still Born Again God."
8. One is reminded of Heidegger's quotation of Hölderlin: "where danger is, grows / The saving power also." Heidegger, *The Question Concerning Technology and Other Essays*, 28.
9. In the *Gay Science* (1882), Nietzsche makes his famous pronouncement of the death of God. Four years later, in *Beyond Good and Evil* (1886), he introduces a conversation on Dionysius, the god of whom he claims to be the last disciple, with the following: "Today, as I have been told, you no longer like to believe in God and gods. Perhaps I shall also have to carry my frankness further in my tale than will always be pleasing to the strict habits of your ears? Certainly the god in question went further, very much further, in dialogues of this sort and was always many steps ahead of me." Nietzsche, *Beyond Good and Evil*, 295.
10. Nietzsche, *Birth of Tragedy*, Preface, 3.
11. Ibid.
12. Ibid., Preface, 5.
13. See "[T]he existence of the world is only justified as an aesthetic phenomenon." Ibid.
14. See the "Chronology of Philosophers" in Blackburn, *The Oxford Dictionary of Philosophy*, 399.
15. Nietzsche, *Birth of Tragedy*, Preface, 5.
16. See Cocchiara, "Aesthetics as First Philosophy: Nietzsche, the Artist, and his Work" (forthcoming, 2018).
17. Nietzsche, *Birth of Tragedy*, 8.
18. See Kearney, "Making God: Theopoetics and Anatheism."
19. Ibid., 7.
20. Ibid., 4.
21. Ibid., 8.

Bibliography

Al-Tabari, Muhammad ibn Jarir. *The History of Al-Tabari* (Albany: SUNY Press, 1987).

Arendt. *Hannah, Men in Dark Times* (San Diego: Harcourt, 1970).

Augustine. *On the Trinity* (Cambridge: Cambridge University Press, 2002).

———. *Confessions* (New York: Vintage, 1998).

———. *City of God* (London: Penguin Classics, 2003).

Boesak, Allan. "Black and Reformed: Contradiction or Challenge?," in *Black and Reformed: Apartheid, Liberation and the Calvinist Tradition* (Johannesburg: Skotaville Publishers, 1984).

Brachtendorf, Johannes. *Augustinus 'Confessiones'* (Darmstadt: WBG, 2005).

Breton, Stanislas. "Kearney's The God Who May Be," in *Research in Phenomenology* 34 (Leiden: Brill, 2004).

Brock, Rita, and Rebecca Anne Parker, eds. *Proverbs of Ashes: Violence, Redemptive Suffering, and the Search for What Saves Us* (Boston: Beacon Press, 2002).

Butler, Judith. *Precarious Life: The Powers of Mourning and Violence* (New York: Verso Books, 2006).

Calvin, John. *Institutes of the Christian Tradition* ed. John T McNeill, trans. Ford Lewis Battles (Westminster John Knox Press: Louisville, 2006).

Caputo, John. "What Do I Love When I Love My God? Deconstruction and Radical Orthodoxy," in *Questioning God* ed. John Caputo, Mark Dooley, and Michael J. Scanlon (Bloomington: Indiana University Press, 2001), 291–317.

———. *The Prayers and Tears of Jacques Derrida: Religion Without Religion* (Bloomington: Indiana University Press, 1997).

———. *The Insistence of God: A Theology of Perhaps* (Bloomington: Indiana University Press. 2013).

Caruth, Cathy. *Literature in the Ashes of History* (Baltimore: Johns Hopkins University Press, 2013).

Chesterton, GK. *St. Francis of Assisi* (Garden City: New York, 1957).

Clifford, William. "The Ethics of Belief," in *Lectures and Essays*, vol. 2 (London: Macmillan, 1879).

Cline, Eric. *1177 B.C: The Year that Civilization Collapsed* (Princeton: Princeton University Press, 2014).

Clooney, Francis. *Theology after Vedanta: An Experiment in Comparative Theology* (Albany: SUNY Press, 1993).

Cocchiara, Bryan. "Aesthetics as First Philosophy: Nietzsche, the Artist, and his Work" in *(mis)reading Nietzsche*, ed. M. Saverio Clemente and Bryan Cocchiara (Eugene, OR: Pickwick Publications, 2018).

Conche, Marcel. "L'humanité d'Homère," in *Essais sur Homère* (Paris: Presses Universitaires de France, 1999).

Corbin Ian Marcus. "An End and a Beginning . . . Richard Kearney on Welcoming Divine Strangers and Writing Divine Words," in *Religion and the Arts*, vol. 14 (Leiden: Brill, 2010), 534–545.

Cornille, Catherine. *The Im-Possibility of Interreligious Dialogue* (New York: Crossroad, 2008).

———. "Empathy and Interreligious Imagination," in *Religion and Arts*, vol. 12 (Leiden: Brill, 2008), 102–117.

Danneels, Godfried Cardinal. "Geloof en moderniteit," in *Hoe dichtbij is de toekomst? Lessen voor de eenentwintigste eeuw* (Louvain: Universitaire Pers, 2005).

Dalferth, Ingolf. "Post-Secular Society: Christianity and the Dialectics of the Secular," in *Journal of the American Academy of Religion* 78, no. 2 (Oxford: Oxford Academic, 2010).

de Gruchy, John, and Steve de Gruchy. *The Church Struggle in South Africa* (Minneapolis: Fortress Press, 2005).

———. *Liberating Reformed Theology: A South African Contribution to an Ecumenical Debate* (Cape Town: David Phillip, 1991).

———. *Led into Mystery: Faith Seeking Answers in Life and Death* (London: SCM Press, 2013).

de Launay, Marc. "L'exigence de la promesse," in *Le sacrifice d'Abraham*, ed. Stéphane Mosès and Olivier Revault d'Allonnes (Paris: Desclée de Brouwer, 2002).

Derrida, Jacques. "Of an Apocalyptic Tone Recently Adopted in Philosophy," trans. John P. Leavey in *Semeia* 23 (1982): 63–98.

———. "Circumfession," in *Jacques Derrida*, ed. Geoffrey Bennington and Jacques Derrida (Chicago: Chicago University Press, 1993), 3–315.

———. *Psyche 2: Inventions of the Other*, ed. Peggy Kamuf and Elizabeth Rottenberg (Palo Alto: Stanford University Press, 2003).

Desmond, William. *Being and the Between* (Albany: SUNY, 1995).

———. *Ethics and the Between* (Albany: State University of New York Press, 2001).

———. *God and the Between* (London: Blackwell, 2008).

———. *Hegel's God: A Counterfeit Double?* (Aldershot: Ashgate, 2003).

———. *Is there a Sabbath for Thought? Between Religion and Philosophy* (New York: Fordham University Press, 2005).

———. "Maybe, Maybe Not: Richard Kearney and God," in *Irish Theological Quarterly*, vol. 68 (Newcastle: SAGE Journals, 2003), 99–118.

Perplexity and Ultimacy (Albany: State University of New York Press, 1995).

———. *Philosophy and Its Others* (Albany: State University of New York Press, 1990).

Doude van Troostwijk, Chris. *Trouvaille. Anamnèses de la critique: Kant, Freud, Lyotard* (Strasbourg: Ianua, 2002).

———. "Phrasing God: Lyotard's Hidden Philosophy of Religion" in *God in France*, ed. Peter Jonkers and Rudd Welten (Leuven: Peeters, 2005).

———. "The Still Born Again God," in *The Art of Anatheism*, ed. Richard Kearney and Matthew Clemente (London: Rowman & Littlefield, 2018).

Dupuis, Jacques. *Christianity and the Religions: From Confrontation to Dialogue* (Ossining, NY: Orbis Books, 2002).

Falque, Emmanuel. *The Metamorphosis of Finitude*, trans. George Hughes (New York: Fordham University Press, 2012).

———. *God, the Flesh, and the Other: From Irenaeus to Duns Scotus*, trans. William Christian Hackettis (Evanston: Northwestern University Press, 2014).

Gerrish, Brian. "Tradition in the Modern World: The Reformed Habit of Mind," in *Toward the Future of Reformed Theology: Tasks, Topics, Traditions*, ed. David Willis and Michael Welker (Grand Rapids: Eerdmans, 1999), 3–20.

Giblin, Charles Homer. "Recapitulation and the Literary Coherence of John's Apocalypse," in *Catholic Biblical Quarterly*, vol. 56 (Washington, DC: Catholic University Press, 1994), 81–95.

Gisel, Pierre. *Qu'est-ce-qu'une religion?* (Paris: Librairie philosophique J. Vrin, 2007).

Gratton, Peter, and John Panteleimon Manoussakis. *Traversing the Imaginary: Richard Kearney and the Postmodern Challenge* (Evanston: Northwestern University Press, 2007).

Gruber, Judith. "Revelatory Alienations: Catholic Tradition and Its Loci Alieni: A Response to Paul Griffiths," in *Studies in Interreligious Dialogue*, vol. 24 (Leuven: Peeters Online Journals, 2014), 46–56.

Gschwandtner, Christina. *Postmodern Apologetics?: Arguments for God in Contemporary Philosophy* (New York: Fordham University Press, 2012).

Haers, Jacques. *De theologen op het matje geroepen* (Averbode: Altiora, 2002).

Hamilton, Kenneth. "Paul Tillich," in *Creative Minds in Contemporary Theology*, ed. Philip Edgcumbe Hughes (Grand Rapids: Eerdmans, 1966), 450–460.

Havel, Vaclav. *The Power of the Powerless: Citizens Against the State in Central Eastern Europe* (London: Routledge, 1985).

Heidegger, Martin. *Holzwege* (Frankfurt: Klostermann, 1980).

———. *The Question Concerning Technology and Other Essays* (New York: Harper Torchbooks, 1977).

Hettema, Theo. *Reading for Good. Narrative Theology and Ethics in the Joseph Story from the Perspective of Ricoeur's Hermeneutics* (Kampen: Kok, 1996).

———. "When the Thin Small Voice Whispers: Richard Kearney's Anatheism and the Postsecular Discernment of Spirits," in *International Journal of Philosophy and Theology* 76, no. 2 (London: Taylor & Francis, 2015), 149–162.

Homer. *The Odyssey* (New York: Perennial Classics, 1999).

James, William. *The Will to Believe* (New York: Dover, 1956).

Janicaud, Dominique and Jean Francois Coutine, *Phenomenology and the "Theological Turn": The French Debate* (New York: Fordham University Press, 2000).

Jantzen, Grace. *Becoming Divine: Toward a Feminist Philosophy of Religion* (Bloomington: Indiana University Press, 1999).

John of the Cross. *The Ascent of Mount Carmel*, trans. David Lewis (New York: Cosimo, 2007).

Jones, Serene. *Calvin and the Rhetoric of Piety* (Louisville: Westminster John Knox Press, 1995).

Jordan, Jeff. *Pascal's Wager: Pragmatic Arguments and Belief in God* (Oxford: Oxford University Press, 2006).

Joyce, James. *Ulysses* (Oxford: Oxford University Press, 1998).

Kant, Immanuel. *Critique of Pure Reason* (New York: St. Martin's Press, 1965).

Kavanagh, Liam. "An Interview with Richard Kearney 'Facing God'," in *Journal of Philosophy and Scripture* (Pennsylvania: Villanova University, 2004), 17–26.

Kavanagh, Patrick. *Collected Poems*, ed. Antoinette Quinn (London: Allen Lane, 2004).

Kearney, Richard. *Anatheism: Returning to God After God* (New York: Columbia University Press, 2010).

———. "Making God: Theopoetics and Anatheism" in *The Art of Anatheism*, ed. Richard Kearney and Matthew Clemente (London: Rowman & Littlefield, 2018).

———. "Diacritical Hermeneutics," in *Hermeneutic Rationality / La Rationalite Hermeneutique*, ed. Maria Luisa Portocarrero, Luis Antonio Umbelino, and Andrzej Wiercinski (Berlin: Lit Verlag, 2012), 177–198.

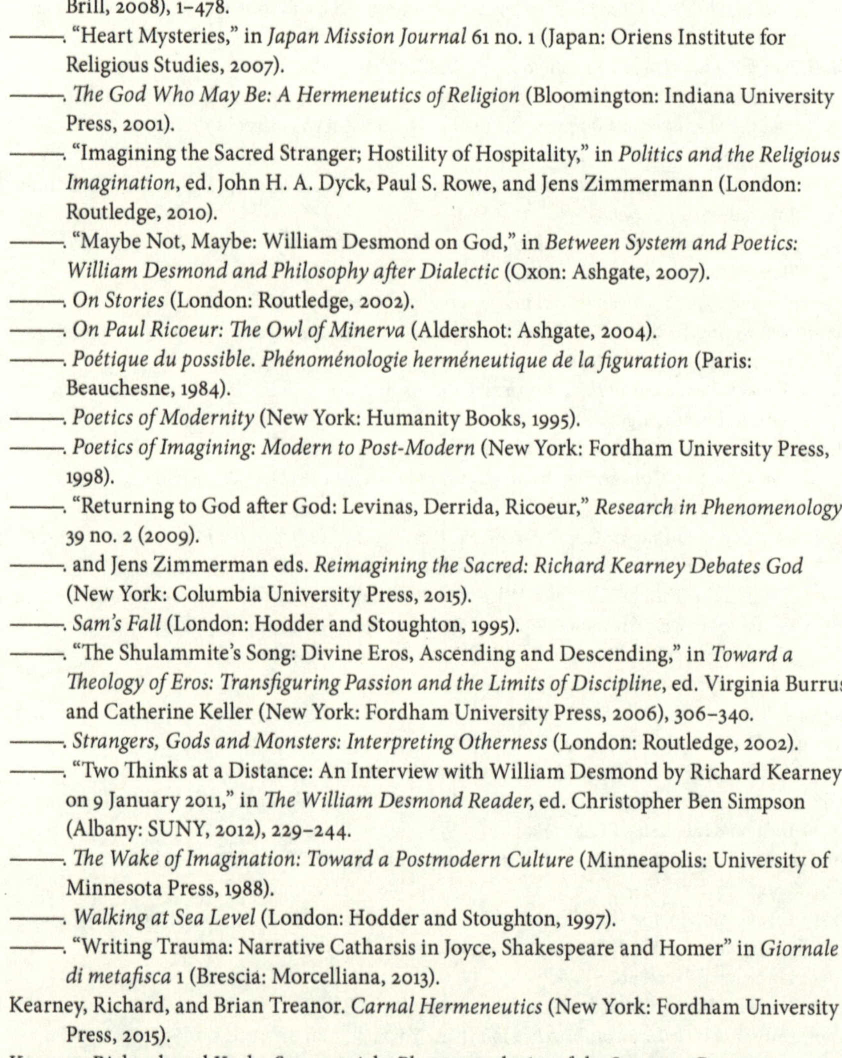

———. ed. "Interreligious Imagination: Special Issue," in *Religion and Arts*, vol. 12 (Leiden: Brill, 2008), 1–478.

———. "Heart Mysteries," in *Japan Mission Journal* 61 no. 1 (Japan: Oriens Institute for Religious Studies, 2007).

———. *The God Who May Be: A Hermeneutics of Religion* (Bloomington: Indiana University Press, 2001).

———. "Imagining the Sacred Stranger; Hostility of Hospitality," in *Politics and the Religious Imagination*, ed. John H. A. Dyck, Paul S. Rowe, and Jens Zimmermann (London: Routledge, 2010).

———. "Maybe Not, Maybe: William Desmond on God," in *Between System and Poetics: William Desmond and Philosophy after Dialectic* (Oxon: Ashgate, 2007).

———. *On Stories* (London: Routledge, 2002).

———. *On Paul Ricoeur: The Owl of Minerva* (Aldershot: Ashgate, 2004).

———. *Poétique du possible. Phénoménologie herméneutique de la figuration* (Paris: Beauchesne, 1984).

———. *Poetics of Modernity* (New York: Humanity Books, 1995).

———. *Poetics of Imagining: Modern to Post-Modern* (New York: Fordham University Press, 1998).

———. "Returning to God after God: Levinas, Derrida, Ricoeur," *Research in Phenomenology* 39 no. 2 (2009).

———. and Jens Zimmerman eds. *Reimagining the Sacred: Richard Kearney Debates God* (New York: Columbia University Press, 2015).

———. *Sam's Fall* (London: Hodder and Stoughton, 1995).

———. "The Shulammite's Song: Divine Eros, Ascending and Descending," in *Toward a Theology of Eros: Transfiguring Passion and the Limits of Discipline*, ed. Virginia Burrus and Catherine Keller (New York: Fordham University Press, 2006), 306–340.

———. *Strangers, Gods and Monsters: Interpreting Otherness* (London: Routledge, 2002).

———. "Two Thinks at a Distance: An Interview with William Desmond by Richard Kearney on 9 January 2011," in *The William Desmond Reader*, ed. Christopher Ben Simpson (Albany: SUNY, 2012), 229–244.

———. *The Wake of Imagination: Toward a Postmodern Culture* (Minneapolis: University of Minnesota Press, 1988).

———. *Walking at Sea Level* (London: Hodder and Stoughton, 1997).

———. "Writing Trauma: Narrative Catharsis in Joyce, Shakespeare and Homer" in *Giornale di metafisca* 1 (Brescia: Morcelliana, 2013).

Kearney, Richard, and Brian Treanor. *Carnal Hermeneutics* (New York: Fordham University Press, 2015).

Kearney, Richard, and Kasha Semonovich. *Phenomenologies of the Stranger: Between Hostility and Hospitality* (New York: Fordham, 2011).

Keller, Catherine. "Richard Kearney's Endless Morning," in *Philosophy & Social Criticism* 30, no. 7 (Newcastle: SAGE Journals, 2004), 890–896.

Kierkegaard, Søren. *Fear and Trembling*, ed. C. Stephen Evans and Sylvia Walsh (Cambridge: Cambridge University Press, 2006).

———. *Either/Or*, vol. 2, trans. Howard V. Hong and Edna H. Hong (New Jersey: Princeton University Press, 1974).

Lacan, Jacques. "The Names of the Father" in *Autres Écrits* (Paris: Éditions du Seuil, 2001).

Lane, Dermot. *Stepping Stones to Other Religions: A Christian Theology of Inter-Religious Dialogue* (Maryknoll: Orbis, 2012).

Lyotard, Jean-François. *The Inhuman: Reflections on Time*, trans. Geoffrey Bennington and Rachel Bowlby (Cambridge: Polity, 1991).

Lyons, George. *Pauline Autobiography: Toward a New Understanding* (New York: Society of Biblical Literature, 1995).

Magliola, Robert. *Facing up to Real Doctrinal Difference: How Some Thought-Motifs from Derrida Can Nourish the Catholic-Buddhist Encounter* (Kettering, OH: Angelico Press, 2014).

Manoussakis, John Panteleimon. *After God: Richard Kearney and the Religious Turn in Continental Philosophy* (New York: Fordham, 2006).

Marion, Jean-Luc. *God Without Being* (Chicago: University of Chicago Press, 1995).

———. "The Privilege of Unknowing," in *The Journal of Religion*, vol. 85 (Chicago: University of Chicago Press, 2005), 1–24.

May, Herbert, and Bruce M. Metzger. *The New Oxford Annotated Bible with the Apocrypha* (New York: Oxford University Press, 1977).

McCarthy, Cormac. *The Road* (New York: Vintage Books, 2006).

Merleau-Ponty, Maurice. *The Primacy of Perception* (Evanston: Northwestern University Press, 1968).

———. *Phenomenology of Perception* (London: Routledge, 1962).

———. *The Visible and the Invisible* (Evanston: Northwestern University Press, 1968).

———. *The Prose of the World* (Evanston: Northwestern University Press, 1973).

———. *Themes from the Lectures at the Collège de France, 1952–1960* (Evanston: Northwestern University Press, 1970).

———. *Nature, Course Notes from the Collège de France* (Evanston: Northwestern University Press, 2003).

Moyaert, Marianne. "Why Are Theologians Annoyed by John Hick," in *Studies in Interreligious Dialogue*, vol. 22 (Leuven: Peeters Online Journals, 2013), 191–208.

———. *In Response to the Religious Other: Ricoeur and the Fragility of Interreligious Encounters* (Lanham: Lexignton, 2014).

———. *Fragile Identities: Towards a Theology of Interreligious Hospitality* (New York: Rodopi, 2011).

———. "Theology Today: Comparative Theology as a Catholic Theological Approach," in *Theological Studies*, vol. 76 (Newcastle: SAGE Journals, 2015), 43–64.

———. "On Vulnerability: Probing after the Ethical Dimensions of Comparative Theology," in *Journal for Academic Study of Religion*, vol. 3 (London: Equinox Publishing, 2012), 1–21. Special issue on European Perspectives on Comparative Theology.

Nancy, Jean-Luc. *Corpus* (Paris: Éditions A.M. Métaillié, 1992).

Newman, Barnett. "The Sublime is Now" in *Art in Theory 1900–1912: An Anthology of Changing Ideas*, ed. Charles Harrison and Paul Wood (Oxford: Blackwell, 1992).

Newman, John Henry. "A Theory of Development in Religious Doctrine," in *Fifteen Sermons Preached Before the University of Oxford Between A.D. 1826 and 1843* (New York: Longmans, 1909).

Nietzsche, Friedrich. *The Gay Science: With a Prelude in Rhymes and an Appendix of Songs* (New York: Vintage, 2010).

———. *Beyond Good and Evil: Prelude to a Philosophy of the Future* (New York: Vintage, 2010).

———. *The Birth of Tragedy and The Case of Wagner* (Vintage, 1967).
Pascal, Blaise. *Pensées* (New York: E. P. Dutton, 1958).
Plantinga, Alvin. "Reason and Belief in God," in *Faith and Rationality: Reason and Belief in God*, ed. Alvin Plantinga and Nicholas Wolterstorff (South Bend, IN: University of Notre Dame Press, 1984), 16–91.
Popkin, Jeremy. *History, Historians, and Autobiography* (Chicago: University of Chicago Press, 2005).
Rambo, Shelley. "Beyond Redemption?: Reading Cormac McCarthy's 'The Road' after the End of the World," in *Studies in the Literary Imagination* 41 no. 2 (Atlanta: Georgia State University, 2008), 99–120.
Ray, Darby Kathleen. *Deceiving by the Devil: Atonement, Ransom, and Abuse* (Pilgrim Press, 1998).
Resseguie, James. *Revelation Unsealed: A Narrative Critical Approach to John's Apocalypse* (Leiden: Brill, 1998).
Ricoeur, Paul. *Living Up to Death* (University of Chicago Press, 2009).
———. *La symbolique du mal* (Paris: Aubier, 1960).
———. "Religion, Atheism and Faith," in *The Conflict of Interpretations: Essays in Hermeneutics*, ed. Don Ihde (Evanston: Northwestern University Press, 1974), 440–467.
———. *The Conflict of Interpretations* (Northwestern University Press, 1974).
———. *The Course of Recognition* (Cambridge: Harvard University Press, 2005).
———. *Freud and Philosophy: An Essay on Interpretation* (New Haven: Yale University Press, 1970).
Ricoeur, Paul, and André LaCocque. *Penser la bible* (Paris: Seuil, 1998).
Rogozinski, Jacob. *The Ego and the Flesh* (Palo Alto: Stanford University Press, 2010).
Schopenhauer, Arthur. *On the Fourfold Root of the Principle of Sufficient Reason* (Lasalle: Open Court, 1997).
Schüssler Fiorenza, Elisabeth. "Composition and Structure of the Book of Revelation," in *Catholic Biblical Quarterly*, vol. 39 (Washington, DC: Catholic University Press, 1977), 358–366.
Sims, James. *A Comparative Literary Study of Daniel and Revelation: Shaping the End* (Lewiston: Mellen Biblical Press, 1995).
Smalbrugge, Matthias. "L'identité sans structure: Le dynamisme de la mémoire," in *Augustiniana*, vol. 64 (Leuven: Peeters Online Journals, 2014), 11–24.
Smit, D. J. "Reformed Theology in South Africa: A Story of Many Stories," in *Essays on Being Reformed: Collected Essays 3*, ed. Robert Vosloo (Stellenbosch: SUN Press, 2009), 201–216.
———. "'Simple and Straightforward'? On Doing Theology," in *Remembering Theologians Doing Theology: Collected Essays 5*, ed. Robert Vosloo (Stellenbosch: SUN Press, 2013), 1–15.
———. "Trends and Directions in Reformed Theology" in *The Expository Times*, vol. 122 (Newcastle: SAGE Journals, 2011), 313–326.
Smith, Christopher, and Anton Powell. *The Lost Memoirs of Augustus and the Development of Roman Autobiography* (Oxford: Oxford, 2009).
Sobrino, Jon. *Christology at the Crossroads: A Latin American Approach* (Eugene: Wipf and Stock, 2002).
Stewart, David. "The Hermeneutics of Suspicion," *Journal of Literature and Theology* 3 (Nov. 1989): 296–307.

Taylor, George. "Ricoeur's Philosophy of Imagination," *Journal of French Philosophy* 16, no. 1 (2006): 93–104.

Thompson, Samantha. "The Confessions of Saint Augustine: Accessory to Grace," in *Autobiography as Philosophy*, ed. Thomas Mathien and D. G. Wright (London: Routledge, 2006), 31–63.

Tillich, Paul. *Systematic Theology* 3 (London: SCM Press, 1963).

Trelstad, Marit A, ed. *Cross Examinations: Readings on the Meaning of the Cross Today* (Minneapolis: fortress press, 2006).

Treanor, Brian. "Blessed are Those Who Have Not Seen and Yet Believe," in *Analecta Hermeneutica* [S.l.], no. 2 (Sep. 2010): 1–17.

———. "The Anatheistic Wager: Faith after Faith," in *Religion and the Arts*, vol. 14 (Leiden: Brill, 2010), 546–559.

Veyne, Paul. *Quand notre monde est devenu Chrétien* (Paris: Albin Michel, 2007).

Vosloo, Robert. "The Displaced Calvin: 'Refugee Reality' as a Lens to Re-Examine Calvin's Life, Theology and Legacy," in *Religion & Theology*, vol. 16 (Leiden: Brill, 2009), 35–52.

Vonnegut, Kurt. *Palm Sunday: An Autobiographical Collage* (New York: Random House Dial Press, 1999).

Westphal, Merold. *Kierkegaard's Concept of Faith* (Grand Rapids: Eerdmans, 2014).

Williams, Delores. *Sisters in the Wilderness: The Challenge of Womanist God-Talk* (Ossining, NY: Orbis Books, 2013).

Wolterstorff, Nicholas. "Can a Calvinist Be Progressive?" in *Hearing the Call: Liturgy, Justice, Church, and World*, ed. Mark Gornik and Greg Thompson (Grand Rapids: Eerdmans, 2011), 249–258.

Index

www.ingramcontent.com/pod-product-compliance
Lightning Source LLC
LaVergne TN
LVHW050150080826
844660LV00002B/146

9780253034007